Dred & Harriet Scott: Their Family Story

Ruth Ann (Abels) Hager

St. Louis County Library
St. Louis, Missouri
2010

Graphics and quotes used with permission from:
Alma (Madison) Miller
Board for Certification of Genealogists
Catholic Cemeteries of the Archdiocese of St. Louis
Centenary Methodist Church Archives
Eugene Field House and St. Louis Toy Museum
Family of John A. Madison, Jr.
Footnote.com
Friends of Greenwood Cemetery
Frontenac Engineering and Pitzman's Company of Surveyors
Joseph T. Hager
Library of Congress
Lincoln University
Missouri History Museum
Museum of Springfield History
National Park Service, Jefferson National Expansion Museum
Saint Louis University Library and Archives
Washington University

Graphic Designer: Marci Donovan
FRONT COVER GRAPHIC: National Park Service, Jefferson National Expansion Memorial
BACK COVER GRAPHIC: Circuit Court, City of St. Louis, in cooperation with the Missouri State Archives and Washington University Digital Library

Graphics and graphics design for this book have been funded in memory of
Pete J. and Agatha (Schieber) Abels and Francis "Mac" and Pauline (Abels) McClary.

Published by:
St. Louis County Library
1640 S. Lindbergh Boulevard
St. Louis, Missouri 63131

ISBN 13: 978-0-615-32762-4

Printed in the United States of America

Second printing

DEDICATION

This book is dedicated to two of Dred and Harriet Scott's great-grandchildren, Alma (Madison) Miller, and her brother, Dr. John A. Madison Jr.

Alma (Madison) Miller graciously shared her unique memories of Lizzie Scott/Marshall. Sharing her memories has helped to preserve Lizzie's story and the unique role she played in their family story. Working with her has been very special.

Dr. John A. Madison Jr. who served as family historian for his entire adult life, deeply inspired me during a brief conversation I had with him. We met on 2 March 2007 in the rotunda of the Old Courthouse following an event for the 150th anniversary of the U.S. Supreme Court's Dred Scott decision. That spring Dr. Madison was able to participate in and enjoy some of the 150th anniversary events and ceremonies during March, April, and May. In early June, his health failed and he died on 26 July 2007.

The efforts of these descendants of Dred and Harriet Scott have greatly enriched this book.

TABLE OF CONTENTS

Dedication iii
Table of Contents v
Letter from Dred Scott Foundation/Madison Family vii
Preface ix
Acknowledgements xi
Introduction xiii
Prologue 1

SLAVERY

- Dred and Harriet (1800–1846) 5
- Suing for Freedom (1846–1852) 17
- Protecting Their Daughters (1852–1857) 25
- A New Suit in Federal Court (1853–1857) 29
- Emancipation (Spring of 1857) 33

FREEDOM

- Together as a Family (1857–1860) 47
- Civil War and its Aftermath (1861–1869) 53
- Harriet's Last Years (1870–1876) 61
- Eliza and Lizzie (1877–1882) 69
- Lizzie and Her Nephews (1882–1912) 75
- John and His Family (1912–1931) 81
- Lizzie's Assistance (1931–1945) 85
- Commemorations (1945–2009) 93
- Epilogue 99

APPENDIX

A: Key Events 101
B: Census 105
C: Maps 113
D: Letters 117
E: Blow and Sanford Families 129
Reference Notes 135
Source List 157
Index 167

November 16, 2010

It is with great delight that I endorse the work on Dred and Harriet Scott's family history done by Ruth Ann Hager. On the day that I received her phone call, introducing herself and asking about past relatives, I had no idea that we would embark on a great fact finding mission that yielded such a rich harvest of information. It was February of 2006 as I was preparing for the 150th anniversary of the Dred Scott Decision in 2007. Providence has a way of knowing and this could not have happened at a better time. Harriet's resting place and her story were about to come to life and she has been further revealed in the pages of this book.

Our continued collaboration, more than work and more than community, has become friendship. Only in this spirit could the end results have come about. I and the Dred Scott family are grateful for the dedication and devotion that went into this work. I thank Ruth Ann and her family as I know the sacrifice of time and effort it required.

I fully support and endorse this as the best real story that can be known today, which Ruth Ann has so faithfully gleaned and compiled. Ruth Ann has nurtured this project with her soul. It has been a joy to work with such a beautiful person and meticulous scholar in her field. It is my great wish that it will inspire others to research their family histories with the intent of remembering not only who they were, but how and why they were. The past can greatly affect our futures for good if we learn the lessons of history. We should never forget, but first we must know.

Lynne M. Jackson
President and Founder
The Dred Scott Heritage Foundation

WWW.THEDREDSCOTTFOUNDATION.ORG P.O. BOX 2009, FLORISSANT, MO 63032-2009 INFO@THEDREDSCOTTFOUNDATION.ORG

PREFACE

Over the last one hundred and fifty years, authors have written about how the U.S. Supreme Court decision, *Scott v. Sandford,* more commonly known as the Dred Scott decision, affected American history. Without question, the role it had in Civil War history and the overall impact it had on the United States was profound.

Very little has been written about how this landmark legal decision changed and affected the lives of Dred and Harriet Scott and their daughters, Eliza and Lizzie. We can now learn more about their family story because of a number of factors.

- Dred and Harriet's great-granddaughter has shared her memories.
- Key resources are more readily available than ever before.
- Indexing of records has made previously untapped sources accessible and easier to use.
- Descendants of one of Dred and Harriet's lawyers donated historic correspondence to the Library of Congress, which is now available to the public.
- Web sites offer digital images of Dred and Harriet's historic legal documents and a wide range of rare out-of-print resources.

This book began in 2006 when Carl Schumacher of the National Park Service called St. Louis County Library's Special Collections Department, which includes both local history and genealogy holdings. He requested a speaker on beginning genealogy for the upcoming program at the Old Courthouse in downtown St. Louis for the 149th anniversary commemoration of the Dred Scott decision. I work extensively with the Julius K. Hunter and Friends African American Research Collection in our department so was chosen to give the talk.

The program commemorated the actions of Dred and Harriet Scott, so I looked for documents about them after their emancipation to show what one might find when tracing ancestors. Research found more records than expected.

Background reading on the Scott family indicated information was vague and brief about the lives of Harriet, Eliza, and Lizzie after Dred's death in 1858. Sources reported Harriet may have died sometime after Dred, sometime during the Civil War, or she may have lived until about 1870. Their daughter, who never married, supposedly died sometime during the Civil War.

This information did not agree with documents I had found. The 1874 St. Louis city directory clearly listed Harriet Scott, widow of Dred, and 1874 was beyond any published estimate of her death. Further, Harriet's death record stated she died 17 June 1876 and was buried in Greenwood Cemetery in St. Louis. Additional research was obviously needed.

Bob Moore, the National Park Service historian for the Old Courthouse, did not think Harriet's death information was public knowledge. He suggested I contact Lynne (Madison) Jackson, Dred and Harriet's great-great-granddaughter, to see if the family knew when Harriet died. Lynne's reply? No, the family did not know Harriet's date of death or place of burial—what had I found?

Thus began a journey of discovery, which has lasted almost four years. It started in 2006 by finding and confirming Harriet's date and place of death and burial. Activities for the commemoration of the 150th anniversary of the Dred Scott decision in 2007 began a new phase of research regarding the family. Slowly the personal story of Dred and Harriet Scott's family emerged.

Ruth Ann (Abels) Hager
2010

ACKNOWLEDGEMENTS

Like a patchwork quilt made from many pieces of fabric, this book would not have been written without the help, support, and sharing of resources, time, and talent by the following individuals and organizations.

DESCENDANTS OF DRED AND HARRIET SCOTT—Lynne (Madison) Jackson, Marsulite (Charleston) and John A. Madison Jr., Alma (Madison) Miller, and Raymond Miller.

NATIONAL PARK SERVICE—Bob Moore, Historian, Jennifer Clark, Archivist, Tom Dewey, Librarian, Charles Schumacher and the other park rangers at the Jefferson National Expansion Memorial.

ST. LOUIS GENEALOGICAL SOCIETY AND ITS MANY VOLUNTEERS—Their published sources and indexes made it possible to access significant St. Louis resources.

GOVERNMENT RECORD OFFICES— CITY OF ST. LOUIS, Mariano Favazza Esq., Circuit Clerk, and Kathy Grillo, Operations/Records Management, Circuit Court; Baxter Leisure, Medical Examiner; Marie Ceselski, Ann Grisham, and Dusty Reese, Recorder of Deeds Archives; Greg Ingram, Probate Court; PULASKI COUNTY, ILLINOIS, Julie Sauerbrunn, County Clerk and Recorder and staff.

ARCHIVES AND RECORDS OF ST. LOUIS—ARCHDIOCESE OF ST. LOUIS ARCHIVES, Audrey Newcomer; BELLEFONTAINE CEMETERY, Jeanie Stephens; CALVARY CEMETERY, Jeanne Besselsen, Associate Director and Mike Campbell; CARONDELET HISTORICAL SOCIETY, Ron Bolte, President; CENTENARY METHODIST CHURCH ARCHIVES, Rev. Kathleen Wilder, Pastor; EPISCOPAL DIOCESE OF MISSOURI ARCHIVES, Sue Rehkopf, Archivist; FRIENDS OF GREENWOOD CEMETERY, Etta Daniels, Executive Director; HARRIS-STOWE UNIVERSITY, Krystal Trice; JEFFERSON BARRACKS PARK, Mark E. Kollbaum, Curator; MERCANTILE LIBRARY, Charles Brown, Assistant Director and Deborah Cribbs, Archivist; MISSOURI HISTORY MUSEUM, Dennis Northcott, Associate Archivist and Dina Young, Associate Archivist; RADFORD FUNERAL HOME, Lois Iverson; RONALD JONES FUNERAL CHAPEL, Ronald Jones; ST. LOUIS PUBLIC LIBRARY, Cynthia Millar, Librarian; WASHINGTON UNIVERSITY LIBRARY, David Straight, Librarian, Andrew Rouner, Director of the Digital Library, and Cassandra Stokes, Digital Projects Librarian.

ARCHIVES, HISTORICAL SOCIETIES, LIBRARIES, AND UNIVERSITIES OUTSIDE OF ST. LOUIS—BELLEVILLE PUBLIC LIBRARY, Belleville, Illinois, Dana Prusacki, Archivist; MUSEUM OF SPRINGFIELD HISTORY, Springfield, Massachusetts, Margaret Humberston, Head of Library and Archives; LIBRARY OF CONGRESS, Bruce Kirby, Manuscript Librarian and Barbara Bair, Ph.D., Historian, Manuscript Division; LINCOLN UNIVERSITY, Jefferson City, Missouri, Carmen Beck, Archivist, Carolyn Cave,

Wanda Harper, and Liz Wilson, Librarian; MISSOURI STATE ARCHIVES, John Dougan, Missouri State Archivist, Patricia Luebbert, Senior Reference Archivist, Mike Everman, Archivist, Local Records Program, and David Snead, Reference Specialist; ILLINOIS REGIONAL ARCHIVES, Carbondale, Illinois, Megan Ditzler; MONROE COUNTY LIBRARY SYSTEM, Rochester, New York, Larry Naukam, Librarian; and Ken Winn, PH.D., Historian and former Missouri State Archivist.

ST. LOUIS COUNTY LIBRARY, ST. LOUIS, MISSOURI—Charles Pace, Director; Barbara Brain, Assistant Director Adult and Support Services; the staff of Special Collections—Joyce Loving, Manager, Scott Holl, Assistant Manager, Mike Bridwell, Jim Brusselback, Kelly Draper, Sharion Duncan, Chris Flesor, Larry Franke, Renee Groeneveld, Lola Kimbrough, Dan Lilienkamp; also Library staff, Sandy Williams, Mildred Rias, Kathy Buckner, and the Interlibrary Loan Department, who found a range of needed sources.

ORDER OF THE EASTERN STAR—Priscilla Harris, Grand Worthy Matron, Harmony Grand Chapter, Missouri; H. Lorraine Jeter, Past Grand Worthy Matron, Illinois; and Vicki Jennings, Past Grand Worthy Matron, Kansas.

RESEARCHERS AND AUTHORS—Adam Arenson, Ph.D., University of Texas at El Paso; Gloria Dettleff, Genealogist; Gary Kremer, Ph.D., Executive Director of the State Historical Society of Missouri; Joe "Red" Menius, Genealogist; and Brett Rogers, Ph.D., William Woods College, Fulton, Missouri.

EDITORS AND ADVISORS—Claire Bettag, CG, CGL; Beth Drescher; Ann Carter Fleming, CG, CGL, FNGS; Kay Haviland Freilich, CG, CGL; Elizabeth Shown Mills, CG, CGL, FNGS, FASG, FUGA; Kris Zapalac, Ph.D.

MANUSCRIPT READERS—Elaine Abels, R.S.C.J., Leo and Carolyn (Skinner) Abels, Mary Berthold, Alexandra and Laurie Cadenhead, Marie Deluca, Viki Fagyal, Sr. Jo Ann Fellin, O.S.B., Sr. Laura Haug, O.S.B., Sr. Janelle Maes, O.S.B., Terri O'Neill, Patricia Walls Stamm, CG, CGL, Alberta Vasarkovy, Sr. Frances Watson, O.S.B., and Sr. Marcia Ziska, O.S.B.

JULIUS HUNTER—who established the Julius K. Hunter and Friends African American Research Collection at St. Louis County Library.

MEMBERS OF THE FRIENDS OF DRED SCOTT COMMITTEE—all fellow committee members, especially Tom Campbell Farnam, Board Member, Eugene Field House and St. Louis Toy Museum; and Louie and Bruce VanReed, Videographers.

Last, and most importantly, my husband, Joseph Hager, for his support, encouragement, and technical expertise; my sister, Elaine Abels, R.S.C.J., and my brother and sister-in-law, Leo and Carolyn (Skinner) Abels, for joining with me to sponsor the graphic layout of this book; my children, Richard and Ruth (Huson) Hager, and Steve and Diane (Hager) Mansfield, and grandchildren, Erin, Ryan, and Nathan Mansfield for their patience and support.

INTRODUCTION

This story of Dred and Harriet Scott, their children, grandchildren, and great-grandchildren is intended for those who want to learn their story from the family perspective. Beyond being legal litigants in one of the most famous court cases in American history, Dred and Harriet were individuals, a husband and wife, parents, and grandparents through several generations down to the present day. Here their lives as individuals are the focal point, and the Dred Scott decision, while dominating their lives, plays a supporting role.

Beyond telling the story, the intent is to encourage examination of the evidence about their lives and act as a catalyst for further research.

Arrangement

Whether read as a story, or used as a reference tool, this book is arranged so that each reader can easily locate material of interest.

Chapters—Told in two parts, slavery and freedom, Dred and Harriet's family story is interwoven with maps, pictures, documents, and charts to help the reader understand, follow, and visualize events and places in their lives.

Text Boxes—Supporting information that goes beyond Dred and Harriet's personal story appears in text boxes. Included are side stories, analyses, evaluation, and comments, such as the status of key locations in 2010. While this material enriches the reader's understanding of Dred and Harriet's personal story, it is not directly part of it. Citations for text box information appear at the end of each text box preceded by a—(dash).

Appendices—Additional information and documents, which the reader may find helpful, are available in one of the following appendices:

A: Key Events

B: Census

C: Maps

D: Letters

E: Blow and Sanford Families

Reference Notes—Source citations in this section document where information was found. For ease of use, they are divided by chapters and appendices.

Source List—Included are all of the sources cited in the "Reference Notes" section as well as other sources used to piece together Dred and Harriet's family story.

Index—Allows readers to more easily use the book as a reference tool.

History through Genealogy

Genealogists research history, one family at a time. Widening the scope of research to include those people with whom they interacted reveals the history of the community, the county, the state, and what was happening at the national level as it affected the family.

Person, Place, and Time

As genealogists research ancestors and their families, they strive to place those individuals in the context of time (history) and place (geography).

DATES—To promote clarity, genealogists write dates as day, month, and year without punctuation. The result is 11 November 2009 rather than November 11, 2009. The day and year are written in digits, the month is spelled out.

NAMES—A woman's maiden name is shown in parentheses ( ).

PLACES—As much as possible, exact locations are included—both historical at the time of the event and current day—so readers may walk in the steps of history and revisit these sites. When the names for locations evolved over time, those changes are reflected in Dred and Harriet's story.

Evaluating Evidence

Only a small amount of information about Dred and Harriet's story has reached the point of proof beyond a shadow of a doubt. The remainder must, therefore, be carefully evaluated and weighed to determine how strong it is, how likely it is true. Conditional words, such as might, could, possible, likely, or probable indicate the evidence described does not by itself prove a fact.

Evidence vs. Proof

Often in research no single document states a specific fact. That situation occured frequently while researching Dred, Harriet, and their descendants. The researcher must then utilize indirect evidence—evidence from a number of sources and documents—in an effort to formulate a convincing argument to prove or disprove that fact.

Genealogists use the Genealogical Proof Standard (GPS), to reach a valid conclusion. To have a valid conclusion, a researcher must have successfully completed the following five steps:

- Conduct a reasonably exhaustive search for all information that is or may be pertinent to the identity, relationship, event, or situation in question;
- Collect and include in the compilation a complete, accurate citation to the source or sources of each item of information used;
- Analyze and correlate the collected information to assess its quality as evidence;
- Resolve any conflicts caused by items of evidence that contradict each other or are contrary to a proposed (hypothetical) solution to the question;
- Arrive at a soundly reasoned, coherently written conclusion.*

---

* The Board for Certification of Genealogists, *The BCG Genealogical Standards Manual* (Orem, Utah: Ancestry, 2000), 1–2. [Used with permission.] Also, Elizabeth Shown Mills, *Evidence Explained* (Baltimore: Genealogical Publishing, 2007), 19.

Even after one has met the GPS standard, it is not the same as proof beyond a shadow of a doubt. Each time new information is found, the original argument must be re-examined to determine whether it is still valid.

Citations

Information is only as good as its source. Citations or source notes documenting information in this book indicate where the information was found enabling others to retrace the research. Original documents, or microfilm or digital images of original documents, were used whenever possible. Many families have nothing published about them, so original documents often make up the bulk of the paper trail left by an ancestral family.

When two or more sources support a piece of information in a single sentence, the citations for those sources are combined in a single reference note. When two or more sources document unique and separate pieces of information within a sentence, a reference note appears directly after the information it supports. In that case, a sentence may contain multiple reference note numbers.

When a source used was not the original copy, the citation includes the format of the source, such as microfilm or a digital image. Microfilm and digital images are wonderful, but in some cases they are not as clear as the original. Occasionally, parts of a document image, such as handwritten notations, which are very small, poorly written, or near the edge of the page, are difficult or impossible to read with any degree of accuracy.

PROLOGUE

As a young child in St. Louis, Missouri, in the early 1930s, Alma stayed with her "Aunt Lizzie" during the week while her widowed mother worked.

Alma felt certain Lizzie was a relative and, after discussing it with her brother John, three years her senior, decided she must be their grandmother. After all, Lizzie was very, very old!

However, Lizzie never told Alma or her siblings who she was. She simply told the children, "Just call me Aunt Lizzie"—and she was not someone to be questioned!

Lizzie, a slender woman who never spoke of the past, at least not to children, walked tall and proud. Yet in her tiny home near the train tracks, a block south of St. Louis Union Station, Lizzie kept heavy drapes pulled across the windows, even in the daytime, and used a kerosene lamp for light. She wanted no one to see into her home or to find out who she was.

Alma never questioned why Lizzie lived as she did. That was just Aunt Lizzie!

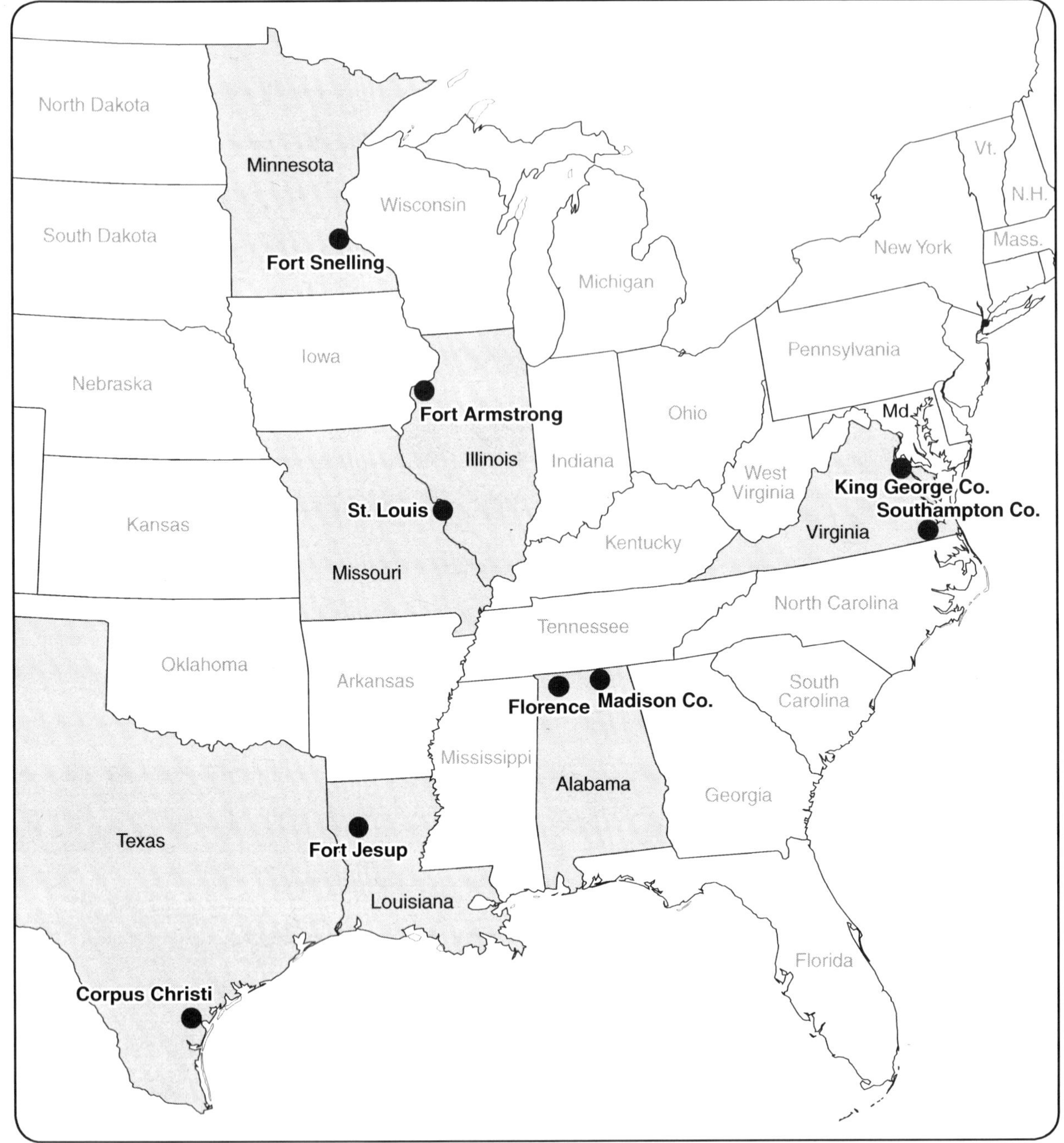

Places in the lives of Dred and Harriet Scott

- Southampton County, Virginia
- King George County, Virginia
- Madison County, Alabama
- Florence, Alabama
- St. Louis, Missouri
- Fort Armstrong, Rock Island, Illinois
- Fort Snelling, Minnesota
- Fort Jesup, Louisiana
- Corpus Christi, Texas

Slavery

Courtesy of the John A. Madison Jr. Family

Harriet and Dred Scott.

DRED AND HARRIET
1800–1846

Dred Scott was born into slavery in Virginia between 1795 and 1809. His first known slave owners were Peter and Elizabeth (Taylor) Blow of Southampton County, Virginia.[1]

The origin of Dred's name is uncertain, but his first and last names were found in Peter and Elizabeth's families. Peter Blow's mother was Mary Scott before her marriage. If Dred was born into the household of Mary Scott's parents, or that of another Scott relative, that could be the source of his last name.[2] Dred's given name may be a shortened form of the name Etheldred, the name of Elizabeth (Taylor) Blow's great-grandfather, Etheldred Taylor, and the middle name of Elizabeth and Peter's middle son, Peter Etheldred Blow.[3]

Peter Blow, the only son of Richard and Mary (Scott) Blow, owned Dred by 1818.[4] Change in the lives of the slave owners brought change to the lives of those they held as slaves. Such was the case for Dred and the Blow family.

Change came to the Blow household in 1818. Three of Peter and Elizabeth Blow's young sons had died and the soil in Virginia was no longer as productive as it once was.[5] Peter sold his property in Virginia that year and moved with Elizabeth, their four daughters, two surviving sons, and their slaves, including Dred, to Madison County in northern Alabama. There Peter purchased land near Huntsville and established one of the region's first cotton plantations.

Their new home was in a sparsely populated area; Alabama would not become a state until the following year. Breaking new ground meant hard work, and living conditions for the Blow family and their slaves were primitive.[6]

Dred's duties in the Blow household were never recorded. He may have worked in the fields, but his size—as an adult he stood five feet, four inches tall—made it more likely that he helped with the children and worked in the house.[7] That could also explain his lifelong closeness to the Blow children, especially the sons whom Dred in later life described as "them boys he was raised with."[8]

DRED AND HARRIET SCOTT AND THEIR FAMILY

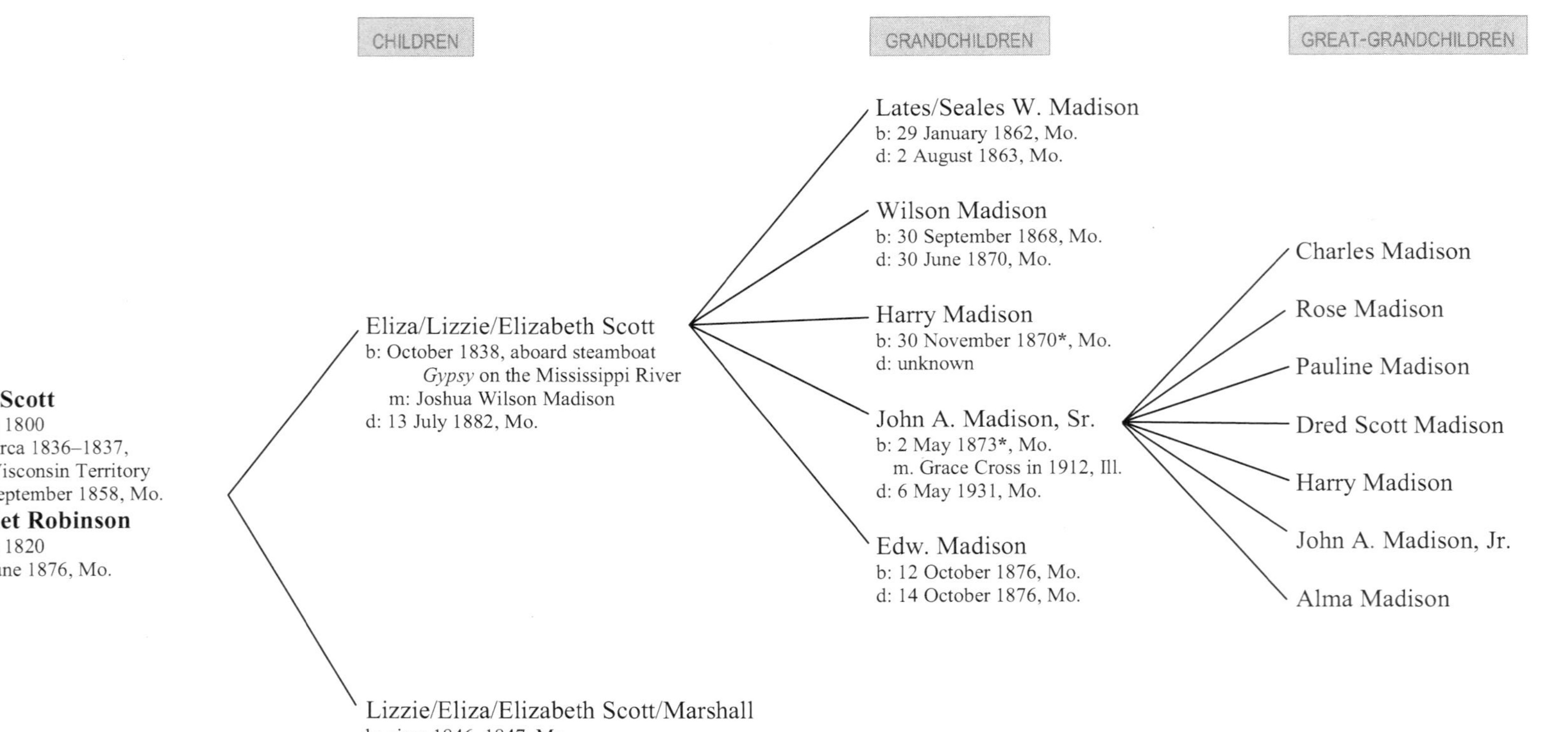

* Birth dates for Harry and John are based on the estimation that they are Eliza and Wilson's unnamed sons born on those dates according to the *St. Louis Birth Register*.

Life in the Blow family carried on despite hard work and hard times. Peter and Elizabeth Blow's oldest daughter, Mary Ann, married John Key on 8 December 1819 in Madison County.[9] The following year Peter's wife Elizabeth gave birth to their tenth child, Taylor Francis Blow, on 26 March 1820.[10]

For Dred, however, life was less stable. Starting a plantation required a lot of money. Peter took out two loans listing his slaves as collateral. If he were unable to repay the loans in cash, he would repay them in slaves. His first loan, from John Jones of Madison County, included Phillis, a young slave woman about Dred's age.[11] Later documents listing Peter's slaves did not include Phillis so it is reasonable to assume she had been sold.[12] In later years, Dred said his first wife had been sold.[13] Could that have been Phillis?

Peter's cotton plantation ultimately failed. In 1821, he sold the land in Madison County, but had little left after paying his debts.[14]

The Blow family and their slaves next moved west to the town of Florence in Lauderdale County, Alabama, just south of the Tennessee and Alabama border. With the help of his family and the labor of his slaves Peter ran the Peter Blow Inn there.[15] Peter and Elizabeth's youngest son, William Thomas, was born there 8 May 1822.[16] Family hardship continued as Mary Ann (Blow) Key died on 7 August 1826, just seven years after her marriage.[17]

BLOW FAMILY IN ST. LOUIS

Peter & Elizabeth Blow

- Elizabeth Rebecca Blow
- Charlotte Taylor Blow
  m: Joseph Charless, Jr.
  (newspaper publisher)
- Martha Ella Blow
  m: Charles D. Drake (lawyer)
- Peter Etheldred Blow
  m 1: Eugenia LaBeaume
  m 2: Sarah Tunstall
- Henry Taylor Blow (served in Mo. Senate & in U.S. House of Representatives)
  m: Minerva Grimsley
- Taylor Francis Blow
  m: Eliza Wahrendoff
- William Thomas Blow
  m: Julia Webster

* For more information about the Blow family, see Appendix E.

In 1830 Peter and Elizabeth Blow, their seven surviving children—Elizabeth, Charlotte, Martha, Peter, Henry, Taylor, and William—and six slaves, Dred still among them, made their final move to St. Louis, Missouri. Charlotte's memoirs, written later in life, recalled their travel on the steamship *Atlantic* and arrival at the St. Louis wharf on 8 May 1830.[18]

Peter may have felt that St. Louis, a large city and hub of steamboat activity, would have more travelers and sufficient business for an inn. He rented a large dwelling at Pine and Main Streets, which the family ran as a boarding house known as the Jefferson Hotel.[19]

Many years later, their daughter Charlotte (Blow) Charless wrote in a letter to her grandchildren about the family's early days in St. Louis.

> "...we had never known what it was to want, until we came to St. Louis. This last move, which was fraught with brilliant hopes, in a monetary point of view, proved most disastrous, and in a few short months, his little [*sic*] all of earthly goods was gone, and his faithful, loving help-meet laid away to sleep in the cold earth, and he himself, declining in health, depressed and discouraged."[20]

Charlotte's mother, Elizabeth (Taylor) Blow, died on 24 July 1831. A few months later, Charlotte married Joseph Charless on 8 November 1831 at the First Presbyterian Church in St. Louis.[21] By then her father had "... become greatly reduced in circumstances and could afford no better preparations for the wedding of his child than such as could be made at home." Charlotte economized by sewing her own wedding dress and her brothers and sisters decorated their parlor.[22]

Once again, changes in the slave-owning family affected the people they held as slaves. Peter Blow's financial problems in Alabama had cost Dred the loss of his first wife. His financial situation in St. Louis was even worse. Consequently, prior to his death on 23 June 1832, Peter sold Dred to Dr. John Emerson, a U.S. Army surgeon, living in St. Louis.[23]

After Peter's death, Charlotte and her new husband took in her orphaned siblings, five younger than she was and ranging in age from ten to twenty years old. She thus kept the family together, and she would later help Dred with his suit for freedom.[24]

Life as Slave of Dr. Emerson

Dred served as Dr. Emerson's personal servant. On 19 November 1833, Dred accompanied Dr. Emerson on assignment at Fort Armstrong at Rock Island, Illinois.[25] In the wake of the War of 1812, the Army had built a fort in 1816 at the foot of Rock Island on the Mississippi River[26] to better protect the region and provide "peacekeeping operations with Indians."[27]

The Mississippi River marks the western boundary of Illinois. The precise boundary is part way across the river separating Illinois from Iowa. Consequently the east part of the river, including Rock Island, belongs to Illinois. That would later be important to Dred because the Illinois state constitution prohibited slavery.[28]

FORT ARMSTRONG

While Fort Armstrong is no longer in existence, a building and a monument, placed in 1901 by the Fort Armstrong Chapter of the Daughters of the American Revolution, currently mark the location of the former fort on Rock Island.

The area, encompassing both the Illinois and Iowa sides of the river to the east and west of Rock Island, is now known as the Quad Cities metropolitan area. It includes Bettendorf and Davenport on the Iowa shore, and Rock Island, Moline, and East Moline on the Illinois side.

— "Fort Armstrong—Rock Island, IL Waymark," *Waymarking.com* (http://www.waymarking.com)

While at Fort Armstrong, Dr. Emerson acquired three pieces of land in Illinois and one across the river in Bettendorf, Iowa.[29] He built a log cabin on the Iowa property to improve the land. As his servant, Dred probably worked on it also.[30]

> **FORT SNELLING**
>
> Although surrounded by wilderness in 1836, Fort Snelling still exists in St. Paul, Minnesota. The Minnesota Historical Society has preserved the fort as an historic site, which visitors in 2010 can tour.
>
> — "Fort Snelling Information," *Minnesota Historical Society* (http://www.mnhs.org/places/sites/hfs)

The army vacated Fort Armstrong in 1836, and Dr. Emerson took Dred to his next assignment at Fort Snelling. The fort was in Wisconsin Territory, located on the west bank of the Mississippi at the juncture with the Minnesota River.[31]

The Missouri Compromise of 1820 prohibited slavery north of parallel latitude 36° 30', except for within the State of Missouri. Slavery was thus not permitted in the Wisconsin Territory.[32] Nevertheless, it was common for Army officers to bring slaves to Fort Snelling as private servants.[33] The fort was in a remote area where living conditions were primitive and harsh. Hired personal servants could choose to leave; slaves had no choice.

Harriet (Robinson) Scott

While at Fort Snelling, Dred met Harriet Robinson, the slave of Major Lawrence Taliaferro, the Indian Agent at St. Peter's Agency, near the fort.[34] Major Taliaferro, born in King George County, Virginia, brought Harriett to Fort Snelling as his slave.[35] Since he was from Virginia, Harriet, born about 1820, might also have been born in Virginia. However, the 1860 federal census for Missouri listed Harriet's birthplace as Kentucky, which was originally part of Virginia.[36]

Dred and Harriet married in a civil ceremony before Major Taliaferro, a justice of the peace. Years later Taliaferro recorded that Harriet was seventeen and Dred was forty when married.[37]

After their marriage, the major arranged for Harriet to become Dr. John Emerson's slave. Having the same slave owner placed the couple in the same household increasing their chance to stay together when Dr. Emerson left for his next assignment. No record of this transfer of ownership has been found to show if it was by sale, transfer, or gift.[38]

The date of their marriage can only be estimated. It would have been between Dred's arrival at Fort Snelling on 8 May 1836, and 14 September 1837, when Lieutenant James L. Thompson's wife arrived and hired Harriet from Dr. Emerson.[39]

Married Life

Dr. Emerson was not satisfied with Fort Snelling and asked for a better assignment. In October 1837, he was assigned to Jefferson Barracks, just south of St. Louis. Having previously served there, and knowing St. Louis was a warmer and more civilized place, Emerson departed leaving Dred, Harriet, and many of his other personal belongings behind. Dred and Harriet continued to work—hired out to officers at Fort Snelling.[40]

> JEFFERSON BARRACKS
>
> In 2010, part of Jefferson Barracks still exists as the Jefferson Barracks Park operated and maintained by the St. Louis County Parks and Recreation Department. Visitors may tour the museum and exhibits in some of the remaining buildings.
>
> — "Jefferson Barracks," St. Louis County. Also, phone conversation between the author and Mark E. Kollbaum, Jefferson Barracks Park curator, 22 April 2009.

Upon arrival at Jefferson Barracks, Emerson received new orders assigning him to Fort Jesup in western Louisiana, along the Texas border.[41] Dr. Emerson arrived at Fort Jesup on 22 November 1837. There, he met twenty-three year-old Eliza Irene Sanford. Irene was visiting her sister, Mary, whose husband, Captain Henry Bainbridge was stationed at the fort.[42] After a brief courtship, Dr. Emerson and Irene married on 6 February 1838, at Natchitoches, Louisiana. C. E. Greneaux, Parish Judge, performed the ceremony and Mary and Henry Bainbridge were among the nine witnesses at their marriage.[43]

Following his marriage, Emerson sent for Dred and Harriet to care for him and his new bride. Dred and Harriet traveled from Fort Snelling and arrived at Fort Jesup in April of 1838.[44]

> FORT JESUP
>
> Situated twenty-two miles southwest of Natchitoches, Louisiana, the U.S. Army built Fort Jesup in 1822. Its purpose was to protect the U.S. border with Texas, which was then part of Mexico, a Spanish colony. Today, Fort Jesup is a Louisiana State Historic Site and a National Historic Landmark. One original and one reconstructed building are open to the public.
>
> — "Fort Jesup," *National Park Serivce* (http://www.nps.gov/history/nr/travel/caneriver/for.htm).

Dr. Emerson's satisfaction with Fort Jesup did not last long and he once again sought a new assignment. He was reassigned to Fort Snelling, which he had not liked previously. Nevertheless, in the fall of 1838, Dred and Harriet returned to Fort Snelling with Dr. Emerson and his bride.[45] Dr. Emerson served at Fort Jesup less than a year. Dred and Harriet spent only a few months there.

Harriet was pregnant on the trips to and from Fort Jesup. In October 1838, journeying upriver to Fort Snelling aboard the steamboat *Gypsy*, Harriet gave birth to their first child, Eliza.[46] Although known as Eliza to her family, records created during her life also listed her as Lizzie and Elizabeth.[47] When Eliza was born the steamboat was on the Mississippi just north of Missouri, headed to Fort Snelling. Thus technically she was born in free territory.[48] Though it was never specifically recorded, her birth aboard the *Gypsy* was a fact agreed upon in 1854 by both sets of lawyers when her parents' freedom suit went before the U.S. Circuit Court in St. Louis.[49]

The Emersons remained at Fort Snelling until 1840 when the doctor's next assignment sent him to Florida for the Seminole War. Rather than accompany her husband, Irene Emerson moved into the home of her father, Alexander Sanford, in rural St. Louis County, Missouri.[50] There her father hired out Dred and Harriet, sometimes as a couple, other times separately.[51]

Alexander Sanford lived in the northwest portion of St. Louis County near the town of Owens Station, later renamed Bridgeton.[52] He owned slaves and his "small plantation" or farm, known as "California," was located about fourteen miles from the city of St. Louis.[53]

Sanford not only owned slaves, he "... worked actively for the 'protection of slave property against the evil designs of abolitionists'."[54] In 1846, he was a vice president of an "Anti-Abolitionist Society in St. Louis," which authorized the employment of "... agents 'to aid in the execution of laws covering slaves'."[55]

Dr. Emerson was discharged from the army in August 1842 while serving in Florida. He then returned to St. Louis, purchased land, and attempted, unsuccessfully, to set up a private medical practice. He had received an honorable discharge from the army, but "... rumors that he had mishandled hospital funds ..." while serving in Florida may have reached St. Louis thwarting his efforts to establish a medical practice.[56]

Dr. Emerson then moved to Davenport, Iowa, where he still owned property.[57] He advertised his professional services in May 1843 issues of the *Davenport Gazette*. He also purchased land in the city of Davenport and started building a home. Irene joined him where they lived in the LeClaire Hotel waiting for the birth of their child and the completion of their home.[58]

SANFORD FAMILY

Alexander Sanford

- John F. A. Sanford
  - m 1: Emelie Chouteau
  - m 2: Isabella Davis
- Charlotte Sanford
  - m: James Barnes
- Henrietta Sanford
  - m: John B. Clark
- Irene Sanford
  - m 1: Dr. John Emerson
  - m 2: Dr. Calvin Chaffee
- Mary Sanford
  - m 1: Henry Bainbridge
  - m 2: Henry S. Humphrey
- Joseph Perry Sanford
  - m: Lydia Ransom
- Virginia Sanford
  - m: Samuel H. Ransom

* For more information about the Sanford family, see Appendix E.

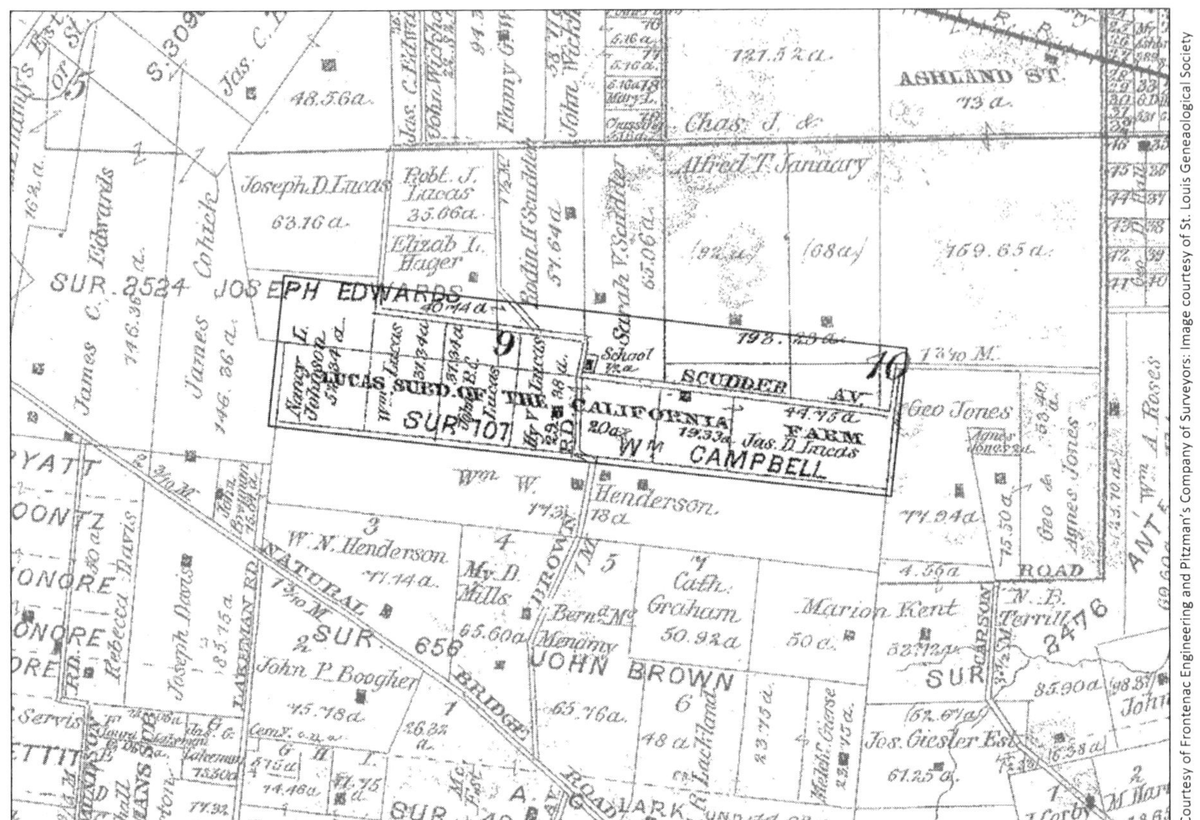

Alexander Sanford's property, the farm "California," identified in Pitzman's 1878 St. Louis atlas.

SANFORD'S FARM

In 2010, the land that was Alexander Sanford's farm is part of Lambert-St. Louis International Airport's east runways and nearby Interstate I-170. Plate 63 of 1878 *Pitzman's New Atlas of the City and County of Saint Louis, Missouri,* shows "Lucas Subd. of the California Farm" located just north of Natural Bridge Road with Brown Road running north to south through the middle of the farm.

The town of Bridgeton is a short distance to the northwest of the farm's location. Kenneth Kaufman said in *Dred Sott's Advocate* (p. 170) that after Alexander's death, James H. Lucas purchased three of his four slaves and his plantation known as California. The property once known as "California Farm" is distinctive and easy to locate on St. Louis County plat maps and atlases showing land ownership for two reasons. First, it was part of "Survey 101," a French land grant confirmed by William Campbell, so is always marked as "Sur [survey] 101 Wm Campbell." Second, the land in Survey 101 is situated at a different angle than some of the surrounding land, which was laid out on the rectangular survey system used by the U.S. federal government.

— *Julius Pitzman, Pitzman's New Atlas of the City and County of Saint Louis, Missouri, Constructed from Actual Surveys and Official Records by Julius Pitzman* (Reprint in CD-ROM format: 1878, St. Louis Genealogical Society, 2005), plate 63.

Dred and Harriet apparently did not accompany the Emersons to Davenport, which was in the Iowa Territory where slavery was prohibited.[59] Just three years earlier, in 1839, the Iowa Supreme Court, *In re Ralph* had declared that Ralph, a slave permitted by his owner to move to Iowa and work to buy freedom, was free. "Once permitted by his owner to establish a residence on Iowa soil he had become free, automatically emancipated by the Missouri Enabling Act."[60]

Whether Dr. Emerson knew about that court case or not, is unknown. That aside there was a financial consideration. Hiring Dred and Harriet out in St. Louis not only avoided the possible complications of their living in a free state; the slave couple's wages produced an income stream for the Emersons.

Dr. Emerson died in Davenport on 29 December 1843, when their newborn daughter, Henrietta, was about one month old.[61] He left his estate, including his slaves, to his widow, Irene, during her lifetime, and after her demise to his daughter.[62]

The widowed Irene and her infant daughter returned to live with her father, Alexander Sanford, in St. Louis County.[63] It is uncertain whether Dred, Harriet, and Eliza lived or worked at Sanford's farm, "California," but it is a possibility.

Dred and Harriet with Captain and Mrs. Bainbridge

In 1843, Irene's brother-in-law, Captain Henry Bainbridge, was transferred from Florida to Jefferson Barracks, south of the city of St. Louis.[64] Much had happened in Irene's life since she visited Mary and Henry Bainbridge at Fort Jesup where she met and married Dr. Emerson. Some time after Mary and Henry's arrival at Jefferson Barracks, Irene loaned or rented to them the services of Dred and Harriet.[65]

Established in 1826, Jefferson Barracks served as a major military installation and gathering point for troops and supplies in the Mexican and later wars. It was in St. Louis County, Missouri, ten miles south of the city of St. Louis and three miles south of the town of Carondelet. Its position on the west bank of the Mississippi River, about twenty miles south of the mouth of the Missouri River, provided excellent transportation for arriving and departing troops.[66]

Events in Texas were building toward the Mexican War. The army sent Captain Bainbridge back to Fort Jesup in 1844 and then into Texas in 1845.[67] In later years, Dred said he was with Captain Bainbridge at the beginning of the Mexican War, although no records confirm this.[68]

Dred may have been with Captain Bainbridge when the American troops gathered at Corpus Christi.[69] However, because court records resulting from his freedom suit show he was hired to Samuel Russell in St. Louis by March 1846, he must have left Corpus Christi before the Mexican War began in April 1846.[70] Whether Mary Bainbridge traveled to Fort Jesup with her husband or stayed at Jefferson Barracks is not known. Harriet and Eliza would probably have been with Mary.[71]

While at Jefferson Barracks with the Bainbridges, Dred and Harriet's second daughter was born.[72] Known as Lizzie to her family, records also list her as Elizabeth and Eliza.[73] Her birth date is uncertain, but if Lizzie was born at Jefferson Barracks, it was before Harriet and Dred left the Bainbridges and were hired out to Samuel Russell in March 1846.[74] That would make Lizzie, the youngest daughter, approximately eight years younger than her older sister, Eliza.

Harriet and Dred also had two sons who died young and their names and birth information are unknown. The boys were likely born sometime between 1838 and 1846 during the seven to eight years after Eliza's birth and before Lizzie's.[75]

Dred Offers To Buy Their Freedom

According to a newspaper interview with Dred, published in 1857, when he returned to St. Louis from Texas in the spring of 1846, he asked Irene Emerson, still living in St. Louis, if he could purchase his freedom and that of his wife and children.[76] He offered to

"... pay part of the money down, and give an eminent citizen of St. Louis, an officer in the army, as security for the payment of the remainder."[77] She refused and in March 1846 Dred and Harriet were hired out to Samuel Russell and his wife who had a grocery at 82 Water Street.[78]

Even though Irene would not allow them to buy their freedom, they had another option. Based on the Missouri State Supreme Court's interpretation in *Winny v. Phebe Whitesides*, they could sue for freedom based on their years of living in free territory.[79]

WINNY v. PHEBE WHITESIDES

In 1819, an enslaved woman named Winny sued her slave owner, Phebe Whitesides, for her freedom. The suit was based on Winny's residence with Whitesides in Illinois, a free state, prior to moving to Missouri.

After an 1822 jury trial in the St. Louis Circuit Court freed Winny, her owner appealed to the newly established Missouri Supreme Court. The court upheld Winny's freedom saying "... that if a slave owner brought a slave to Illinois and took up residence, the slave would be freed under the terms of the Northwest Ordinance, even if the slave were returned to slave territory."

— Robert Moore, "A Ray of Hope, Extinguished," *Gateway Heritage* 14 (1993–1994), 10.

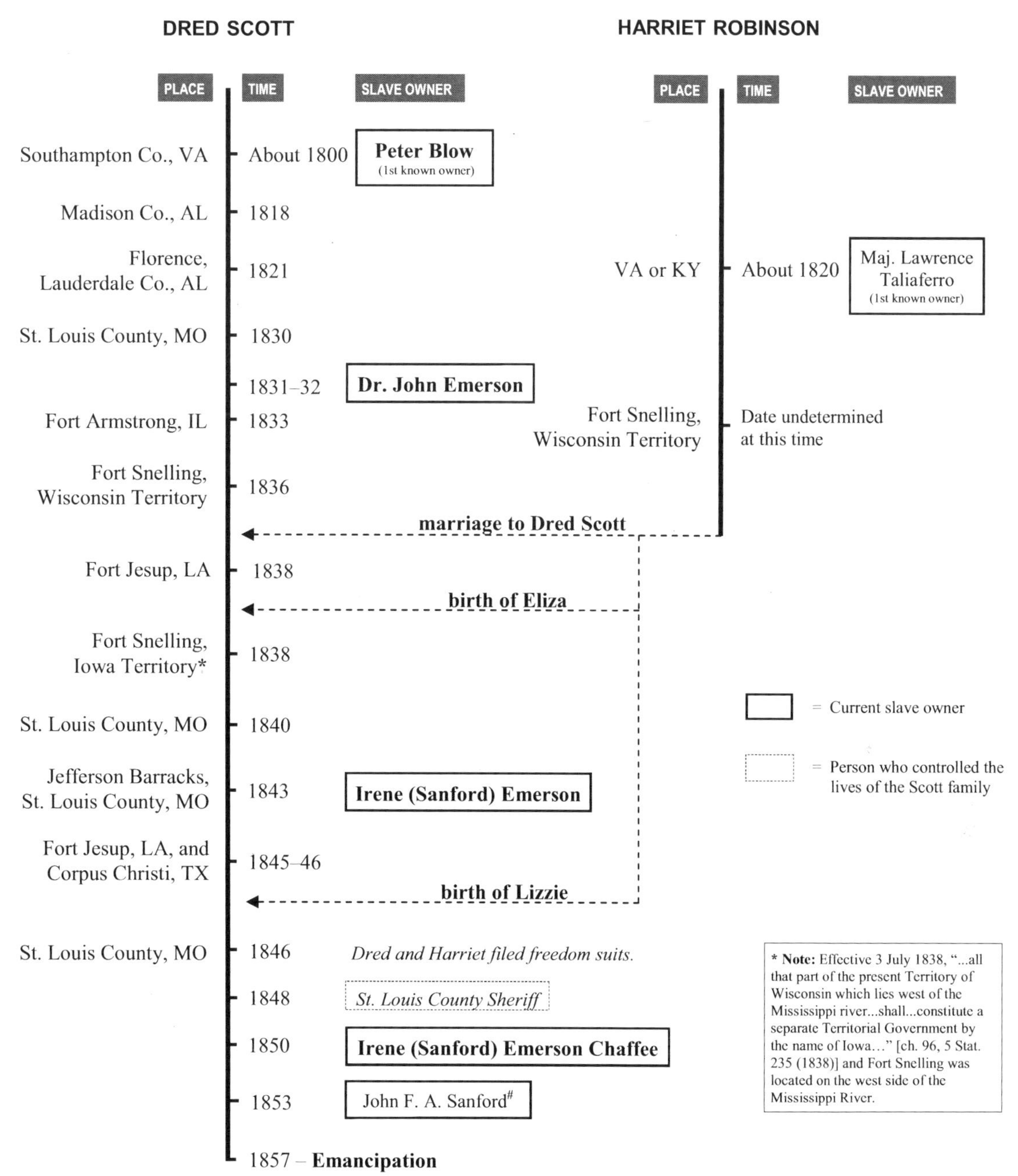

Dred and Harriet Scott's Slave Owners
DRED SCOTT
HARRIET ROBINSON
PLACE
TIME
SLAVE OWNER
Southampton Co., VA
About 1800
Peter Blow
(1st known owner)
Madison Co., AL
1818
Florence, Lauderdale Co., AL
1821
St. Louis County, MO
1830
1831–32
Dr. John Emerson
Fort Armstrong, IL
1833
Fort Snelling, Wisconsin Territory
1836
marriage to Dred Scott
Fort Jesup, LA
1838
birth of Eliza
Fort Snelling, Iowa Territory*
1838
St. Louis County, MO
1840
Jefferson Barracks, St. Louis County, MO
1843
Irene (Sanford) Emerson
Fort Jesup, LA, and Corpus Christi, TX
1845–46
birth of Lizzie
St. Louis County, MO
1846
Dred and Harriet filed freedom suits.
1848
St. Louis County Sheriff
1850
Irene (Sanford) Emerson Chaffee
1853
John F. A. Sanford#
1857 – Emancipation
VA or KY
About 1820
Maj. Lawrence Taliaferro
(1st known owner)
Fort Snelling, Wisconsin Territory
Date undetermined at this time
= Current slave owner
= Person who controlled the lives of the Scott family
* Note: Effective 3 July 1838, "...all that part of the present Territory of Wisconsin which lies west of the Mississippi river...shall...constitute a separate Territorial Government by the name of Iowa…" [ch. 96, 5 Stat. 235 (1838)] and Fort Snelling was located on the west side of the Mississippi River.
# Although John F. A. Sanford was the defendant in the U.S. Supreme Court case, Scott v Sandford, no evidence has been found showing that he owned the Scott family.

To the Hon. John M. Krum, Judge of the St Louis Circuit Court

The Petition of Harriet, a woman of color states, that she is claimed as a slave by one Irene Emerson, of the County of St Louis in the State of Missouri, widow of the late Dr John Emerson, surgeon in the United States army, now dec'd: That about eleven years ago, petitioner was brought from the State of Virginia, by one Major Talliaferro, and carried to Fort Snelling on the St Peters river in the territory of Iowa, that after living there, doing labor & service to the said Talliaferro, for about three years, he the said Talliaferro, sold your petitioner to the said Dr John Emerson, then also stationed at Fort Snelling, who kept and retained her there for about a year after he became the owner of her, part of the time in his own charge and part of the time in charge of Maj. Plimpton, and a Mrs Anderson; That afterwards said Emerson was ordered to Fort Jessup in Louisiana, and having married there, he had petitioner removed to that post from Fort Snelling. After remaining at Fort Jessup, about 6 months, the sd Emerson went back to Fort Snelling on the St Peters river in Iowa territory and took petitioner with him where she remained with him as a servant about a year longer, and from thence was brought to St Louis in the County aforesaid, where he left her in charge of his wife, while he proceeded to Florida. That said Emerson is now dead and his widow the said Irene, claims property in her as a slave, but believing, that under this state of facts, that she is entitled to freedom, she prays your honor to allow her to sue in said Court the said Irene Emerson in order to establish her right to freedom and she will pray &c.

Harriet her + mark of Color

Petition of "Harriet, a woman of color" to sue for her freedom.

SUING FOR FREEDOM
1846–1852

The view from the east steps of the St. Louis County courthouse included the Mississippi River and the flat lands of Illinois across the river. Standing on the east courthouse porch, four blocks from the river, visitors could see steamboats docked up and down the levee. St. Louis was a busy hub for steamboats loading and unloading passengers, livestock, dry goods, and other cargo. Beginning or ending their journeys in St. Louis, or just stopping along the way, boats made the St. Louis riverfront a busy place.

The courthouse played an important role in the lives of St. Louis residents. Men might go there to record land transactions or be naturalized as United States citizens. Other men, women, and children were sold as slaves on the courthouse steps by order of the court.

For much of their time in St. Louis, Dred and Harriet lived within a few blocks of the courthouse. For them, it was the starting point in their quest for freedom.

Filing Freedom Suits

On 6 April 1846, Dred and Harriet initiated separate freedom suits signing petitions with an "X" because they could not write. Each petition summarized "... the circumstances of their residence on free soil and requesting permission to bring suit against Irene Emerson in order to establish their right to freedom."[80] Their lawyer, Francis B. Murdoch, filed the petitions in the Missouri Circuit Court in St. Louis and the judge granted their petitions to sue for freedom.[81]

> **ST. LOUIS COURTHOUSE**
>
> The citizens of St. Louis built their first courthouse in 1828 on a hilltop four blocks west of the Mississippi River. Land for the courthouse was donated by Auguste Chouteau, a founding father of St. Louis, and Judge John B. Lucas. The population of St. Louis grew quickly and in 1839, construction was begun on a new and larger courthouse on the same city block of land, right beside the existing courthouse. Construction continued for twenty-three years and was mostly complete by 1862.
>
> — Donald F. Dosch, *The Old Courthouse* (St. Louis, Missouri: Jefferson National Expansion Historical Association, 1979), 18, 52.

Dred had lived as Dr. John Emerson's slave at Fort Armstrong, in Rock Island, Illinois, and at Fort Snelling, in Wisconsin Territory. That was the basis of his suit.[82] The Illinois constitution outlawed slavery.[83] The Wisconsin Territory was formed from the Northwest Territory, which outlawed slavery by the 1787 Northwest Ordinance.[84]

Harriet based her suit on her time at Fort Snelling in Wisconsin Territory, as the slave of Major Taliaferro.[85] Both contended that living where slavery was illegal made them free. Their time in free territory was unquestionable. Legally there was no reason their suits should not succeed, yet suing their slave owner must have been daunting and frightening for them.[86]

Beyond wanting freedom for its own sake, Dred and Harriet's suits were a way to protect their children and keep their family together. As slaves, any of them could be sold at any moment. Their youngest daughter, Lizzie, was born about the time the Scotts filed their freedom suits. Her birth may have influenced their decision to initiate their suits then. Proximity to the courthouse and contact with lawyers willing to take their case might also have affected the timing.

SLAVERY INHERITED FROM THE MOTHER

Harriet's suit for freedom was vital for the future of her daughters because, in the U. S., slavery was hereditary through the mother. This was based upon the principle of *partus sequitur vetrum,* which translates to "what is born follows the womb."* If the mother was a slave at the moment of birth, the child was also a slave; if the mother was free when she gave birth to a child, then that child was also free.

Harriet gave birth to both Eliza and Lizzie after she lived at Fort Snelling in free territory and, according to her freedom suit, had earned her freedom. Because of that, the girls' status as slave or free depended on the outcome of Harriet's suit.

— *Robert Moore Jr., "A Ray of Hope, Extinguished: St. Louis Slave Suits for Freedom," *Gateway Heritage*, 14 (1993–94): 9.

— George M. Stroud, *A Sketch of the Laws Relating to Slavery in the Several States of the United States of America with Some Alterations and Considerable Additions* (Philadelphia: No publisher, 1856), 96; digital images, *Google Book Search* (http://books.google.com).

Murdoch carried out another important action on behalf of Dred and Harriet; he signed a bond required by law "... accepting responsibility for costs that might accrue in the case."[87] Without bonds, their suits could not have gone forward. Although Murdoch's help early on was critical, it was also short lived. In 1847 he moved to California.[88]

After Murdoch's departure Charles Drake (the Blows' brother-in-law) became their attorney. He took important testimony from Samuel Russell regarding hiring out Dred and Harriet. Drake then moved to Cincinnati in May or early June of 1847, so Dred and Harriet had to find yet another attorney. This time, Samuel Mansfield Bay took their case. It was Bay who finally represented them when the case was heard on 30 June 1847.[89]

Dred and Harriet's hopes for a quick, favorable decision were dashed when they lost their case on a technicality. Bay used Samuel Russell's testimony, but it did not hold up in court. Questioning revealed that Russell had not actually hired the Scotts. His wife had hired them—and she had given no testimony. Bay requested a new trial, which Judge Alexander Hamilton of the Missouri Circuit Court granted on 2 December 1847.[90]

RACHEL v. WALKER

Dred and Harriet may have had confidence they would win their freedom suits because of the case of *Rachel v. Walker*, which was very similar to their own situation. Rachel had been held as the slave of Stockton, an Army officer, at St. Peters [close to Fort Snelling], while he was assigned to Fort Snelling for a year. He later sold Rachel and her son to William Walker in St. Louis. She sued for freedom in 1834, based on her residence at St. Peters where slavery was outlawed by the 1787 Northwest Ordinance. She lost her initial case but appealed to the Missouri Supreme Court where she won freedom for herself and her son.

— "Before Dred Scott: Freedom Suits in Antebellum Missouri, *Rachel v. William Walker* (1836)," *Missouri State Archives* (http://www.sos.mo.gov/archives/education/aahi/beforedredscott/rachelV.asp).

Changes for Dred and Harriet

Before Dred and Harriet's case came to trial, a significant change occurred in their lives. As had happened with the sale of Dred's first wife, and his own sale to Dr. Emerson, difficulties in the slave-owning family affected their slaves' lives. This time, the death of Irene Emerson's father, Alexander Sanford, in February 1848 altered the lives of Dred, Harriet, and their daughters.[91]

Irene and her daughter had lived with her father since John Emerson left her widowed in 1843. After her father's death, Irene's brother John sold the farm "California" to settle his father's debts.[92] Irene lost her home, and apparently received nothing from her father's estate.[93]

Evidently the death of Irene's father left her next closest male relative, her brother John F. A. Sanford, in charge of the Scott family's suit. By 1848 John lived in New York City representing the business interests of Chouteau and Sanford, but he visited St. Louis regularly on business.[94]

Irene needed to find a new home. Her older sister and brother-in-law, Charlotte and James Barnes, lived in Springfield, Massachusetts, and she could go there.[95] However, she could not take her slaves to a free state. Neither could she likely sell slaves with freedom suits in progress, which they were likely to win in the near future. If and when that happened, their owners would lose a significant investment.

Just one month after her father's death, Irene's lawyers filed a motion on 14 March 1848 for the St. Louis County sheriff to take custody of Dred and Harriet.[96] Judge Hamilton granted the motion, and the sheriff assumed custody of the couple, and presumably their daughters.[97] This solved Irene's dilemma. Her slaves could continue to be hired out, and the sheriff would be responsible for them and would hold their wages pending the outcome of the suits.[98]

In the Sheriff's Custody

When the sheriff had custody of a slave suing for freedom, he usually housed the slave in the county jail whenever he or she was not hired out.[99] No mention of this happening to Dred, Harriet, and their daughters has been found. However, since it was established procedure, it seems likely they spent some time in the county jail.

For unknown reasons, in March 1848, Dred and Harriet had yet another change in lawyers. Alexander P. Field and David N. Hall, who had worked with Samuel Bay on the Scott's case for awhile, became their only lawyers.[100]

Initially placed on the docket for February 1849 their retrial was moved to May 1849. It was delayed again partly because of catastrophic events in St. Louis that spring. In May 1849, fire broke out on a steamboat on the waterfront and spread, engulfing other boats and destroying a large section of the city. Fortunately, the courthouse survived the fire. Cholera struck in St. Louis in early 1849, and with the arrival of warmer weather in late May, the death toll from the disease increased significantly. By the end of the month, it claimed the lives of 539 people. Cholera accounted for 1,820 deaths in June and 1,917 in August.[101] Some residents fled the city and some rural county residents refused to enter the city—even for court.[102]

Although it is uncertain where Dred, Harriet, and their daughters lived during the fire and cholera epidemic of 1849, records indicate to whom Dred was hired during that crucial time. According to a sworn statement, St. Louis County Sheriff Louis LaBeaume hired Dred's services to his attorney, David N. Hall, for $5 per month. His service began on 17 March 1849, and ended when the attorney died in March 1851.[103]

Hall likely had Dred clean either the law office he shared with his law partner, Alexander P. Field, or his residence. In 1848 Hall's office was at the corner of Third and Pine streets and he lived at 176 Market.[104] Although no 1849 city directory was published, Dred probably lived within walking distance of his work place, so he likely lived in the city of St. Louis. The person to whom Harriet was hired is unknown, but Dred, Harriet, Eliza, and Lizzie safely survived the fire and the cholera epidemic.

FREEDOM SUITS

Freedom suits were neither new nor out of the ordinary in St. Louis. Between 1814 and 1860, people held in slavery filed at least 300 legal petitions for freedom in St. Louis courts. Of those, less than half won their suits.

— "Freedom Suits," Jefferson National Expansion Memorial, *National Park Service* (http://www.nps.gov/jeff/historyculture/freedom-suits.htm).

Dred and Harriet's retrial, moved to December 1849, was finally called on 12 January 1850.[105] This time with the needed testimony from Mrs. Russell, the jury found in favor of Dred and Harriet and declared them free—at least on paper.[106] Many slave owners would have accepted the St. Louis Circuit Court decision, but that did not happen in this case.

On 5 June 1850, Chouteau and Company paid $69 to satisfy court costs for the two 12 January 1850 judgments against Irene Emerson, Dred's suit and Harriet's suit.[107] Pierre Chouteau Jr., was the business partner and former father-in-law of John F. A. Sanford, who was handling Irene's legal affairs related to the Scott's suits.[108] A powerful and influential member of the St. Louis founding family, Chouteau adamantly supported slavery.

From a slave owner's viewpoint, freedom suits were bad business. They cost legal fees, time in court, public embarrassment of being sued by one's slave, and after all that, the possible loss of a valuable asset—the slave. Furthermore, freedom suits challenged their rights as slave owners.

Missouri Supreme Court

On 14 February 1850, one month after a jury found the Scotts free, Irene's lawyers appealed her case to the Missouri Supreme Court.[109] Irene's appeal meant that freedom for the Scott family was on paper, but did not change their personal lives for the better. They remained in the sheriff's custody. However, one legal change did take place. The attorneys and the court combined the Scott's lawsuits into a single case, *Dred Scott v. Emerson.* The decision in Dred's case would apply to Harriet and their daughters.[110]

Combining the suits almost hid Harriet's role as an equal partner in their legal battle for freedom. The original St. Louis Circuit Court documents, though, confirm that Harriet filed her own freedom suit on 6 April 1846 as "Harriet, a woman of color."[111]

Ten months after lawyers appealed her case to the Missouri Supreme Court, Irene married her second husband, Dr. Calvin Chaffee, on 21 November 1850 in Springfield, Massachusetts.[112] Chaffee held strong beliefs about the evils of slavery.[113] Evidently he did not know Irene owned slaves and that her lawyers in St. Louis were working so she could continue holding Dred, Harriet, and their daughters in slavery. Irene's second marriage was crucially important to the Scott family because, ironically, it was Dr. Chaffee's entrance into this drama that later set into motion events leading to emancipation for Dred, Harriet, Eliza, and Lizzie.

For the Scott family, who may have been assured of an easy victory by their attorneys when their cases were filed in 1846, the tension must have grown with each passing month. Though the jury had declared them free, their status had not changed because the case was under appeal.

At last, on 22 March 1852, the Missouri State Supreme Court announced its decision in *Scott v. Emerson,* finding in favor of Irene Emerson. It said that when Dred Scott voluntarily returned to Missouri from free territory, Missouri law applied, and he was once again a slave.[114]

Missouri Supreme Court Justice William Scott's Opinion of the Court explained the reversal of the court's previous "once free, always free" reasoning. He said "Times now are not as they were, when the former decisions on this subject were made."[115] This decision returned Dred, Harriet, and their daughters to slavery.

Following the Missouri Supreme Court decision in Irene's favor, the St. Louis Circuit Court would ordinarily have handed Irene custody of the Scott family, along with their wages held by the St. Louis County Sheriff. Irene's lawyers filed a motion to do just that—end the sheriff's custody

PIERRE CHOUTEAU JR.

Pierre Chouteau Jr. was one of the most powerful men in St. Louis. When he ran for election as a delegate to Missouri's first constitutional convention in 1820, he placed a notice in the *Missouri Gazette* saying "Should I be elected a member of the convention, any attempts to prevent the introduction of slaves, or any other species of property (lawfully held in any other state of the nation) into the state of Missouri, will meet my warmest opposition."

Chouteau had owned seven part-Indian slaves, members of the Scypion family, who had tried but failed to legally gain their freedom from a prior slave owner. In 1825, they sought their freedom from Pierre Chouteau Jr. because the law no longer allowed Indians to be held as slaves. Although he hired a team of St. Louis lawyers to defend his ownership, he lost the case. He appealed the decision to the U.S. Supreme Court and was unsuccessful when that court ruled that it lacked jurisdiction. Although Chouteau had no further legal recourse, he was a proud man, and it is unlikely that he forgot the experience.

Including the Scypion family, people enslaved by Pierre Chouteau Jr. or other individuals with the Chouteau surname, initiated a total of eleven freedom suits against their slave owners between 1821 and 1845. Of those eleven suits, the Chouteau family member won three court cases and lost six others. The results of two are unknown.

If Chouteau gave advice to John Sanford regarding Irene's legal affairs, based on Chouteau's outspoken attitude towards slavery, his personal experience with slaves suing for freedom, and his actions as a power broker in St. Louis events, it seems likely that he advised Sanford to pursue the suit until he won it.

— Shirley Christian, *Before Lewis and Clark: The Story of the Chouteaus, the French Dynasty That Ruled Amercia's Frontier* (New York: Farrar, Straus and Giroux, 2004), 233, 245–247.

— "Suits for Freedom, St. Louis, 1804–1865," *National Park Service, U.S. Department of the Interior, Jefferson National Expansion Memorial* (http://www.nps.gov/jeff/historyculture/people.htm). [African-American Life in St. Louis, 1804–1865.]

of the Scott family and reclaim their wages—but Judge Alexander Hamilton denied it. Judge Hamilton's atypical decision preserved the Scott family intact for the moment. An 1854 court notation records the case as "continued by consent, awaiting decision of Supreme Court of the United States."[116]

Reestablishing custody would have allowed Irene to sell Dred, Harriet, or their daughters. That may have been her intention because she no longer had family in St. Louis who could arrange to hire out Dred and Harriet and collect their wages; she could not bring them to Massachusetts where slavery was illegal; and she probably did not want her husband who opposed slavery to know about them.

ST. LOUIS CIRCUIT COURT FREEDOM SUITS INVOLING A CHOUTEAU FAMILY MEMBER		
Court Sesstion	Case	Freedom Won: Yes, No or Unknown
April 1821	*Marie v. Auguste P. Chouteau*	Yes
February 1824	*Ellen Chevalier (deceased) v. Pierre Chouteau*	Yes
July 1825	*Marguerite v. Pierre Chouteau Sr.*	Yes
March 1827	*Francois La Grange alias Isador v. B. Pratt and Chouteau*	No
July 1827	*Theotiste alias Catiche v. Pierre Chouteau Jr. and C. J. Hempstead*	Unknown
March 1828	*Aspasia v. Francois Chouteau and Pierre Menard*	Yes
11 February 1834	*Charles v. Pierre Chouteau*	Unknown
16 July 1835	*Sally v. Henry Chouteau*	Yes
November 1842	*Pierre v. Gabriel Chouteau*	No
April 1844	*Louis Chouteau v. Gabriel S. Chouteau*	Yes
24 May 1845	*Mary Charlotte v. Gabriel Chouteau*	No
Data extracted from "Suits for Freedom. St. Louis, 1804–1865," compiled by staff of the Missouri State Archives, available on the Jefferson National Expansion Memorial website.		

Courtesy of National Park Service, Jefferson National Expansion Memorial

Lizzie and Eliza Scott, ca 1857.

PROTECTING THEIR DAUGHTERS
1852–1857

Until Dred and Harriet's cases, including appeals, were finally settled, they could not be sold. Beyond legal restraints though, the mere existence of their suits or the possibility of further appeals challenged Irene's clear title of ownership. Few would risk buying a slave under such circumstances.

In later years, a story in the 3 April 1857 issue of the *St. Louis Republican* said Irene Chaffee had "… offered to Dred Scott his own freedom if he would buy it with the slavery of his daughters & the discontinuance of his suit."[117] The story did not indicate when that might have occurred, and no evidence has been found to support or disprove the story.

After the 1852 Missouri Supreme Court's decision against Dred, the Scott family had one last protection from sale. They were still in the sheriff's custody because Judge Hamilton had denied Irene's request to reclaim them. Nevertheless, the possibility of one or both of the girls being sold lingered. By 1852, Eliza was about thirteen or fourteen years old and female slaves of child-bearing age commanded higher prices. If she or Lizzie were intentionally sold quickly, and transported elsewhere, the possibility of Dred and Harriet ever seeing them again would not be good.

Sending Their Daughters Into Hiding

After their suits failed in Missouri, Dred and Harriet had another way to protect Eliza and Lizzie. They sent the girls into hiding "while the decision of Dred's position was in doubt …"[118]

What little information exists about the girls' time in hiding did not emerge until after the Dred Scott decision in 1857 when interest was high and many newspapers ran articles. The *St. Louis Daily Evening News* published an article, dated 3 April 1857, stating that Eliza and Lizzie "... took advantage of the absence of restraint on their movements, a year or two since, to disappear, and their whereabouts remains a mystery."[119] Other newspapers beyond Missouri later duplicated the information, or a variation of it.

Eliza and Lizzie likely went into hiding sometime between 1852 and 1856 when the risk of being sold was greatest. In 1852, the Missouri Supreme Court had confirmed the Scotts as slaves; by 1856, Dred's suit was before the U.S. Supreme Court. All expected a relatively quick decision, and chances of the Scott family winning freedom did not look good.[120]

The identity of those who hid the Scott daughters, and their location while in hiding, are unsolved mysteries. Many runaway slaves sought safe havens in northern states, or possibly in Canada. Either might have held safety for Eliza and Lizzie. However, they might also have been closer to home, maybe even in St. Louis.

An article in the *St. Louis Daily Evening News* on 26 May 1857—the day of emancipation for the Scott family—said of Eliza and Lizzie that "Their father knew where they were, and could bring them back at any moment. He will doubtless recall them now."[121] That suggests Dred had some communication with his daughters or their protectors.

If the girls went into hiding sometime between 1852 and 1856, Lizzie would have been at the time between six and ten years old and Eliza between fourteen and eighteen. While Eliza probably understood much of what was happening and what she needed to do, the situation must have been quite confusing for young Lizzie.

Eliza and Lizzie's safety, and that of those hiding them, depended upon the girl's ability to be silent and as invisible as possible. If they were seen at all, Eliza's appearance in a new household might have been easier to explain than Lizzie's. A teenager, Eliza could pass as extra help. However, the presence of Lizzie, eight years younger, might raise questions. Possibly the sisters—one or both—were hidden so they rarely, or never, saw the light of day.

Isolating the girls from anyone they knew, and even from each other, would have been one way to prevent their saying anything to betray their parent's identities. Whether Eliza and Lizzie lived in the same household, or in the same community, the experience of going into hiding apparently traumatized young Lizzie.

Behavior patterns Lizzie may have learned in hiding—telling no one who she really was, drawing no attention to herself, fading into the background as much as possible, making no friends who might want to know something about her—defined how she would live the rest of her life.

While sending the girls into hiding must have been difficult for Dred and Harriet, it also protected the girls' possible freedom—regardless of the outcome of Dred's case. If Dred were to win his case and the family declared free, Eliza and Lizzie could return home and live with their parents as free persons of color. If Dred were to lose the case, and he and Harriet remained enslaved, Eliza and Lizzie could remain free as long as the law or slave catchers did not find them. The price of freedom in that case would be the girls' permanent separation from their parents.

WHICH DAUGHTER IS ELIZA AND WHICH IS LIZZIE?

Both Eliza and Lizzie's names are variations of the name Elizabeth, which has caused tremendous confusion. However, their parents may have had little or no control over the names of their children. Dr. Emerson's wife's name was Eliza Irene and that may have influenced what Dred and Harriet named their daughters.

Following Eliza and Lizzie's life stories is challenging because records exist for each of the daughters under the three names of Elizabeth, Lizzie, and Eliza. Therefore, a name alone does not define which daughter was being discussed. To decide which daughter a record describes, supporting information such as her age, occupation, household occupants, location of the home, and with whom she was living must also be considered.

The time span between their ages is the element that most clearly defines one daughter from the other. Three documents contain information on both girls, including their ages. Together these records provide an estimate of the difference in their ages, even though they do not agree on the exact number of years.

- The 1854 "Agreed Statement of Facts" listed Eliza as fourteen (born about 1840) and Lizzie as seven (born about 1847) and showed a difference of about seven years between the sisters.
  [The attorneys representing Dred Scott and John F. A. Sanford agreed upon certain facts in 1854 and filed the resulting "Agreed Statement of Facts" document in the St. Louis Circuit Court. While both sides accepted these facts, this does not mean they were proven facts.]

  — Walter Ehrlich, *They Have No Rights: Dred Scott's Struggle for Freedom (*1979; reprint, Bedford, Massachusetts: Applewood Books, 2007*)*, 189.

- The 1857 "Writ of Emancipation" listed Eliza as nineteen (born about 1838) and Lizzie as ten (born about 1847), which showed an age difference of about nine years between the sisters.
  [This document, filed by Taylor Blow in the St. Louis Circuit Court in 1857, freed the Scott family.]

  — "The Revised Dred Scott Collection," *Washington University* (http://digital.wustl.edu/d/dre). [Use search term "Taylor Blow."]

- The 1860 U.S. census for St. Louis showed Eliza [listed as Elizabeth] living with her husband, Wilson "Maddison," as being twenty-one (born about 1839). A few houses away, that census showed Lizzie [listed as Elizabeth] in her mother's household as being fifteen (born about 1845). In this record, there was a difference of about six years between the sisters.

  — To view these two census records, side-by-side, see Appendix B.

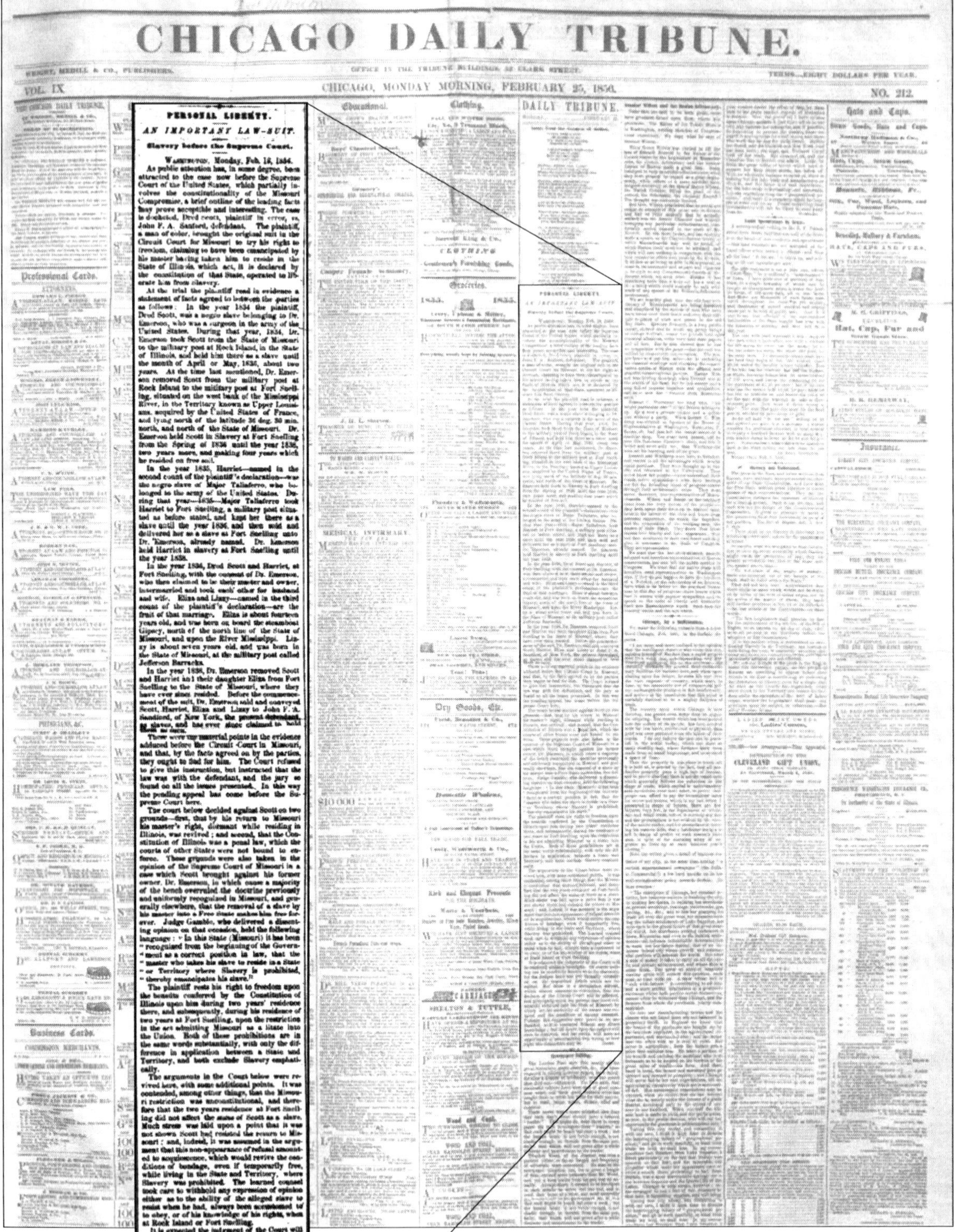

CHICAGO DAILY TRIBUNE.

VOL. IX. CHICAGO, MONDAY MORNING, FEBRUARY 25, 1856. NO. 212.

PERSONAL LIBERTY.

AN IMPORTANT LAW-SUIT.

Slavery before the Supreme Court.

WASHINGTON, Monday, Feb. 18, 1856.

As public attention has, in some degree, been attracted to the case now before the Supreme Court of the United States, which partially involves the constitutionality of the Missouri Compromise, a brief outline of the leading facts may prove acceptible and interesting. The case is docketed, Dred Scott, plaintiff in error, vs. John F. A. Sanford, defendant. The plaintiff, a man of color, brought the original suit in the Circuit Court for Missouri to try his right to freedom, claiming to have been emancipated by his master having taken him to reside in the State of Illinois, which act, it is declared by the constitution of that State, operated to liberate him from slavery.

At the trial the plaintiff read in evidence a statement of facts agreed to between the parties as follows: In the year 1834 the plaintiff, Dred Scott, was a negro slave belonging to Dr. Emerson, who was a surgeon in the army of the United States. During that year, 1834, Dr. Emerson took Scott from the State of Missouri to the military post at Rock Island, in the State of Illinois, and held him there as a slave until the month of April or May, 1836, about two years. At the time last mentioned, Dr. Emerson removed Scott from the military post at Rock Island to the military post at Fort Snelling, situated on the west bank of the Mississippi River, in the Territory known as Upper Louisiana, acquired by the United States of France, and lying north of the latitude 36 deg. 30 min. north, and north of the State of Missouri. Dr. Emerson held Scott in Slavery at Fort Snelling from the Spring of 1836 until the year 1838, two years more, and making four years which he resided on free soil.

In the year 1835, Harriet—named in the second count of the plaintiff's declaration—was the negro slave of Major Taliaferro, who belonged to the army of the United States. During that year—1835—Major Taliaferro took Harriet to Fort Snelling, a military post situated as before stated, and kept her there as a slave until the year 1836, and then sold and delivered her as a slave at Fort Snelling unto Dr. Emerson, already named. Dr. Emerson held Harriet in slavery at Fort Snelling until the year 1838.

In the year 1836, Dred Scott and Harriet, at Fort Snelling, with the consent of Dr. Emerson, who then claimed to be their master and owner, intermarried and took each other for husband and wife. Eliza and Lizzy—named in the third count of the plaintiff's declaration—are the fruit of that marriage. Eliza is about fourteen years old, and was born on board the steamboat Gipsey, north of the north line of the State of Missouri, and upon the River Mississippi. Lizzy is about seven years old, and was born in the State of Missouri, at the military post called Jefferson Barracks.

In the year 1838, Dr. Emerson removed Scott and Harriet and their daughter Eliza from Fort Snelling to the State of Missouri, where they have ever since resided. Before the commencement of the suit, Dr. Emerson sold and conveyed Scott, Harriet, Eliza and Lizzy to John F. A. Sandford, of New York, the present defendant, as slaves, and has ever since claimed to hold them as such.

These were the material points in the evidence adduced before the Circuit Court in Missouri, and that, by the facts agreed on by the parties, they ought to find for him. The Court refused to give this instruction, but instructed that the law was with the defendant, and the jury so found on all the issues presented. In this way the pending appeal has come before the Supreme Court here.

The court below decided against Scott on two grounds—first, that by his return to Missouri his master's right, dormant while residing in Illinois, was revived; and second, that the Constitution of Illinois was a penal law, which the courts of other States were not bound to enforce. These grounds were also taken in the opinion of the Supreme Court of Missouri in a case which Scott brought against his former owner, Dr. Emerson, in which cause a majority of the bench overruled the doctrine previously and uniformly recognized in Missouri, and generally elsewhere, that the removal of a slave by his master into a Free State makes him free forever. Judge Gamble, who delivered a dissenting opinion on that occasion, held the following language: "In this State (Missouri) it has been "recognized from the beginning of the Govern-"ment as a correct position in law, that the "master who takes his slave to reside in a State "or Territory where Slavery is prohibited, "thereby emancipates his slave."

The plaintiff rests his right to freedom upon the benefits conferred by the Constitution of Illinois upon him during two years' residence there, and subsequently, during his residence of two years at Fort Snelling, upon the restriction in the act admitting Missouri as a State into the Union. Both of these prohibitions are in the same words substantially, with only the difference in application between a State and Territory, and both exclude Slavery emphatically.

The arguments in the Court below were revived here, with some additional points. It was contended, among other things, that the Missouri restriction was unconstitutional, and therefore that the two years residence at Fort Snelling did not affect the status of Scott as a slave. Much stress was laid upon a point that it was not shown Scott had resisted the return to Missouri; and, indeed, it was assumed in the argument that this non-appearance of refusal amounted to acquiescence, which would revive the conditions of bondage, even if temporarily free, while living in the State and Territory, where Slavery was prohibited. The learned counsel took care to withhold any expression of opinion either as to the ability of the alleged slave to resist when he had, always been accustomed to obey, or of his knowledge of his rights, when at Rock Island or Fort Snelling.

It is expected the judgment of the Court will be rendered within a fortnight. Of course nothing can be positively known as to its character, for the Judges have not yet formally consulted on the important points which are involved. But there is a speculation abroad, which almost amounts to conviction, that the decision of the Circuit Court will be affirmed, and principally upon the reason that Scott voluntarily returned into the State of Missouri, by which act the authority of the owner was restored and the condition of slavery resumed. Perhaps this suggestion may prove to be unfounded, as it is ventured without any direct knowledge; but all doubt upon the subject will soon be removed, and the public will have an opportunity of ascertaining how wrong or how right this conjecture may be.

INDEX.

Dred Scott's case Scott v. Sandford *became national news by February of 1856.*

A NEW SUIT IN FEDERAL COURT
1853–1857

After the shocking reversal by the Missouri Supreme Court, influenced by politics and the increasing arguments over slavery, Dred and Harriet's efforts for freedom had little chance of success. Their case was no longer about their right to be free; it represented a major national issue.

Dred received support with his freedom suit from Blow family members, in-laws, and associates.[122] Over the years, needed bonds were signed by Taylor Blow, Henry T. Blow, Joseph Charless, Louis T. LaBeaume, and Charles Edmund LaBeaume.[123] His attorney at one point was Charles Drake, husband of Martha Blow.

After the Missouri Supreme Court decision, Dred needed help at the federal level. Charles Edmund LaBeaume, an attorney and Peter E. Blow's brother-in-law, contacted St. Louis attorney Roswell Field. The issues, which Dred's case represented, were of major importance to the country, and Field agreed to work on the case at no charge.[124]

Filing a New Suit

On 2 November 1853, Dred's lawyer, Roswell Field, brought suit in federal court in St. Louis against Irene's brother, John Sanford.[125] In this new suit Field accused Sanford, "a citizen of the state of New York," of illegally assaulting, holding, and imprisoning Dred Scott, "a citizen of Missouri," Harriet Scott, and their daughters Eliza and Lizzie.[126]

Photo by T. C. Farnam Courtesy of Eugene Field House and St. Louis Toy Museum, St. Louis

Roswell Field

Whether this suit was against John Sanford because he had purchased Dred and his family, because he was acting on Irene's behalf as her brother, or because he was an executor of Dr. Emerson's estate is unclear. However, Roswell Field could file the case in federal court because the two parties involved, Sanford and Dred, were from different states.

ROSWELL FIELD

Roswell M. Field, born in Newfane, Vermont, on 22 February 1807 graduated from Middlebury College at the age of fifteen. As a student, he mastered Latin and Greek and later learned French, Spanish, and German. His father, Martin Field, was a lawyer, and Roswell followed in his footsteps. Roswell was admitted to the bar as a lawyer in Vermont in 1825 at the age of eighteen. In 1839, he moved to St. Louis and by 1842, the *St. Louis City Directory* listed him as an attorney at 42 Chestnut Street.

Roswell Field was also the father of Eugene Field, the beloved American children's poet who wrote such classics as "Little Boy Blue," "The Duel" (The Gingham Dog and the Calico Cat), and "Wynken, Blynken, and Nod."

— Kenneth C. Kaufman, *Dred Scott's Advocate: A Biography of Roswell M. Field* (Columbia, Missouri: University of Missouri Press, 1996), 14, 27, 30, 35, 94.

— *The Saint Louis Directory for the year 1842*; microfilm reprint, *United States City Directories through 1860, St. Louis, Missouri*, fiche 1334: 1, 1842 (No place: no publisher, no date), 44.

As expected, Dred lost the case because the judge's instructions to the jury were based upon the findings of the Missouri Supreme Court: Dred's slavery was dormant while in free territory, but revived when he returned to Missouri.[127] Because Dred lost this new suit, his attorney could appeal the case to the U.S. Supreme Court, and that is what Field did on his behalf.[128]

While this new suit in the U.S. Circuit Court continued the Scotts' efforts to secure their freedom, there were some important differences from Dred and Harriet's original freedom suits. When they initially sued in 1846, they did so as individuals. Dred and Harriet each had a separate suit and there was no indication that they were husband and wife. Her initial petition to sue described Harriet only as "... Harriet, a woman of color ..."[129] Their 1853 U.S. Circuit Court suit acknowledged them as a family. It listed Harriet as "Harriet Scott, then and still the wife of the plaintiff." The suit further recorded Eliza and Lizzie by their full names, Eliza Scott and "Lizzy" Scott, and listed them as "... daughters of Dred and Harriet Scott."[130]

Montgomery Blair—Attorney

Dred's cause next needed an attorney who had experience pleading cases before the U.S. Supreme Court. To fill that role, Field asked Montgomery Blair, a resident of Washington, D.C., and former resident of St. Louis, to argue Dred's case before the Supreme Court.[131]

Courtesy of Prints and Photographs Division, Library of Congress, Washington, D.C.

Montgomery Blair

Blair, a more experienced attorney than Field, had moved to the nation's capital by 1853. He had the needed experience and his family had powerful connections. Blair agreed to take Dred's case and waive his legal fees. Gamaliel Bailey, editor of the antislavery newspaper, the *National Era*, agreed to raise money for court costs and other expenses.[132]

U.S. Supreme Court

When the case went to the U.S. Supreme Court, the clerk spelled John Sanford's last name as "Sandford," a common spelling variation for Sanford, so the case was titled *Dred Scott v. Sandford.*[133]

On 11 February 1856, arguments began in the case of *Scott v. Sandford* before the U.S. Supreme Court with Montgomery Blair arguing Dred's case. Two days later on 13 February 1856, newspapers beyond Washington, D.C. began to report on the case.[134] It was not until 6 March 1857, more than a year later, that the court handed down its decision.

Read from the bench by Chief Justice Roger Taney, the decision went beyond denying Dred, Harriet, Eliza, and Lizzie their freedom. It also said that no person of African descent could be a citizen of the U.S. It nullified the Missouri Compromise and said that Congress did not have the right to keep slavery out of the territories.[135] This outraged the opponents of slavery and divided the country on the question of slavery even more.

MONTGOMERY BLAIR

Born in Kentucky, the son of a slave owner, Montgomery Blair supported emancipation, but only if it was tied to colonizing freed African Americans outside the United States to Central or South America. His support of the Scott's claim to freedom was not about abolition and human rights.

When Montgomery Blair worked with Dred's case, he lived in a house owned by his parents, Francis Preston and Eliza (Gist) Blair, which was across the street from the White House. It is now known as Blair House, the official guest house of the President of the United States.

— "Blair, Francis Preston, "*American National Biography Online* (http://www.anb.org).

— "Blair, Montgomery," *American National Biography Online.*

— Leon F. Litwack, *North of Slavery: The Negro in the Free States, 1790–1860* (Chicago, University of Chicago Press, 1961), 272.

Dred and Harriet's eleven years of legal efforts to be free to live their lives as a family had ended in failure. What would happen to them?

One Last Possibility

Dred's lawyers had exhausted all court enforced avenues for freedom. However, there was one other way for the Scott family to obtain freedom—and it was legal.

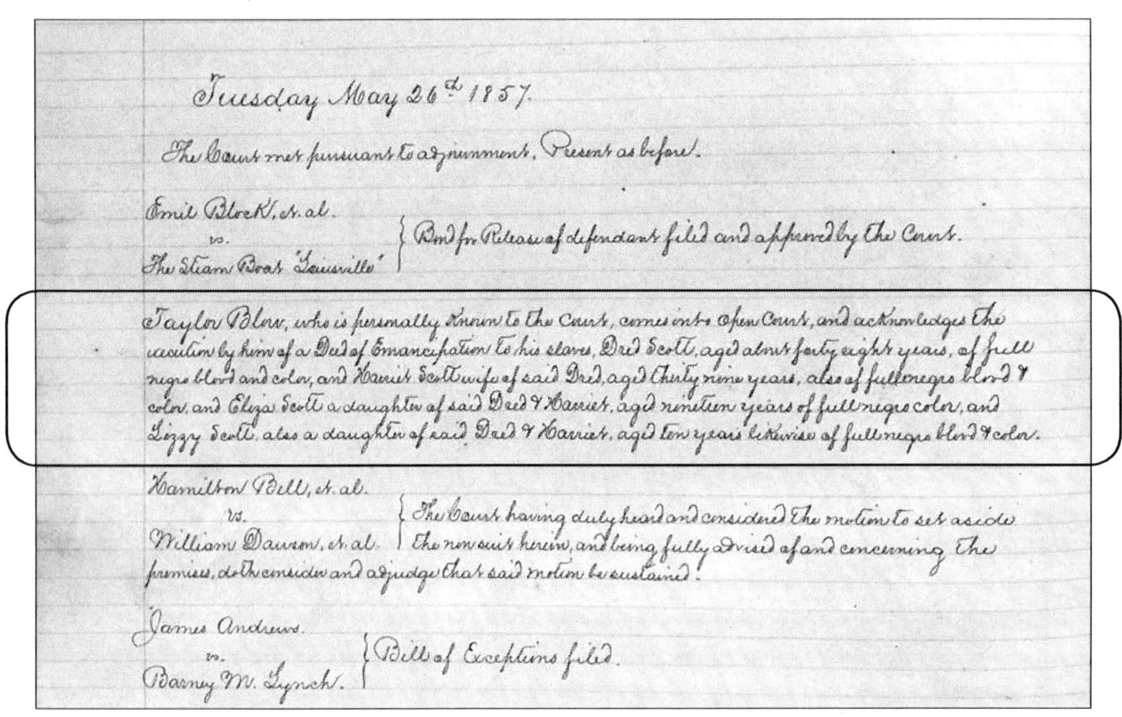

Tuesday May 26th 1857.

The Court met pursuant to adjournment. Present as before.

Emil Block, et. al.
vs.
The Steam Boat "Louisville" } Bond for Release of defendant filed and approved by the Court.

Taylor Blow, who is personally known to the Court, comes into open Court, and acknowledges the execution by him of a Deed of Emancipation to his slaves, Dred Scott, aged about forty eight years, of full negro blood and color, and Harriet Scott wife of said Dred, aged thirty nine years, also of full negro blood & color, and Eliza Scott a daughter of said Dred & Harriet, aged nineteen years of full negro color, and Lizzy Scott, also a daughter of said Dred & Harriet, aged ten years likewise of full negro blood & color.

Hamilton Bell, et. al.
vs.
William Dawson, et. al. } The Court having duly heard and considered the motion to set aside the non suit herein, and being fully advised of and concerning the premises, doth consider and adjudge that said motion be sustained.

James Andrews.
vs.
Barney M. Lynch. } Bill of Exceptions filed.

This deed of emancipation, filed in St. Louis Circuit Court, freed Dred, Harriet, Eliza, and Lizzie Scott on 26 May 1857.

EMANCIPATION
SPRING 1857

The 1857 Dred Scott decision left Dred, Harriet, and their daughters slaves. However, news coverage of the decision set into motion unexpected events that led to their freedom.

Irene and Calvin Chaffee

Irene (Sanford) Emerson Chaffee had gone to great lengths to keep the Scott family enslaved. Ultimately and ironically though, when she married her second husband, Dr. Calvin Chaffee in 1850, she opened the door to their eventual freedom. Chaffee had been a widower with two children, twelve-year-old Emma and nine-year-old Clemens.[136]

Chaffee later wrote of the evils of slavery and how he had opposed the institution for many years.[137] However, when he married Irene, apparently he "… innocently marched up the aisle with his Southern bride, unaware that his betrothed was soon to be unmasked as one of the most famous slave masters on the continent."[138]

Irene's legal efforts to retain ownership of the Scotts continued after she married Chaffee. In 1852, two years after their marriage, Irene won the Missouri Supreme Court case, *Scott v. Emerson* that reversed the earlier St. Louis Circuit Court ruling and confirmed her ownership of the Scott family slaves.

In 1855, the American Party nominated Chaffee to fill a vacated seat in the U.S. House of Representatives and he won.[139] He ran for re-election as a Republican and served two terms representing his district from 4 March 1855 to 3 March 1859.[140] His service as an elected official brought with it more scrutiny than he would have experienced as a private citizen.

IRENE (SANFORD) EMERSON IN MASSACHUSETTS

For many years, researchers thought that Irene went to live with her sister and brother-in-law, Charlotte (Sanford) and James Barnes in Springfield, Massachusetts, after the death of her father. It seems more likely that she and her daughter, Henrietta, moved east to live near them.

Neither Irene nor her daughter, Henrietta Emerson, is listed in the James Barnes household in the 1850 census. However, that year's census includes a household in Springfield with Irene's widowed sister, Henrietta (Sanford) Clark, as head-of-household. Beyond two of her own children, Clark's household includes ten-year-old Henrietta Emerson, and Mary Sanford, but not Irene.

Census takers were instructed to record a person's name in a household only if that individual actually resided there, so the presence of Irene's ten-year-old daughter, Henrietta Emerson, in the home of her aunt meant that was where the young girl lived. Because Irene has not been found elsewhere in the 1850 census listings, the census listing for Henrietta Clark's household bears further study.

On the line above young Henrietta Emerson's census entry is a Frank Emerson, described as thirty-eight years of age, male, and born in Virginia. Since Widow Emerson is not found in the census elsewhere, this could be Irene enumerated with her daughter and living in her sister's home. The census taker did not record an occupation for any adult woman on that census page and every adult male on the page included an occupation—except for Frank Emerson. Census takers, being human, have been known to record information incorrectly and make some truly outrageous mistakes. If that happened in this case, then the entry for Frank might really be describing Irene.

As a widow of limited financial means, with a young child, Irene might well have sought a home with a widowed sibling. Because Frank Emerson is in the Clark household with the right surname, age, birthplace of Virginia, and lacks an occupation, the household of her sister Henrietta Clark offers a likely candidate for Irene's census entry for that year, hidden under an incorrect name and information.

Of further interest in that same household is Mary Sanford, fifty-eight years of age, and born in Pennsylvania, listed on the line just below young Henrietta Emerson. Mary is probably the widow of Alexander Sanford and possibly Irene's mother, but that is uncertain.

— Fehrenbacher, *The Dred Scott Case*, 256. Also, Ehrlich, *They Have No Rights*, 55.

— 1850 U.S. census, Hampden County, Massachusetts, population schedule, City of Springfield, page 104 (stamped), dwelling 1613, family 1762, James and Virginia Barnes household.

— 1850 U.S. census, Hampden County, Massachusetts, population schedule, Springfield, p. 234 (penned), family 1817, dwelling 1986, Henrietta Clark household.

Who Really Was Dred's Owner?

It was unclear who owned Dred Scott at the time of the U.S. Supreme Court decision in 1857, and the question remains to this day. In the earlier Missouri court cases, Irene Emerson was named as the owner of Dred, Harriet, and their daughters. However, in the U.S. Circuit Court in 1853, Roswell Field filed suit on behalf of Dred against Irene's brother, John Sanford not against Irene.

Courtesy of Springfield Photograph Collection, Archives of the Lyman & Merrie Wood Museum of Springfield History, Springfield, MA

Irene (Sanford) Emerson Chaffee

During the ensuing legal process at the federal level, Sanford acknowledged the Scotts as his slaves. Nevertheless, historians have found no document of his legal relationship to Dred.[141] Even if Sanford acted as his sister's agent to help her after her marriage to Chaffee, Irene would still have been their owner.

Breaking News—March 1857

On 4 March 1857, two days before the Supreme Court handed down the Dred Scott decision, Calvin Chaffee took his seat for his second term in the U.S. House of Representatives. Within days after the decision was handed down, the *Springfield Argus,* a newspaper in Chaffee's hometown broke the news. The real owner of Dred Scott was Mrs. Calvin Chaffee, the wife of U.S. Congressman Calvin Chaffee of Massachusetts![142]

Newspapers across the country reprinted the story. Many people saw Chaffee as an abolitionist who owned the most famous slave in America—an unforgivable and hypocritical position in the view of many. Quite possibly Chaffee did not know Irene owned the Scott family until the *Springfield Argus* announced it to the world. One has to wonder, though—how he would not know! A plausible answer is simply that she never told him.

For Chaffee, the revelation spelled a political disaster. Irene made no public statements about owning the Scotts. It was her husband, an elected official who was abruptly thrust into the national spotlight, who was forced to deal with the outrage and fury of the press and face public embarrassment and humiliation.

To answer questions, Chaffee wrote a letter on 14 March to his local newspaper, which published it on 16 March. His published letter was reprinted in many other papers. In it he said

> "... the defendant [John Sanford] was and is the only person who had or has any power in the matter, and neither myself nor any member of my family were consulted in relation to or ever knew of the existence of that suit till after it was noticed for trial, when we learned it in an accidental way ..."[143]

Courtesy of Springfield Photograph Collection, Archives of the Lyman & Merrie Wood Museum of Springfield History, Springfield, MA

Dr. Calvin Chaffee

Chaffee may have learned about it in an accidental way, but did Irene truly not know about the case and her role in it?

While most newspapers ridiculed Chaffee, the *Bangor Daily Whig & Courier* in Maine, wrote that "Dr. Chaffee will of course give Dred his freedom, for he would no more claim property in a fellow man, than he would sell one of his own children by public auction."[144] Also, the *Union and Advertiser* newspaper, in Nunda, New York, where he had once lived, quoted a Democratic editor in Livingston County as having said that Calvin Chaffee had been "the most ultra abolitionist in that town."[145]

Responding to questions and accusations, Chaffee wrote in a letter to his local paper in Springfield.

> "I have lived to little purpose, if, after more than twenty years service in the anti-slavery cause, it is now necessary that I should put in a formal disclaimer of my own participation in the sin and crime of slaveholding."[146]

Chaffee's Solution

On 1 April 1857 Chaffee wrote to Montgomery Blair, Dred's lawyer who had pleaded the case before the U.S. Supreme Court. Chaffee's letter said his wife "... desires to know whether she has the legal power and right to emancipate the Dred Scott family."[147] This was critical because ownership of Dred was uncertain and by the spring of 1857, John Sanford was mentally incompetent and unable to answer.[148]

Ten days later, on 11 April, Chaffee again wrote to Blair requesting proof of his wife's ownership of Dred and his family. He also requested the necessary papers to free them. Chaffee wrote quite eloquently that "My whole soul utterly loathes & abhors the whole system of slavery ..."[149] In a 6 May letter to Blair, Chaffee described the Dred Scott suit as a "... suit which has made humanity grieve and all true Americans blush."[150]

Irene had specifically asked Chaffee to direct all questions to Montgomery Blair in Washington, D.C. Then, as needed, Blair forwarded Chaffee's letters to Roswell Field in St. Louis.*

---

* To read Chaffee's letters to Blair, and their transcriptions, see Appendix D.

Freeing a Slave in Missouri

Missouri law allowed slave owners to free slaves. They could do it either while alive or through a will. However, the law also stated that the owners—or their estates—were still financially responsible for the slaves if they were

1. not of sound body and mind
2. over the age of forty-five
3. a male under the age of twenty-one
4. a female under the age of eighteen.[151]

In those situations, the emancipating person or their estate continued to bear financial responsibility in case the freed slaves could not support themselves or pay taxes and fees. If necessary, the owner's property could be sold to obtain the needed funds.

The Missouri law controlling the emancipation of slaves had more than one purpose. It prevented slave owners from granting freedom simply to avoid supporting slaves too old or ill to be productive. In effect, it discouraged increasing the population of free persons of color whose growing numbers were viewed by slave owners as destabilizing control of their "slave property."[152]

A Missouri resident had to be responsible for every emancipated slave in one of the four categories defined by law. Dred Scott was over the age of forty-five and Lizzie was under the age of eighteen. If they were emancipated, the law required a Missouri resident to be responsible for them.

Looking for Eliza and Lizzie

While arrangements for freedom for the Scott family were underway, Eliza and Lizzie, still slaves, remained in hiding. Newspaper articles, published in the spring of 1857 following the Supreme Court decision, provided clues about Eliza and Lizzie in hiding.[153] Many articles repeated the same basic information, but an article in the 3 April 1857 *St. Louis Republican* newspaper told a unique story.

Deep within the lengthy article was this statement. "… and two weeks since … the agent of Mrs. Chaffee dispatched a policeman to hunt down the daughters of Dred Scott empowered by the decision of the Supreme Court of the United States …"[154] While no known evidence supports this story, it is possible that the sheriff initiated a search for the girls, at least in the St. Louis area if not beyond.

It is important, however, to evaluate written accounts before accepting them as fact. Several points are relevant regarding this story of the sheriff's search.

- Irene's lawyers had successfully motioned to place Dred and Harriet in the custody of the St. Louis County Sheriff in 1848. The sheriff was responsible for keeping them in the area. Probably custody also extended to Eliza and Lizzie, Harriet's daughters and Irene's slaves.
- After the U.S. Supreme Court handed down its decision, Judge Hamilton could conclude the *Scott v. Emerson* case, which was still open in St. Louis Circuit Court. Because of the Dred Scott decision, the judge found in favor of Irene. That gave her the right to do two things: file for back wages of Dred and Harriet and take possession of the Scott family as her slaves.
- If and when Irene or her attorneys requested the return of the Scott family to her custody, the St. Louis County Sheriff would have to hand over Dred, Harriet, Eliza, and Lizzie. The problem was, he didn't know where Eliza and Lizzie were.

The sheriff's obligation to enforce the law should have led to a search for Eliza and Lizzie, even if limited in time and area. The news that Irene's husband was a congressman from Massachusetts who opposed slavery and denied her ownership of the Scott family minimized the chances that she would actually collect slaves her husband insisted she did not own.

Process of Emancipation

No records reveal when Dred and Harriet found out that Chaffee planned to emancipate them. To free them he would have to fulfill the necessary requirements of Missouri law regarding emancipation. He had a problem though: the identity of their owner was unclear.

The U.S. Supreme Court case was *Scott v. Sandford*, so John Sanford would have been the logical person to explain who owned the Scotts. However, John Sanford's deteriorating mental and physical condition rendered him incapable of helping or of clarifying who actually owned the Scott family. Sanford's death on 5 May 1857 left Irene as Dred and Harriet's obvious owner.[155]

JOHN F. A. SANFORD

Although John Sanford had a mental breakdown in the early part of December 1856, his condition improved. In fact, "... on February 21, 1857, Pierre Chouteau Jr. wrote that Sanford was perfectly well and leaving soon for Europe." However, sometime after that, Sanford had a relapse and died in New York in an insane asylum on 5 May 1857.

— Le Roy Reuben Hafen and Scott Eckberg, *Fur Traders, Trappers, and Mountain Men of the Upper Missouri* (Lincoln, Nebraska: University of Nebraska Press, 1995), 59.

Missouri law regarding emancipation of slaves required ownership of the Scott family to be passed to someone in the state. A notation on the back of Chaffee's letter of 11 April indicates that Dred himself possibly made one of the decisions for their freedom. The last sentence of the notation said, "Let Dred select the person to whom the transfer shall be made."[156] Whom did Dred trust to be his and his family's temporary slave owner? He selected Taylor Blow, son of his original slave owner.

On 13 May, eight days after John Sanford's death, Irene and Calvin Chaffee, and her daughter, Henrietta Emerson, signed a quit claim deed. By this carefully worded document, they gave up any possible claim of ownership to Dred, Harriet, Eliza and Lizzie—without actually acknowledging ownership in the first place.

> "... C. C. Chaffee, Eliza Irene Chaffee, & Henrietta S. Emerson claim no such Interest and are desirous to do whatever may be in their power to remove all ground for such Representations and all pretense for calling said persons Slaves ..."[157]

They ceded any possible claims to Taylor Blow, a Missouri resident, for the specific purpose of freeing the Scott family.[158] Even though Chaffee avoided acknowledging ownership of the Scott family in this quit claim, it was sufficient for Taylor Blow to assume their ownership and fulfill the requirements of Missouri law to emancipate them.

The next day, Chaffee wrote to Blair enclosing with it the executed papers necessary for the Scott family's freedom. In his letter, Chaffee told Blair "... if they are not as speedily emancipated as possible, the papers will be withdrawn & other means used to effect that object [freedom]." He went on to say that "... there should be no publicity given, the subject, beyond strict legal necessity."[159]

Freedom

Dred, Harriet, Eliza, and Lizzie were legally freed on 26 May 1857. For them, emancipation required two steps, and both took place that day.

- Taylor Blow recorded the quit claim deed in the St. Louis Recorder of Deeds office giving him legal ownership of the Scott family—and thus the right to free them.[160]
- Blow then went to the St. Louis Circuit Court and formally acknowledged his "Deed of Emancipation" for Dred, Harriet, Eliza, and Lizzie. That made 26 May 1857 their day of freedom.

Whereas it has been represented that C. C. Chaffee of Springfield in the County of Hampden & State of Massachusetts has in right of his wife Eliza Irene Chaffee some right title or Interest in or to certain persons now resident in St Louis in the County of St Louis & State of Missouri, described as negro Slaves and named Dred Scott, Harriet Scott his wife and Eliza & Lizzy their daughters, and whereas it has been represented that the said Eliza Irene Chaffee & Henrietta S. Emerson both of said Springfield have some right title or Interest in & to the said persons under or by virtue of the last will and testament of Dr John Emerson late of Davenport in the State of Iowa deceased, and whereas the C. C. Chaffee, Eliza Irene Chaffee & Henrietta S. Emerson claim no such Interest and are desirous to do whatever may be in their power to remove all ground for such Representations and all pretence for calling said persons Slaves: & whereas they are informed that this object can be best effected by the following Conveyance: Now Therefore for the consideration above mentioned and for the further consideration of one dollar paid to us to our full satisfaction by Taylor Blow of said St Louis We the said C. C. Chaffee, Eliza Irene Chaffee & Henrietta S. Emerson have quit claimed released and assigned and do by these presents quit claim release & assign to the said Blow all the Right title & Interest which we the said grantors or either of us have or are supposed to have, or which any person has or claims to have for the benefit of us or either of us in & to the said Dred Scott, Harriet Scott his wife & Eliza & Lizzie their daughters or either of them & to their services for all periods of time past, present & future so that the said Taylor Blow may be entitled to all the rights which we or either of us have in and to the said persons or each of them, To the Intent & purpose that the said Taylor Blow shall with all convenient speed, make & execute all deeds & other Instruments & do all acts that may be necessary & proper under the laws of the State of Missouri to effect the emancipation of the said persons and remove all pretence so far as may be in our power for the representation that the said persons or either of them are Slaves or that we or either of us have any claim upon them. Witness our hands & seals this thirteenth day of May A.D. 1857.

C. C. Chaffee (Seal) Eliza I. Chaffee (Seal)
Henrietta S. Emerson (Seal)

Commonwealth of Massachusetts
Hampden County ss. At Springfield the fourteenth day of May A.D. 1857.

Then and there personally appeared before me Clerk of the Supreme Judicial Court of said Commonwealth for the County of Hampden the same being a Court of record, C. C. Chaffee Eliza Irene Chaffee his wife and Henrietta S. Emerson personally known to me to be the same persons whose names are subscribed to the foregoing Instrument of writing as parties thereto and severally acknowledged the same Instrument to be their act and deed for the purposes therein mentioned; and the said Eliza Irene Chaffee being by me first made acquainted with the contents of said Instrument acknowledged on an examination apart from her husband that she executed the same Instrument voluntarily without the compulsion or undue influence of her husband and freely of her own accord. (Seal) In testimony whereof I have hereunto subscribed my name & set the Seal of said Court the day & year above mentioned. George B. Morris Clerk

Filed & Recorded May 26. 1857 C Keemle Recorder

Courtesy of St. Louis Recorder of Deeds Office, St. Louis, MO

Document which passed any possible ownership of the Scott family to Taylor Blow so he could emancipate them.

TRANSCRIPTION

Whereas it has been represented that C.C. Chaffee of Springfield in the County of Hampden & State of Massachusetts has in right of his wife Eliza Irene Chaffee some right title or Interest in or to certain persons now resident in St. Louis in the County of St. Louis & State of Missouri, described as negro Slaves and named Dred Scott, Harriet Scott his wife and Eliza & Lizzy their daughters; and whereas it has been represented that the said Eliza Irene Chaffee & Henrietta S. Emerson both of said Springfield have some right title or Interest in & to said persons under or by virtue of the last will and testament of Dr John Emerson late of Davenport in the State of Iowa deceased, and whereas the C.C. Chaffee, Eliza Irene Chaffee & Henrietta S. Emerson claim no such Interest and are desirous to do whatever may be in their power to remove all ground for such Representations and all pretense for calling said persons Slaves: & whereas they are informed that this object can be best effected by the following Conveyance: Now Therefore, for the Consideration above mentioned and for the further Consideration of one Dollar paid to us to our full satisfaction by Taylor Blow of said St Louis We the said C.C. Chaffee, Eliza Irene Chaffee & Henrietta S. Emerson have quit claimed released and assigned and do by these presents quit claim release & assign to the said Blow all the Right title & Interest which we the said grantors or either of us have or are supposed to have, or which any person has or claims to have for the benefit of us or either of us in & to the said Dred Scott, Harriet Scott his wife & Eliza & Lizzie their daughters or either of them & to their services for all periods of time past, present & future, so that the said Taylor Blow may be entitled to all the rights which we or either of us have in and to the said persons & each of them; To the Intent & purpose that the said Taylor Blow shall with all convenient speed, make and execute all deeds & other Instruments & do all acts that may be necessary & proper under the laws of the State of Missouri to effect the emancipation of the said persons and remove all pretense so far as may be in our power for the representation that the said persons or either of them are Slaves or that we or either of us have any claim upon them.

Witness our hands & Seals this thirteenth day of May A D. 1857.

C. C. Chaffee (Seal)   Eliza I. Chaffee (Seal)
Henrietta S. Emerson (Seal)

Commonwealth of Massachusetts
Hampden County   SS.   At Springfield the fourteenth day of May A D. 1857.
Then and there personally appeared before me Clerk of the Supreme Judicial Court of said Commonwealth for the County of Hampden the same being a Court of record, C.C. Chaffee, Eliza Irene Chaffee his wife and Henrietta S. Emerson personally known to me to be the same persons whose names are subscribed to the forgoing Instrument of writing as parties thereto and Severally acknowledged the same Instrument to be their act and deed for the purposes therein mentioned; and She the said Eliza Irene Chaffee being by me first made acquainted with the contents of said instrument acknowledged on an Examination apart from her husband that she executed the same Instrument voluntarily without the compulsion or undue influence of her husband and freely of her own accord. (Seal) In Testimony whereof I have hereunto subscribed my name & set the seal of said Court the day & year above mentioned, George B. Morris Clerk

Filed & Recorded May 26, 1857   C Keemle Recorder

—Land Records Book 186, page 199, Archives, Recorder of Deeds, City of Saint Louis, State of Missouri

The deed of emancipation court record reads:

> "Taylor Blow, who is personally known to the court, comes into open court, and acknowledges the execution by him of a Deed of Emancipation to his slaves, Dred Scott, aged about forty eight years, of full negro blood and color, and Harriet Scott wife of said Dred, aged thirty nine years, also of full negro blood & color, and Eliza Scott a daughter of said Dred & Harriet, aged nineteen years of full negro color, and Lizzy Scott, also a daughter of said Dred & Harriet, aged ten years likewise of full negro blood & color."[161]

BLACK REPUBLICANS

At this time in history, Democrats used the term "Black Republican" to inaccurately describe members of the newly formed (1854) Republican Party as supporters of abolition and black equality. They did this in order to instill in voters fear of Republican candidates as a threat to white supremacy.

— Leo F. Litwack, *North of Slavery: The Negro in the Free States, 1790–1860* (Chicago: University of Chicago Press, 1961), 268.

Newspapers spread the word of Dred's emancipation, usually crediting Taylor Blow with the action since his name was on the emancipation deed. Because Chaffee had transferred ownership to Taylor Blow, some acknowledged Chaffee's role in granting freedom. However, *The Daily Ohio Statesman* newspaper ran a small article, credited to the *New Haven Register*, which presented a different and probably more accurate opinion. It said that

> "The emancipation of 'Dred Scott and family,' the Missouri slaves, by Dr. Chaffee the Black Republican member of congress from Massachusetts, should be credited to the editor of the Springfield Argus, rather than to the Doctor."[162]

It made the point that the revelation in the *Springfield Argus* article opened the way for Chaffee to free Dred, Harriet, and their daughters. The article certainly focused national scrutiny on anything Chaffee said or did regarding ownership of the Scott family.

Release of Back Wages

Dred and Harriet's wages, earned since 1848 when they were placed in the custody of the St. Louis County Sheriff, had been collected and held pending the outcome of their suit. After the Supreme Court decision, their legal case was over and the wages could be paid out to the winner of the suit. Judge Hamilton of the St. Louis Circuit Court closed the case of *Scott v. Emerson*. Those wages collected and held by the St. Louis County Sheriff since 1848 came to about $750.[163]

When Irene's attorneys claimed Dred and Harriet's wages amassed over nine years, the claim amounted to an acknowledgement she owned the Scott family. Although her husband had gone to great lengths to refute her ownership in the press, only their slave owner would have had the right to their wages.[164]

For whatever reason, no St. Louis newspaper mentioned Irene's motion to collect back wages when reporting on the activities of the St. Louis Circuit Court for that day.[165] That may explain why the national press never reported it. It is uncertain if Irene actually received the money, how that might have happened, or whether her husband ever found out about it.

Fallout for Chaffee

Irene's apparent failure to inform her husband of her slave-holding status and the existence of her slaves' freedom suits against her cost Chaffee dearly. Newspapers across the country subjected him to scathing ridicule and criticism just as he was beginning his second term in the House of Representatives. His colleagues' response to his involvement with the Dred Scott case would affect their dealings with him in Congress.

One news article sarcastically said that Chaffee's reputation was now "... known by this time by every gentleman who will be honored by a seat with him in the next Congress. He will have a comfortable time of it in Washington, next winter."[166]

Some politicians would have resigned under the circumstances, but Chaffee did not. He served out his second term (March 1857–March 1859) in the U.S. House of Representatives.[167] In the fall of 1858 he ran for re-election, but lost.[168] From 1860 to 1862 he served as the librarian of the House of Representatives and then practiced medicine in Washington, D.C. until 1876.[169]

As with many American families, the Civil War impacted Chaffee's family. His only son, Clemens, secured an appointment to West Point Military Academy in 1858 and graduated in 1862.[170] He fought for the Union in the Civil War serving as an engineer. Never married, he died on 5 July 1867 as a result of consumption contracted during the siege of Vicksburg.[171]

One can only wonder how the Dred Scott decision affected Irene and Calvin Chaffee's marriage. Calvin Chaffee died on 8 August 1896 in Springfield, Massachusetts; Irene died in Springfield on 11 February 1903.[172]

Success or Failure?

After eleven years the legal system failed Dred and Harriet. They remained enslaved and in an interview reported in *Frank Leslie's Illustrated Newspaper,* Dred said the suit had cost him "... $500 in cash, beside labor to nearly the same amount." Bills still needed to be paid and the article went on to say that his lawyer would "... receive and apply any money contributed for Dred's benefit."[173]

Because the Supreme Court decision left the family in slavery, some considered their legal fight for freedom a total failure—but was it? The outcome of their legal fight may have been a failure, but in the end, they gained their freedom. The intense news coverage surrounding Dred's Supreme Court case was the catalyst for the exposé revealing Irene, and by marriage, her husband Calvin Chaffee, as the owners of the Scott family.

Chaffee's embarrassment and ridicule in newspapers across the country left Irene with really no choice except to go along with his decision to free the Scott family. The tremendous pressure placed on Irene is important because it is unlikely that she would have signed papers to free the Scott family—whom she had just spent eleven years trying to hold in slavery—if she felt she had any other choice in the matter.

Freedom

FRANK LESLIE'S ILLUSTRATED

NEWSPAPER

Entered according to Act of Congress, in the year 1857, by FRANK LESLIE, in the Clerk's Office of the District Court for the Southern District of New York. (Copyrighted June 22, 1857.)

No. 82.—VOL. IV.] NEW YORK, SATURDAY, JUNE 27, 1857. [PRICE 6 CENTS.

TO TOURISTS AND TRAVELLERS.

We shall be happy to receive personal narratives, of land or sea, including adventures and incidents, from every person who pleases to correspond with our paper.

We take this opportunity of returning our thanks to our numerous artistic correspondents throughout the country, for the many sketches we are constantly receiving from them of the news of the day. We trust they will spare no pains to furnish us with drawings of events as they may occur. We would also remind them that it is necessary to send all sketches, if possible, by the earliest conveyance.

VISIT TO DRED SCOTT—HIS FAMILY—INCIDENTS OF HIS LIFE—DECISION OF THE SUPREME COURT.

WHILE standing in the Fair grounds at St. Louis, and engaged in conversation with a prominent citizen of that enterprising city, he suddenly asked us if we would not like to be introduced to Dred Scott. Upon expressing a desire to be thus honored, the gentleman called to an old negro who was standing near by, and our wish was gratified. Dred made a rude obeisance to our recognition, and seemed to enjoy the notice we expended upon him. We found him on examination to be a pure-blooded African, perhaps fifty years of age, with a shrewd, intelligent, good-natured face, of rather light frame, being not more than five feet six inches high. After some general remarks we expressed a wish to get his portrait (we had made efforts before, through correspondents, and failed), and asked him if he would not go to Fitzgibbon's gallery and have it taken. The gentleman present explained to Dred that it was proper he should have his likeness in the "great illustrated paper of the country," overruled his many objections, which seemed to grow out of a superstitious feeling, and he promised to be at the gallery the next day. This appointment Dred did not keep. Determined not to be foiled, we sought an interview with Mr. Crane, Dred's lawyer, who promptly gave us a letter of introduction, explaining to Dred that it was to his advantage to have his picture taken to be engraved for our paper, and also directions where we could find his domicile. We found the place with difficulty, the streets in Dred's neighborhood being more clearly defined in the plan of the city than on the mother earth; we finally reached a wooden house, however, protected by a balcony that answered the description. Approaching the door, we saw a smart, tidy-looking negress, perhaps thirty years of age, who, with two female assistants, was busy ironing. To our question, "Is this where Dred Scott lives?" we received, rather hesitatingly, the answer, "Yes." Upon our asking if he was home, she said,

"What white man arter dad nigger for?—why don't white man 'tend to his own business, and let dat nigger 'lone! Some of dese days dey'll steal dat nigger—dat are a fact."

ELIZA AND LIZZIE, CHILDREN OF DRED SCOTT.

DRED SCOTT. PHOTOGRAPHED BY FITZGIBBON, OF ST. LOUIS.

HIS WIFE, HARRIET. PHOTOGRAPHED BY FITZGIBBON, OF ST. LOUIS.

TOGETHER AS A FAMILY
1857–1860

Beyond freeing Dred, Harriet, Eliza, and Lizzie, the emancipation deed made it safe for Eliza and Lizzie to come out of hiding. They could celebrate freedom as a family.

National publicity resulting from their Supreme Court case placed Dred and Harriet in the public spotlight in a way that must have been a shock to them. According to *Frank Leslie's Illustrated Newspaper*, the publicity made Dred Scott's name recognized across the country. He was even approached by a man offering him a thousand dollars a month to travel through the North so people could see him. Dred declined the offer. Harriet was concerned someone might try to steal him away from the family.[174]

A reporter from *Frank Leslie's Illustrated Newspaper* obtained an interview with Dred and Harriet at their home in the alley near Carr Street between 6th and 7th.[175] Beyond an interview, the newspaper wanted a daguerreotype portrait* made of Dred, but he hesitated.[176] Encouraged by Arbra Crane, a lawyer working with Roswell Field, the reporter convinced the entire family to have their portraits made at Fitzgibbon's Gallery in St. Louis. Separate portraits of Dred and Harriet, and a single one of Eliza and Lizzie together appeared on the front page of the 27 June 1857 issue of *Frank Leslie's Illustrated Newspaper*, along with a lengthy article.[177]

That article, published shortly after Eliza and Lizzie's arrival home, provides the most well-known description and portraits of the family. It said Dred had "... a shrewd, intelligent, good-natured face, of rather light frame, being not more than five feet six inches high."[178] After that, more people recognized him and stopped to talk with him on the streets of St. Louis or where he worked—probably as a porter—at Barnum's Hotel at Walnut and 2nd Streets.[179]

---

* A daguerreotype was an early type of photograph made on a silver coated copper plate.

Courtesy of the Geography and Map Division, Library of Congress, Washington, D.C.

Some St. Louis city blocks had homes and businesses in the interior portion of the block. This is St. Louis city block 140, bordered by 6th and 7th, Wash and Carr Streets, as shown in Camille Dry's Pictorial St. Louis, the Great Metropolis of the Mississippi Valley: A Topographical Survey Drawn in perspective A.D. 1875. *This may be the block where Harriet lived in 1859 as the city directory listed her residence as the alley near Carr between 6th and 7th.*

The article went on to mention that Harriet was his second wife and that he and Harriet had also had two boys who had died.[180] She was a laundress and Dred delivered laundry for her. The writer described Harriet as "… neat, industrious, and devotedly attached to her husband and children, an acceptable member of the church, and would evidently be satisfied with obscurity and repose."[181]

Approximately one month elapsed between the family's emancipation on 26 May and the publication of their pictures in *Frank Leslie's Illustrated Newspaper* on 27 June. That establishes a time frame for Eliza and Lizzie's return home and suggests a date for these famous portraits. The girls' return home and reunion with their parents probably would have taken place either in late May or early June. Additional time would have been needed to take the portraits, send them to New York, and publish them. The remaining time suggests the daguerreotypes were made in early June 1857.

Eliza and Lizzie had returned home only a week or two before they sat for their picture. In the portrait Lizzie, left, looks scared and frightened. Eliza appears to be reassuring her sister, with her right arm around Lizzie's shoulder, and her left hand on Lizzie's hand. This picture gives a glimpse of the frightened young girl that oral tradition reports Lizzie had become during her time in hiding.

How people live in their older years often reveals a certain "comfort zone" established in childhood. In her later years, Lizzie lived with heavy drapes pulled across her window, presumably fearing someone would see in and find out who she was.

Free Negro Licenses

On 4 May 1858, almost a year after their emancipation, Dred and Harriet each signed an "X" mark on a one-thousand-dollar bond for good behavior while living in Missouri. Taylor Blow again helped them by signing as security for their bond.[182]

Courtesy of the National Park Service, Jefferson National Expansion Memorial

Lizzie and Eliza Scott ca 1857. The newspaper incorrectly identified the daughters, reversing their names.

That day each also received from the St. Louis County Court the required "Free Negro License," which permitted them to live as free people of color in the state of Missouri "... during good behavior."[183] Without the licenses, they would have had to leave the state. The license also covered their children younger than twenty-one years of age, so the girls did not yet need licenses of their own.[184]

Dred's Death

For Dred, freedom lasted little more than a year. Freed on 26 May 1857, Dred died of tuberculosis in St. Louis on 17 September 1858. He was buried at Wesleyan Cemetery, at Grand and Laclede Avenues. Henry Blow, another son of Dred's former owner, Peter Blow, and others paid for his burial.[185]

Dred's death left Harriet, Eliza, and Lizzie alone. They were free women of color during slave times, and they were the family of Dred Scott. One can only wonder how much the notoriety of the Dred Scott decision complicated their lives.

Eliza and Wilson Madison

Eliza, the older daughter, married Wilson Madison also listed in city directories as Joshua W. Madison.[186] He was born in Pennsylvania on 26 September 1837.[187] Records consistently listed him as a cook, but one city directory called him a pastry cook and another a river cook.[188] His census records listed him as a cook or a riverman, so he may have been a cook on a steamboat.[189]

Where Wilson and Eliza met is unknown, but since she and Lizzie were in hiding until 1857, they may have met while she was in hiding. If so, one wonders when Wilson learned of her true identity. No St. Louis marriage record has been found for Eliza and Wilson, but since Wilson worked on the river they could have married up or down the river.

1860 Census

The 1860 *St. Louis City Directory* listed Harriet as living in a home in the alleyway of city block no. 253, bounded by Franklin, Wash, 7th, and 8th Streets. The 1860 census listed "Harriote Scott" as a forty-year-old black woman, born in Virginia. Fifteen-year-old Elizabeth Scott, also listed as black, lived with Harriet and listed her birth place as Missouri. The third woman in the household, Ellen Knox, was fifty years of age, female, mulatto, and born in South Carolina. All three women worked as laundresses.[190] No kinship or connection to Ellen Knox is known except that they shared the same occupation and residence. Twelve doors away from Harriet lived twenty-five-year-old "Wilson Maddison," a cook, and twenty-one-year-old "Elizabeth."[191]

Each household included a young woman named Elizabeth, but it is her last name, age, and with whom she was living that defines her. Fifteen-year-old Elizabeth Scott is listed as living in Harriet's household and twenty-one-year-old Elizabeth Madison is part of Wilson's household. This seems to indicate that Wilson married the older of the two Scott daughters—known to her family as Eliza. Further, if Wilson and Eliza lived twelve doors away from Harriet, and Harriet's home was in the alleyway between Franklin Avenue, Wash Street, and 7th and 8th Streets, then it is likely they lived in the same block or in an adjoining block.

ST. LOUIS CITY BLOCK 253

While Harriet and Lizzie's 1860 home is no longer in existence, block 253 where they lived can still be pinpointed on a 2010 map. Wash Street was later renamed Cole Street and the St. Louis Convention Center is located on the south side of Cole Street at 701 Convention Plaza in downtown St. Louis. Within the Convention Center, "Hall 5" is built on city block no. 253 where Harriet and Lizzie lived in 1860.

Courtesy of Ancestry.com

Wilson and Elizabeth "Maddison" living in dwelling 408 in 1860 U.S. Census, ward 7, City of St. Louis, St. Louis County, Missouri.

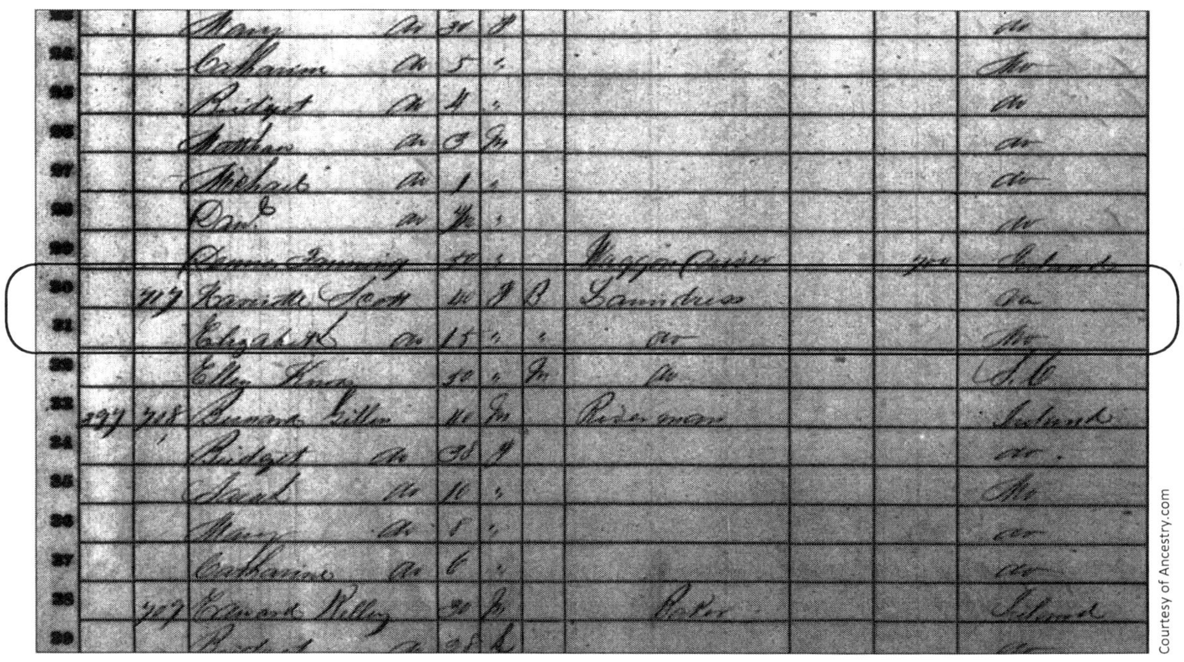

Courtesy of Ancestry.com

"Harriotte" and Elizabeth [Lizzie] Scott living in dwelling 396 in 1860 U.S. census, ward 7, City of St. Louis, St. Louis County, Missouri.

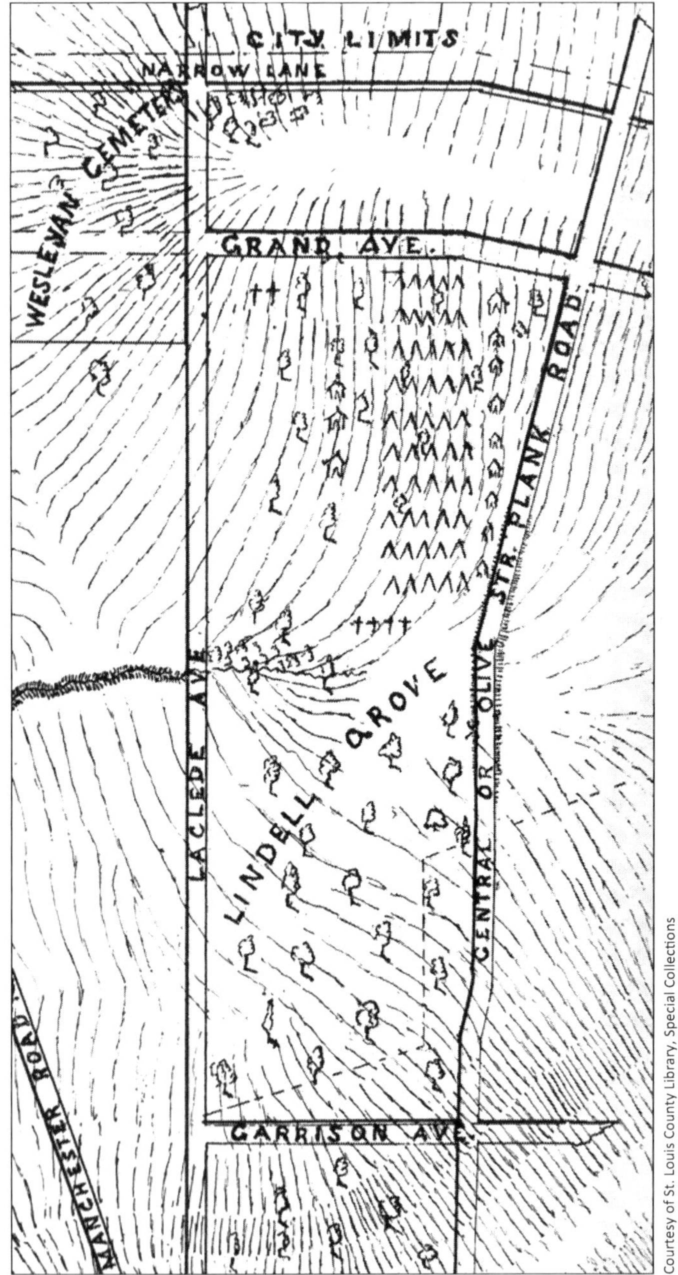

Temporarily named "Camp Jackson," Lindell's Grove was the site of the first Civil War military action in St. Louis. Wesleyan Cemetery, where Dred was originally buried, was just across the street from Lindell's Grove as shown in this map from Robert J. Rombauer's The Union Cause in St. Louis in 1861.

CIVIL WAR AND ITS AFTERMATH
1861–1869

The Dred Scott decision profoundly intensified the chasm dividing Americans opposing and those supporting slavery. The shots fired on Fort Sumter on 12 April 1861 ignited the Civil War. One wonders what it was like for Harriet, Eliza, and Lizzie during that time, whether people blamed them, and if it was even safe for them to go about their daily tasks during the war.

For years newspapers and books reported incorrectly that both Harriet and her unmarried daughter died during the Civil War. Both lived much longer than that.[192] The Scott family may have led such a quiet life that people thought Harriet and Lizzie died shortly after Dred or during the Civil War. Or, perhaps the community allowed the misconception of their deaths to continue, uncorrected, hoping to give the women some anonymity, privacy, and possibly safety.

The War Limits Activities

To maintain order in the city, the St. Louis police board published a series of orders on 10 April 1861 in the local press. One directly affecting the three Scott women said that "Churches for negroes, or churches wherein negroes or mulattoes officiate as preachers, will not be allowed to open unless an officer of the police is present ..." Another order said "... that 'all free negroes' found within the city limits without a 'license' would be dealt with according to the law."[193]

On 15 April, five days later, another published notice in the press further restricted the movements of the family. "It stated that 'all negroes found in the street after the hour of ten o'clock without a proper pass will be arrested and brought before the recorder'."[194] Missouri State Statutes already severely restricted the activities of slaves and free people of color, so these notices were perhaps just reminders of what was and was not permitted.[195]

Eliza's Free Negro License

Harriet already had a license and Lizzie, being younger than twenty-one years old, did not need one. However, the 1860 census listed Eliza as twenty-one, so if she had not already obtained a license, she would have needed one. On 23 April 1861, five women with the occupation "washer" received free Negro licenses with Samuel Simmons as bondsman.[196] One was an Elizabeth Scott described as five feet, five and a quarter inches tall.[197]

Was she the wife of Wilson Madison and the older daughter of Dred and Harriet Scott? It seems possible. The 1860 census listed Eliza as twenty-one and this application is dated less than two weeks after the notice ordering free Negroes in St. Louis to have licenses. Further research may reveal whether this license was for Dred and Harriet's daughter or for someone else.

It is uncertain why Eliza's application might have named her Elizabeth Scott rather than Elizabeth Madison. The St. Louis County Court issued more free Negro licenses in a short period than did other venues, possibly as a result of the published police orders, so less attention may have been given to each. The person writing the record may not have known her married name and simply recorded Eliza's name as he knew it, Elizabeth Scott. No record has been found of Wilson Madison's application for a free Negro license.

Civil War Begins in St. Louis

Less than two weeks later, in early May of 1861, the Missouri State Militia held its annual encampment and drill just west of St. Louis in Lindell's Grove, temporarily called "Camp Jackson." The Union feared pro-Confederate Governor Claiborne Jackson would direct the militia to capture the U.S. Arsenal in St. Louis and its store of weapons. To prevent that, Union volunteers under the command of Captain Nathaniel Lyon surrounded the militia in Camp Jackson on 10 May 1861 and demanded its surrender. As Union volunteers marched the captured militia prisoners towards the U.S. Arsenal, a crowd of angry civilians gathered. Shots rang out. Civilians were among the nearly three dozen casualties and many more were wounded.[198]

> LINDELL'S GROVE AND WESLEYAN CEMETERY
>
> Lindell's Grove and Wesleyan Cemetery (the 1861 location) are now part of the campus of Saint Louis University. An historical marker commemorating Camp Jackson and telling its story is located on the campus.
>
> — "Saint Francis Xavier College Church: History of the College Church," *Saint Louis University* (http://www.slu.edu/departments/church/history.html).

Wesleyan Cemetery, where Dred was laid to rest in September 1858, was west of Lindell's Grove at Grand and Laclede Avenues. During the "Camp Jackson Affair," as the incident came to be known, some of the soldiers may have walked past Dred's grave in Wesleyan Cemetery.

Conditions in St. Louis

Major-General J. C. Fremont declared martial law in St. Louis County on 14 August 1861. He appointed Major J. McKinstry provost marshal in charge of the military police.[199] About two weeks later, Fremont placed all of Missouri under martial law because of the state's

> "... disorganized condition, the helplessness of the civil authority, the total insecurity of life, and the devastation of property by bands of murderers and marauders, who infest nearly every county of the State, and avail themselves of the public misfortunes and the vicinity of hostile force to gratify private and neighborhood vengeance ..."[200]

St. Louis was in a border state—a slave state that remained in the Union—but just across the Mississippi River from Illinois, where slavery was illegal. Although Missouri did not secede, many St. Louisans supported the Confederacy. Distrust ran high, and even an unwise statement could provoke an encounter with the provost marshal or his staff.

Even Dred's strongest supporter, Taylor Blow, left conflicting evidence about his political leanings. He signed an oath of loyalty to the Union in early 1862. In 1863 he was charged with disloyalty (dropped two days later), because of remarks made while out drinking one night, and he refused to take another oath of loyalty in 1865.[201]

Eliza—As Mother

Lates W. Madison was born on 29 January 1862.[202] The name appears only twice in known records. Because of the difficulty of interpreting the nineteenth century handwriting, the name may also be interpreted as Seales W. Madison.[203]

Lates, listed as "colored" in the St. Louis death register, died on 2 August 1863 at the age of one year, six months, and four days.[204] No record indicates if Lates was a boy or a girl, but the middle initial "W" may have stood for Wilson.

When young Lates died, Wesleyan Cemetery reopened Dred Scott's grave and buried this child in it.[205] Records show it was not uncommon for two people to share a grave plot in that cemetery, although regulations or customs allowing for that are unknown.[206]

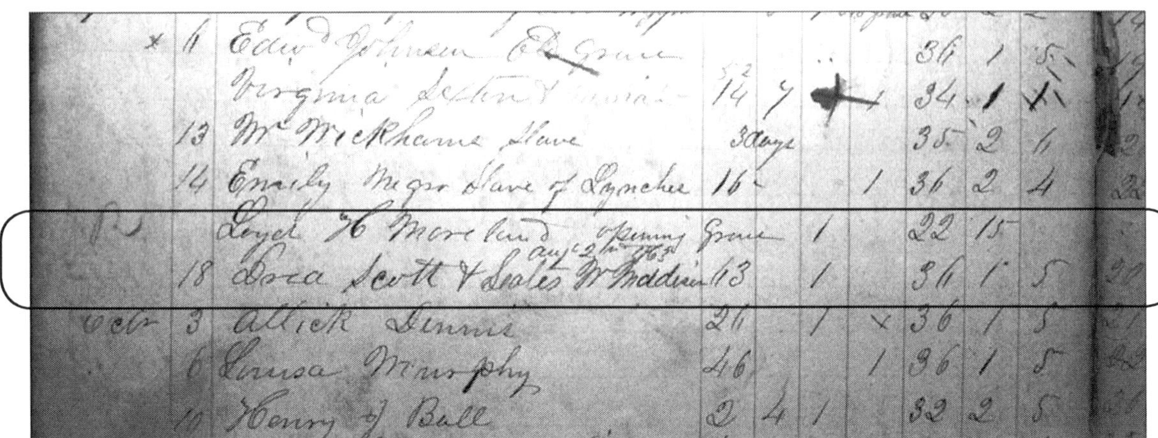

	11	Edw Johnson ... Grave				36	1	5
		Virginia Sexton	14	7		34	1	
	13	Mc Mickhams Slave	3 days			35	2	1
	14	Emily Negro Slave of Lynches	16		1	36	2	4
		Loyd H Moreland opening Grave		1		22	15	
	18	Drea Scott & Seales W Maddin (aug 2nd 1865)	13	1		36	1	5
Oct	3	Allick Dennis	21	1		36	1	5
	6	Louisa Murphy	46		1	36	1	5
	10	Henry J Ball	2	4	1	32	2	5

Courtesy of Wesleyan Cemetery Archives, Centennary Methodist Church

Wesleyan Cemetery burial record for Dred Scott and Lates/Seales W. Madison.

July	31	John Parker	Unknown
Aug	2	Ross Mahoney	"
"	"	John Fenton	"
"	"	Lates W. Madison	"
"	"	Mary Samuel	"
"	3	Willie Langford	"

Drowned
Eclampsia
Small pox
Hooping Cough
Teething
Hydrocephalus
Infirmities of old age
Old age
Still Born

Courtesy of St. Louis County Library, Special Collections

St. Louis death register for Lates W. Madison.

Although no record states who Lates was, indirect evidence suggests an identity. It is unlikely that Harriet or the Blow family would allow anyone except immediate family to be buried in Dred's grave. Lates carried the last name of Dred's married daughter. A child with the surname Madison and close to Dred was probably his grandchild and thus the child of Eliza and Wilson Madison.

Dred's Remains Moved to Calvary Cemetery

On 26 October 1867, Taylor Blow purchased lot 177 in section 1 of Calvary Cemetery, a large Catholic cemetery in North St. Louis City.[207] As Catholics, Taylor, his family, and their servants were eligible for burial there. He paid twenty-five dollars for the 100 square foot lot, large enough to bury three people. One month later, on 27 November 1867, Taylor moved Dred's remains from Wesleyan Cemetery to the recently purchased grave in Calvary Cemetery. Dred was buried in the center of the three lots; the other two remain unused. There is no evidence that the new grave was marked at that time.[208]

SECTION	LOT NO.	SQ. FEET	NAME OF LOT OWNER	PHONE NO.
I	177	100	TAYLOR BLOW	

DATE OF PURCHASE 10-23-1867 ADDRESS

GR. NO.	NAME OF INTERRED	DATE OF BURIAL	CONTAINER
1.	Dred Scott	11/27/67	

W. N.

Courtesy of The Catholic Cemeteries of the Archdiocese of St. Louis

Calvary Cemetery burial card for Dred's reburial there in 1867.

When Dred was reburied in Calvary Cemetery, Taylor Blow, a widower with dependent children was facing failing health and had financial problems. In particular his daughter, Fannie, must have had special needs; he described her as "afflicted" in his last will and testament. On 27 May 1868, six months after Dred's reburial, Taylor Blow declared bankruptcy.[209]

Despite failing health and financial problems, Taylor Blow spent the time, energy, and money to purchase the new gravesite and rebury Dred there. Why? It has been suggested that Taylor moved Dred's remains because Wesleyan Cemetery was either closing or being abandoned.[210] However, he may have had other reasons.

On 28 March 1874, a full seven years after Dred's removal to Calvary Cemetery, Wesleyan Cemetery Association amended its charter to dispose of the cemetery at Grand and Laclede where Dred was initially buried. The amendment allowed the removal of bodies to a new location beyond the St. Louis city limits.[211] The Missouri law amending Wesleyan Cemetery's charter cited the following reasons for the cemetery's move:

- the city and its population had grown, and by 1874, the cemetery was within the city limits
- the cemetery was "offensive to the people residing near it"
- it was depreciating the value of the property in the area thus decreasing the tax revenue that property would otherwise generate.[212]

Taylor Blow may have anticipated a need to move Dred in 1867. However, the "old" Wesleyan cemetery at Grand and Laclede did not close until 1878—eleven years after Dred's removal to Calvary.[213] Did Taylor move Dred to Calvary for a reason other than Wesleyan's future closing, and if so why? Although we may never know for certain, there are possible clues.

One oral tradition in the Madison family was that "someone" was planning to desecrate Dred's grave.[214] Taylor may have arranged to move Dred's remains to avoid such a possibility. Dred had taken care of Taylor as a child and moving the grave may have been Taylor's final effort to care for him in return. The new unmarked grave gave Dred the anonymity to rest in peace.

Anger directed towards Dred's grave would have also affected the family. Wilson Madison was not listed in the city directories from 1866 to 1871 and Harriet was not listed from 1868 through 1873.[215] The lack of listings for those years may have been just a coincidence. However, for protection or other personal reasons, the family may have intentionally kept a low profile during the years after the Civil War.

Available evidence is sparse and inconclusive. Perhaps future research will shed more light on the events and social history that the Scott and Madison families experienced in the post-war years.

TAYLOR BLOW

On 20 August 1869, Taylor Blow died at his home in St. Louis. He was buried beside other Blow family members in the Charless family lot in Bellefontaine Cemetery, a large non-denominational cemetery. Calvary Cemetery, where he had reinterred Dred two years earlier, lies directly across the street from Bellefontaine Cemetery.

— John A. Bryan, "The Blow Family and Their Slave Dred Scott: Part II," *Missouri Historical Society Bulletin*, 5 (1948): 28.

— Bellefontaine Cemetery Office (St. Louis, Missouri) Burial diagram for Lot 240, owned by Joseph Charless; photocopy courtesy of Bellefontaine Cemetery.

Reburial of Baby Lates?

Another question regarding Dred's removal to Calvary Cemetery concerns the remains of Lates W. Madison. The child was buried in Dred's Wesleyan grave in August 1863. Calvary Cemetery records do not show the baby's reinterment with Dred, so the family will probably never know. At least in theory, if not in reality, Lates still lies at rest with Dred.

The Family Grows

Catherine Madison, was born on 7 February 1867. She died 26 December 1867, at the age of ten months and nineteen days and was buried in Wesleyan Cemetery.[216] Although no evidence specifically links Catherine to Eliza and Wilson, it is possible that she too was their child. Her last name was Madison, her race was listed as "colored," and the address where she died, 921 B Franklin Avenue and Wash Street, was close to the other locations where Eliza and Wilson Madison lived. Also, her life span from conception to birth does not overlap any other of Eliza and Wilson's known or probable children.

On 30 September 1868, Eliza and Wilson had a son named Wilson.[217] Little Wilson died on 30 June 1870, just short of his second birthday. He also was buried at Wesleyan Cemetery.[218]

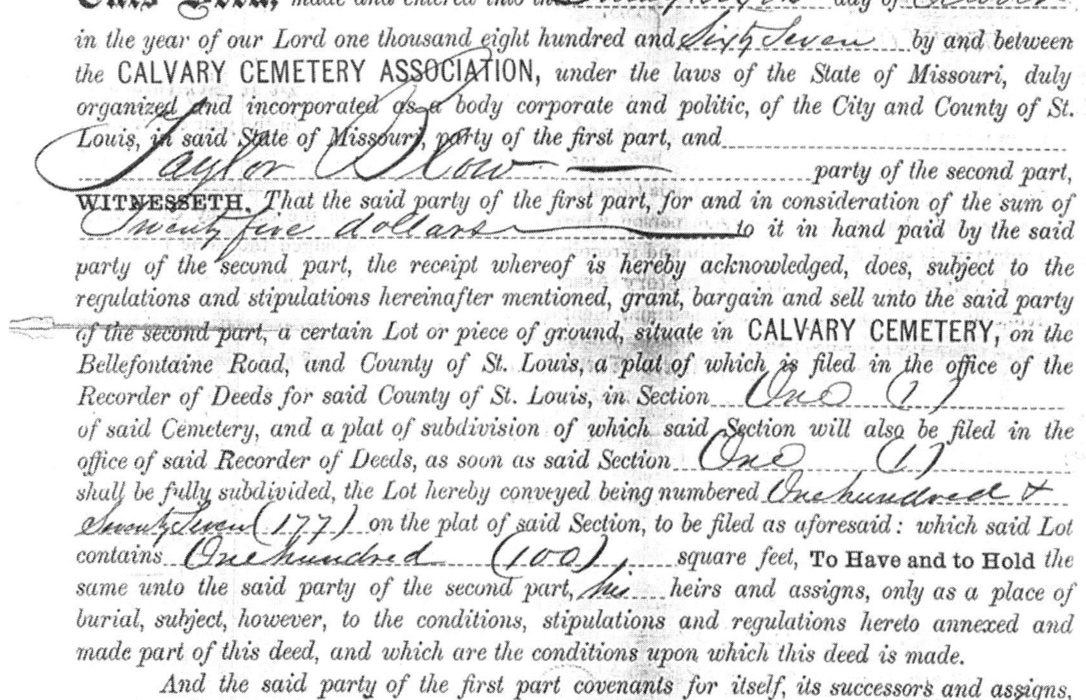

This Deed, *made and entered into this* Twenty Sixth *day of* October *in the year of our Lord one thousand eight hundred and* Sixty Seven *by and between the* CALVARY CEMETERY ASSOCIATION, *under the laws of the State of Missouri, duly organized and incorporated as a body corporate and politic, of the City and County of St. Louis, in said State of Missouri, party of the first part, and* Taylor Blow *party of the second part,* **WITNESSETH,** *That the said party of the first part, for and in consideration of the sum of* Twenty five dollars *to it in hand paid by the said party of the second part, the receipt whereof is hereby acknowledged, does, subject to the regulations and stipulations hereinafter mentioned, grant, bargain and sell unto the said party of the second part, a certain Lot or piece of ground, situate in* CALVARY CEMETERY, *on the Bellefontaine Road, and County of St. Louis, a plat of which is filed in the office of the Recorder of Deeds for said County of St. Louis, in Section* One (1) *of said Cemetery, and a plat of subdivision of which said Section will also be filed in the office of said Recorder of Deeds, as soon as said Section* One (1) *shall be fully subdivided, the Lot hereby conveyed being numbered* One hundred & Seventy Seven (177) *on the plat of said Section, to be filed as aforesaid: which said Lot contains* One hundred (100) *square feet,* **To Have and to Hold** *the same unto the said party of the second part,* his *heirs and assigns, only as a place of burial, subject, however, to the conditions, stipulations and regulations hereto annexed and made part of this deed, and which are the conditions upon which this deed is made.*

And the said party of the first part covenants for itself, its successors and assigns, that it shall and will, upon the faithful compliance by said party of the second part, his *heirs, executors, administrators and assigns, of the said stipulations and regulations,* **Warrant and Defend** *the title to the premises to* him *and them, the said party of the second part,* his *heirs, executors, administrators and assigns, against the lawful claims and demands of all persons whatsoever.*

In Witness Whereof, *The said party of the first part has caused these presents to be executed under the seal and signature of* Joseph O'Neil *its President, hereto*

Taylor Blow's deed for Dred Scott's grave at Calvary Cemetery.

Courtesy of Catholic Cemeteries of the Archdiocese of St. Louis

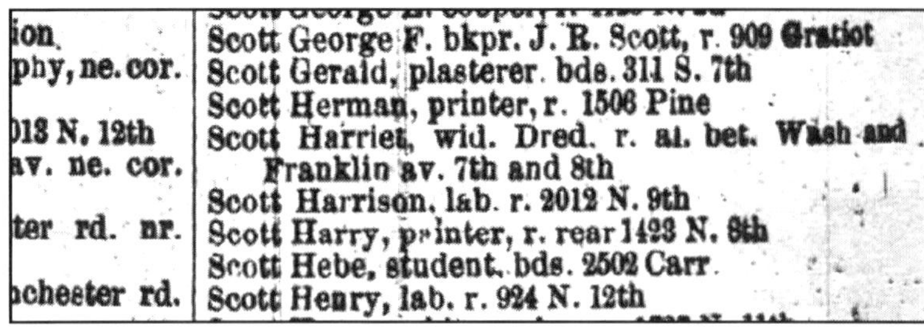

ion. | Scott George F. bkpr. J. R. Scott, r. 909 Gratiot
phy, ne. cor. | Scott Gerald, plasterer. bds. 311 S. 7th
Scott Herman, printer, r. 1506 Pine
013 N. 12th | Scott Harriet, wid. Dred. r. al. bet. Wash and Franklin av. 7th and 8th
av. ne. cor. |
Scott Harrison, lab. r. 2012 N. 9th
ter rd. nr. | Scott Harry, printer, r. rear 1423 N. 8th
Scott Hebe, student. bds. 2502 Carr.
chester rd. | Scott Henry, lab. r. 924 N. 12th

Schweppe Herman, lab. Levi Ashbrook & Co
Schweppe William, lab. r. rear 2117 N. 12th
Schweppenstede Henry, grocer. 1318 N. 10th
Schwer William, plumber, r. 1806 Hebert
Schwerdt Sophie, dressmkr. 1331 Chestnut
Schwerdtfeger August (Broeker & Schwerdtfeger), r. 2409 N. 16th
Schwerg Henry, butcher, bds. ns. Louisa, nr. De Kalb
Schwering Bernard H. r. Elizabeth, nr. Russell av.
Schwering Louisa, dressmkr. 2806 N. 15th
Schwerling Anthony, cooper, r Salisbury, ne. cor. 12th
Schwermann Bernard. blksmith, r. rear 2608 N. 18th
Schwersinger Francis, wid. Michael, r. 516 S. 3d
Schwerzler John, grocer, 1504 and 1506 S. 7th
Schwetje Frederick, lab. r. 3916 B'way
Schwetz Albert, cooper, r. Emmett, nr. 10th
Schwickmann Henry, lab. r. 3507 N. 12th
Schwidde August, moulder. r. 1304 Monroe
Schwidde John H. flour and feed, ws. 14th, nr. Warren, r. Warren, se cor. 14th
Schwidde William, mechanic. r 1422 Wright
Schwide Herman, lab. Levi Ashbrook
Schwieder John, lab. P. Danerrheim & Co. Cardt
Schwieker Charles, news carrier, r. 1823 North Market
Schwiekert Thomas, lab. r. es. Julia, nr. Chouteau av.
Schwienehorst Joseph, watchmkr. bds. 417 Duchouquette
Schwier Hermann (Habighorst & Co.), r. 2915 Cardt av.
Schwiering Anna M. wid. Christian, r. 1405 Benton
Schwiering John, driver, bds. 1405 Benton
Schwietering Bernard, blksmith. bds. 1108 Emmet
Schwietering Henry. blksmith, 1901 S. 11th, r. 1108 Emmet
Schwille Charles. finisher, r. 1108 Marion
Schwilley John J. salesman, r. Mullanphy, ne. cor. 14th
Schwimley Ricka, wid. John, r. rear 1013 N. 12th
Schwind Albert, painter, bds. Cardt av. ne. cor. Marine av.
Schwindker Christ, lab, r. Manchester rd. nr. Clayton rd.
Schwindker Frederick, lab. bds. Manchester rd. nr. Clayton rd.
Schwingemann Henry, cook, r. 1502 Columbus
Schwininger Maria, r. 214 Poplar
Schwion Dietrich driver, r. rear 1013 Sidney
Schwitte William, sawyer, r. 1422½ Wright
Schwitzer Carl, stonecutter, r. 1041 North Market
Schwitzer Jacob, peddler, r. Cass av, ne. cor. Glasgow av.
Schwitzer Samuel, porter, r. 1931 N. 16th
Schwob Christian, sawmkr. bds. 2716 N. 16th
Schwoebel Gabriel, mason, bds. 112 Elm
Schworm Simon, stonedresser, r. ns. Cherokee, nr. Lemp av.
Schworz Fred, clk. Theo Kalb, r. 206 Plum
Schyerr Philip, tinner, bds. 2115 N. 13th
Scied Katrina, butcher, ws. Main, 8 N. Randolph, Cardt
Scilear Frederick, lab. r. 3715 N. 12th
Scipey John, bartender, r. 723 Morgan
Sclaff Peter, r. 1109 Angelrodt
Sclerath John, tinner, r. 2018 Christy av.
Scobee Johanna, wid. George, r. 3709 N 9th
Scofield E L. Rev. 720 N. 4th, r. Jennings Station, St L K C & N R R.

Sceles Richard, blksmith, r. ws. Columbus, nr. Anna
Scollar Michael, riverman. bds. 1220 B'way
Scollard Patrick F. porter, r. 202 Cass av.
Scollay Charles, molder, 1009 St. Charles
Scollay James, painter, r. 1009 St. Charles
Scolly Edmond, lab. 1825 S. 2d
Score William J. treas. Excelsior Shoe Co. r. 615 Wash
Scotia Iron Co. Rufus J. Lackland, pres. Thomas Howard, vice-pres. Robert Anderson, sec. and treas. 306½ Olive
Scott Adam, teamster, r. ws. Mercer, nr. Gratiot
Scott Allen, lab. r. 3109 Elizabeth
Scott Andrew, river, bds 736 S. Main
Scott Annie, r. rear 1615 N. 7th
Scott Arthur L. clk. Scott, Collins & Co. r. 1820 Washington av.
Scott Ashley D. (Scott, Collins & Co.), r. 2026 Pine
Scott Augustus, dry goods, r. 1411 Olive
Scott Benjamin, lab r. Grand av. s. of Meramec
Scott Charles, expressman, r. 308 Poplar
Scott Charles, lab. r. 1517 N. 9th
Scott Charles, porter, r. 412 S. 2d
Scott Charles J. bkpr. Smith & Woods, bds. St. Clair Hotel
Scott Charles M. pilot, bds. Columbus House
Scott Charles S. *Republican*, r. 12 N 11th
Scott Clingan, com. mer. 9 Locust. r. 2045 Pine
Scott Collins, lab. r. ns. Illinois, nr. 8th, Cardt
SCOTT, COLLINS & CO. (Ashley D. Scott, Samuel S. Scott and Nelson R. Collins), provisions and fancy groceries, 518 and 326 N. 2d
Scott Cornelia, wid. William, r. 1229 Chouteau av.
Scott Daniel, lab. bds. 711 N. Levee
Scott David, clk. Parker, Russell & Co. r. Oak Hill
Scott Dudley, hand express, r. 1118 N. 12th
Scott Edward, clk. Benton House
Scott Edward, waiter, bds. 2012 N. 9th
Scott Edward J. steamfitter, r. 923 N. 6th
Scott Edward P. physician, bds. 2721 Lucas av.
Scott Elisha, lab. r. al. rear 2412 Morgan
Scott Elizabeth M. wid. William C. bds. 2045 Pine
Scott Ellen, wid. Alexander, r. 1713 Franklin av.
Scott Emerson W. with Scott, Collins & Co. r. 2026 Pine
Scott Francis, teamster, r. 1514 N. 10th
Scott Francis W. egg packer, r. 1117 N. 5th
Scott Frankie, dressmkr. r. 1415 B'way
Scott George, correspondent, Dodd, Brown & Co. 2945 Dayton
Scott George E. cooper, r. 4125 N. 2d
Scott George F. bkpr. J. R. Scott, r. 909 Gratiot
Scott Gerald, plasterer. bds. 311 S. 7th
Scott Herman, printer, r. 1506 Pine
Scott Harriet, wid. Dred. r. al. bet. Wash and Franklin av. 7th and 8th
Scott Harrison, lab. r. 2012 N. 9th
Scott Harry, printer, r. rear 1423 N. 8th
Scott Hebe, student. bds. 2502 Carr
Scott Henry, lab. r. 924 N. 12th
Scott Henry, whitewasher, r. 1727 N. 11th
Scott Henry L. riverman, r. 1233 O'Fallon
Scott Honora, wid. James, r. 944 B'way
Scott Howard, printer, bds. 811 Washington av.
Scott Hugh, huckster, 14 Lucas Market, r. 1108 Chestnut
Scott Humphrey F. r. 824 Walnut
Scott H. tel operator, bds. 1609 Washington av.
Scott Isabella, r. 310 S. 5th
Scott James, huckster, r. 1103 Chestnut
Scott James, teamster, r. ws. 8th, nr. Nebraska, Cardt

Harriet Scott's 1874 St. Louis City Directory entry.

HARRIET'S LAST YEARS
1870–1876

By 1870 Wilson and Eliza lived in the 8th ward of St. Louis city. Wilson was a "riverman" and Eliza, this time recorded as "Lizzie," was keeping house. The federal census enumerator visited their home on 20 July 1870, less than a month after little Wilson's death, yet listed the deceased child as part of their household. The census taker's instructions included directions to record everyone who lived in the household as of 1 June 1870 and the little boy did not die until 30 June.[219] If other children were born to Eliza and Wilson between Lates' birth in 1862 and the 1870 census, they did not survive. Young Wilson was the only child listed in the family's 1870 census record.

The 1870 census for St. Louis listed a Harriet Scott, perhaps the widow of Dred Scott. The Harriet Scott in question was recorded by the census taker as black, female, and working as a domestic

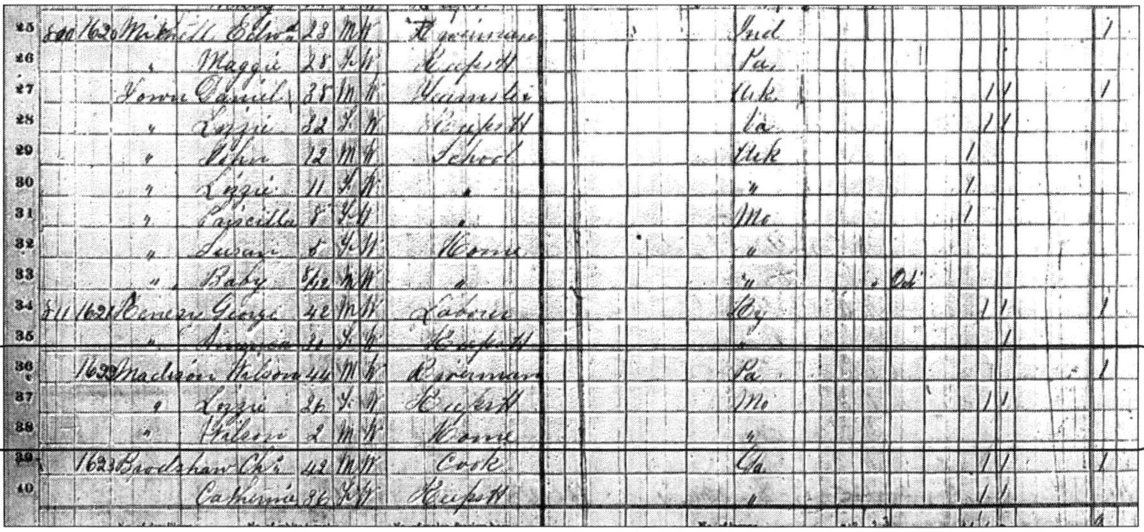

Courtesy of Mid-Continent Public Library, Independence, MO

Wilson, Lizzie [Eliza], and young Wilson Madison, U.S. 1870 census, ward 8, City of St. Louis.

servant. She was listed in the household of civil engineer William Werden.[220] The census taker was to record only members of a household, so Harriet's listing in the Werden household implied she lived and worked there.

2229 Scott Street. Residence of Wm. Werden family in 1870 census.

Block 181 where Harriet died in 1876.

1905 *Atlas of the City of St. Louis*

The 1870 census did not record house addresses, but the St. Louis city directory for that year listed a William Werden at 2229 Scott Street.[221] His neighbors on the same 1870 census page also lived in the 2200 block of Scott.[222] That address was distant from Harriet's previous residences. so being a live-in domestic would have been logical.

Why would Harriet work as a live-in domestic rather than as a laundress? The latter was physically demanding and would have been more difficult as she grew older. Also, working as a live-in domestic would provide room and lodging. This might have been a way to support herself rather than be a burden on her daughters.

Also, as previously speculated, anger was perhaps directed at Dred Scott after the Civil War. As his widow, Harriet may have found shelter and anonymity living in someone else's home. Residing in someone's home might also account for Harriet's absence in the St. Louis city directories from 1868 through 1873.

If the Harriet Scott in the Werden household was not Dred's widow, then where was she? An 1870 census listing for Lizzie Scott, if recorded, has not been found. Thus, Harriet may have lived with Lizzie and their household was simply not recorded.

Birth of Unnamed Grandchildren

Five months after their son Wilson died, Eliza and Wilson welcomed another son into the world on 30 November 1870.[223] This child's birth record listed "Elizabeth" Madison as the mother, her maiden name as Scott, and the father as Wilson Madison. Clearly, this child was one of Dred and Harriet's grandchildren. The baby's first name was not recorded, but that was not unusual for that time. This infant was born at 505 6th Street, and according to the birth record, was the sixth child born to Eliza.

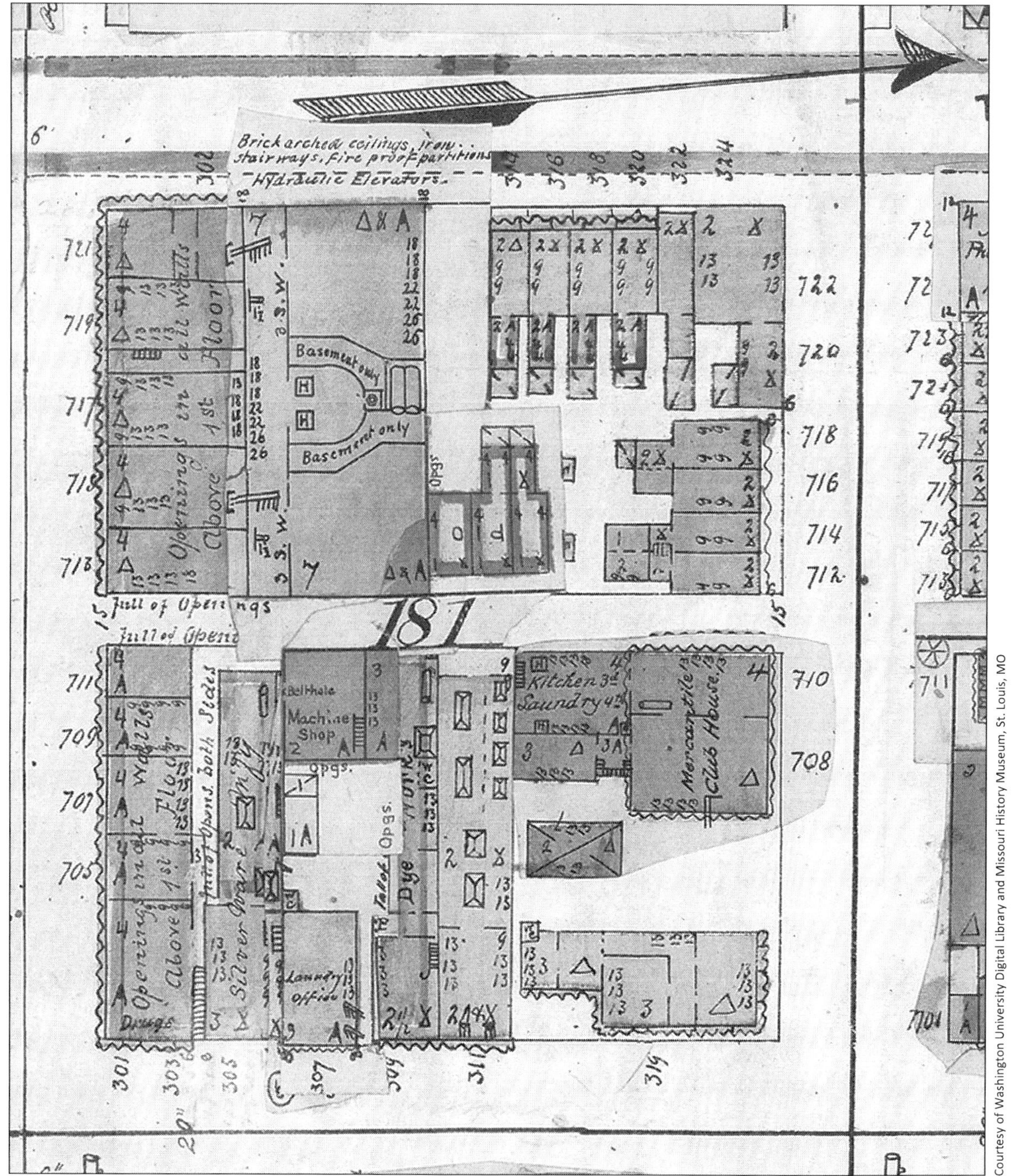

This 1876 Whipple Fire Insurance *map of block 181, bounded by 7th & 8th and Locust & Olive, does not identify the exact location of No. 6 Hicks Alley where Wilson and Eliza Madison lived.*

Courtesy of Washington University Digital Library and Missouri History Museum, St. Louis, MO

Another unnamed son was born to Wilson and "Elizabeth" Madison on 2 May 1873.[224] The clerk recording the births that month failed to record complete information for the babies and their parents. As a result the address where he was born and the number of children to whom the mother had previously given birth is unknown.

Harriet's Death

The 1874 city directory listed Harriet as Dred's widow, living in the alleyway between Wash and Franklin, 7th and 8th.[225] One year later, the 1875 city directory listed a Harriet Scott living at the rear of 712 Wash, which would be a more specific description of a residence in the alley between Wash and Franklin, 7th and 8th.[226] These two records are probably for the same Harriet.

No single document says when and where Harriet, widow of Dred Scott, died. The information can be inferred, however, from several documents.

1. Eliza and Wilson Madison were living at 6 Hicks alley in 1876, in St. Louis city block 181.[227]
2. Harriet Scott, a sixty-year-old black woman, died on 17 June 1876, in St. Louis. Her place of death was listed as alley no. 6 between 7th and 8th, Locust and Olive.[228]
3. The street directory section of the 1876 St. Louis city directory states that Hicks Alley is "N. to S., 752 Locust to 751 Olive in block 181.[229]

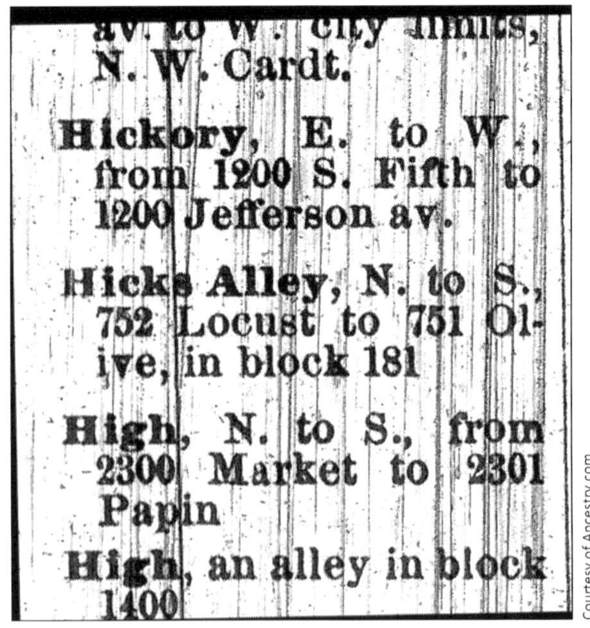

N. W. Cardt.

Hickory, E. to W., from 1200 S. Fifth to 1200 Jefferson av.

Hicks Alley, N. to S., 752 Locust to 751 Olive, in block 181

High, N. to S., from 2300 Market to 2301 Papin

High, an alley in block 1400

Courtesy of Ancestry.com

1876 street directory listing for Hicks Alley.

Registry of Deaths in the

City of St. Louis, 20th June–21st 1876. 131

Courtesy of St. Louis County Library, Special Collections

Left side (top) and right side (bottom) of Harriet Scott's St. Louis death register entry showing her place of death as "Alley, No. 6 betw. 7th & 8th and Locust & Olive str."

If Eliza and Wilson lived at No. 6 Hicks Alley (the alley in block 181), and this Harriet Scott died at No. 6 in the alley of block 181, then this Harriet died in the same house where Eliza and Wilson lived. She also had the same name, approximate age, and race as Dred's widow. It is probable, therefore, that Harriet Scott who died 17 June 1876, was Eliza's mother and Dred's widow. It is possible she was someone else, but not probable. No newspaper article mentioning Harriet's death has been found, but her death occurred about two weeks before the 100th birthday of the United States. News of the day revolved around politics and the country's centennial celebration.

Harriet belonged to the 8th Street Baptist Church in St. Louis, and its church history says her funeral was from there.[230] Harriet was buried in section C of Greenwood Cemetery in St. Louis County. Her grave cost five dollars, one of the more expensive graves in that cemetery.[231] The cost of her grave suggests that someone beyond the immediate family may have paid for part or all of the funeral expenses. By 1876, both Henry and Taylor Blow were deceased, so possibly one of the other Blow family members, such as Henry's daughter, Susan Blow, may have purchased the grave. [232] The cemetery did not record the location and number of Harriet's grave. Also, all tombstones in section C were removed, probably by the end of the 1800s, so there is no way to know the exact location of her grave within that section.[233]

Grandchild, Edw. Madison

Born on 12 October 1876, Edw. Madison died two days later on 14 October.[234] Harriet Scott had died four months earlier and her grave in Greenwood Cemetery was reopened for the burial of this infant.[235] Again pertinent is the same question asked when Lates was buried in Dred's grave—for whom would the family allow Harriet's grave to be reopened? It would probably only happen for someone very close to Harriet, most likely a family member. It is logical to believe that a newborn bearing the last name of Madison and sharing the same grave was Harriet's grandchild.

The St. Louis death register listed the place of death for Edw. as "Nick St"—yet there is no Nick Street according to the St. Louis street directory for that year.[236] Should the entry have read "Hick St.?" A close look at the death register for Edw. Madison is helpful.

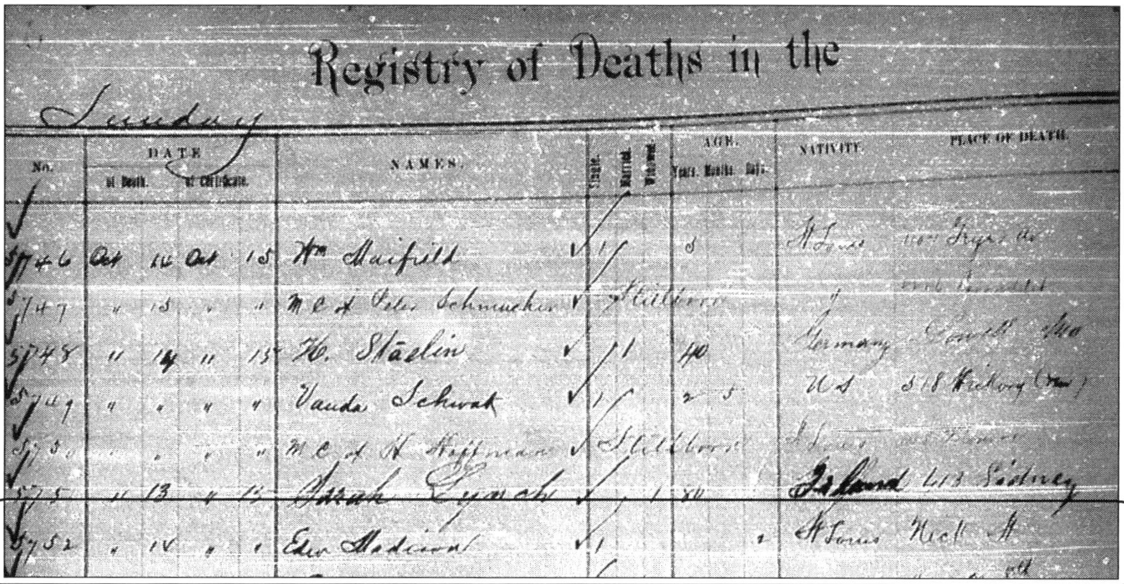

Registry of Deaths in the

No.	DATE of Death.	of Certificate.	NAMES.	Single. Married. Widowed.	AGE. Years. Months. Days.	NATIVITY.	PLACE OF DEATH.
5746	Oct 14	Oct 15	Wm Maifield			St Louis	
5747	" 15	" "	Mc & Peter Schmucker	Stillborn			
5748	" 14	" 15	H. Staslin		40	Germany	
5749	" "	" "	Vanda Schwak			US	518 Hickory
5750	" "	" "	Mc & H Hoffman	Stillborn			
5751	" 13	" 15	Sarah Lynch		80	Ireland	413 Sidney
5752	" 14	" "	Edw Madison			St Louis	

Courtesy of St. Louis County Library, Special Collections

St. Louis death register listing for Edw. Madison who was buried in the same grave with Harriet Scott.

ST. LOUIS CITY/COUNTY SPLIT OF 1876

In 1876, the City of St. Louis split off from St. Louis County and became an independent city. The "Great Divorce," as it is often called, resulted in the City of St. Louis and St. Louis County having separate governing bodies, court and record keeping systems after 1876. The resulting confusion, especially for those unaware of the historic split, continues to this day.

— William N. Cassella Jr., "City-County Separation: The 'Great Divorce' of 1876," *Missouri Historical Society Bulletin* 15 (January 1959) 85–104.

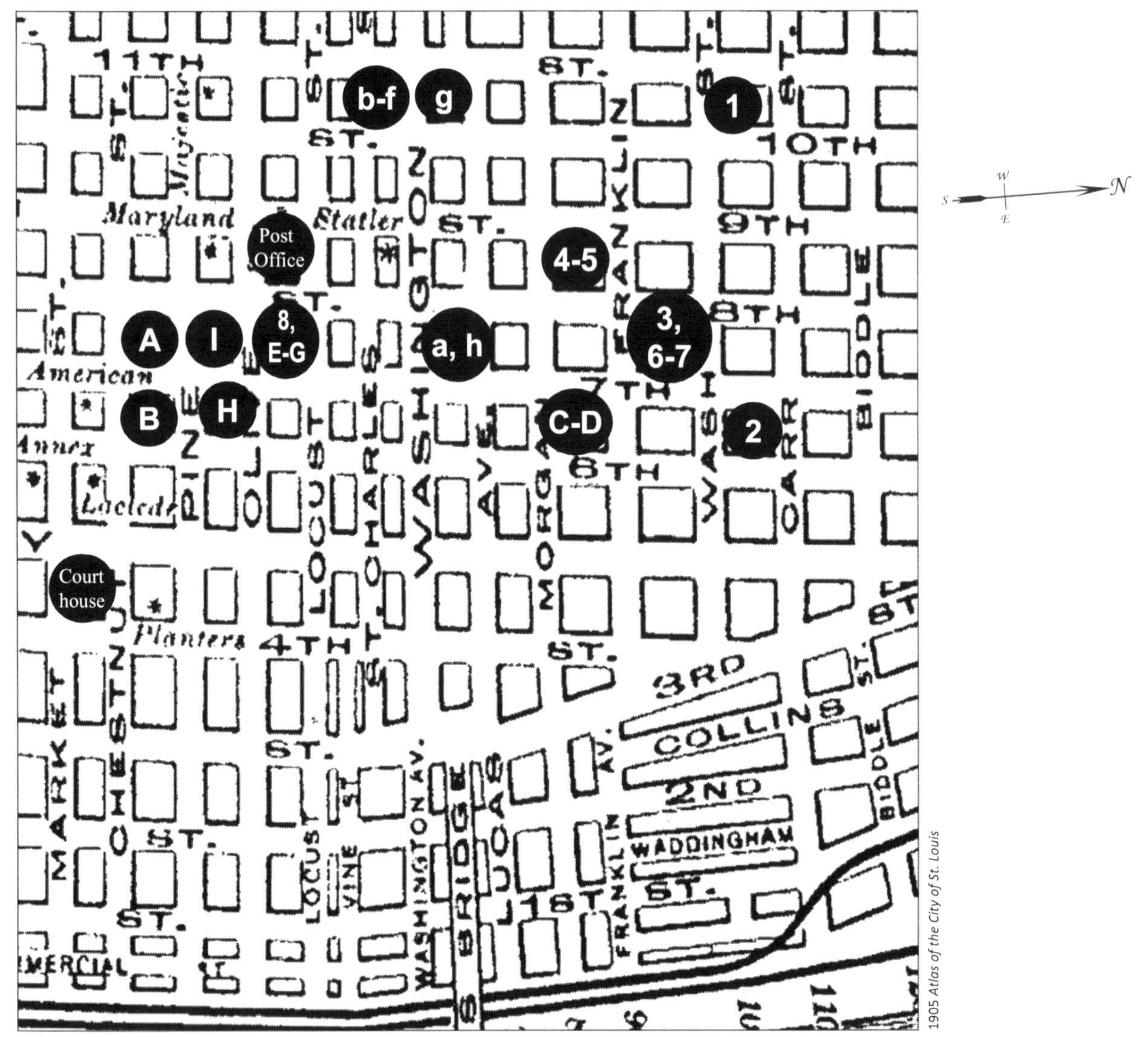

1905 *Atlas of the City of St. Louis*

Scott Family Places of Residence, 1854–1888

Addresses were often vague, so locations are approximate

Harriet & Dred Scott

1. 1854–5
2. 1859: Harriet a widow
3. 1860
4. 1864–65
5. 1866–67
6. 1874
7. 1875
8. 1876: Harriet died

Eliza & Wilson Madison

A. 1864–65
B. 1872–73
C. 1874
D. 1875
E. 1876
F. 1877
G. 1879
H. 1881: Wilson died
I. 1882: Eliza died

Lizzie/Eliza Scott

a. 1872–73
b. 1879
c. 1880
d. 1881
e. 1882
f. 1883–84
g. 1886–87
h. 1887–88

ELIZA AND LIZZIE
1877–1882

Apparently traumatized by her childhood time in hiding, Lizzie lived as a recluse. Hence, her story is understandably the most difficult to uncover.

The 1872 city directory lists a Lizzie Scott, a "colored" washerwoman, residing at 719 Washington Avenue in the middle of the neighborhood where Harriet and Eliza's family lived. By 1879, the city directory lists an Eliza Scott at 1010 Washington. She was at that address in each directory through 1881. In one of those years, she was listed as a laundress. In 1882 and 1883, a laundress living at 1010 Washington is listed as Lizzie Scott rather than Eliza Scott. It seems likely that the records for 1879 through 1883 are all for the same person.[237]

More information about this young resident of 1010 Washington Avenue comes from her listing in the 1880 St. Louis federal census. Two schedules were enumerated for St. Louis that year— one in June that was rejected, and the second in November, that was accepted.

Listed as Eliza Scott in the June census and as Lizzie Scott in November, she was recorded both times as a black, single washerwoman rooming at 1010 Washington. She was thirty years of age in June and only twenty-five in November, but that discrepancy may be because someone else gave the information, possibly a neighbor.[238] Her residence at 1010 Washington Avenue was only a few blocks from the places where Eliza and Wilson lived from 1879 until their deaths.[239]

> **10TH AND WASHINGTON AVENUE**
>
> The "shanties" on the south side of Washington Avenue between 10th and 11th were torn down to make way for the construction of a new building for Liggett & Myers Tobacco sometime after 1884. That building, which was completed in 1888, still stands today and is known as the Merchandise Mart.
>
> — Joann Lucas Conrad, "Building on a Grave-Yard," *St. Louis Genealogical Society Quarterly*, 42 (2009): 17.

The 1880 census shows Charles Scott and his wife, Polly, were Lizzie's next-door neighbors. Charles was as a cook on a steamboat.[240] While they share the same last name of Scott, no connection to Dred and Harriet's family is known.

Despite two St. Louis enumerations for 1880, no census record has been found for Wilson and Eliza and their family. They may have been missed; some census takers were more diligent than others. Or their entries may simply be unreadable as many pages are severely faded and the faint handwriting is difficult or impossible to read.

Deaths of Wilson and Eliza

Records with facts about Dred and Harriet's family after 1880 are scarce. However, references that do exist for Wilson and Eliza from 1876 until their deaths in 1881 and 1882, respectively, provide a better picture of the couple. Separately, these records are confusing because of the variations in their first names. But as a group, the records yield helpful information.

- The same place of residence, 6 Hicks Alley, and common occupation as a cook for Wilson Madison in the 1876 city directory and for Joshua W. Madison in the 1877 city directory imply that they were one and the same person.[241]
- Wilson's place of death, listed in his 1881 St. Louis death register as the "rear of 615 Pine," is the same address listed for Joshua Madison, cook, in the 1881 city directory.[242]

These facts make it probable that Joshua W. Madison, Joshua Madison, and Wilson Madison were name variations for the same man.

Eliza Scott, Eldest Daughter.
Courtesy of Missouri History Museum, St. Louis, MO

Eliza Scott, Eldest Daughter. St. Louis Globe-Democrat *newspaper article, 10 January 1886 on Dred Scott's family.*

The St. Louis death register describes Wilson Madison as "colored," married, forty-three years of age, and a cook when he died on 18 May 1881. His place of death, the "rear of 615 Pine," was also his residence in the 1881 city directory, so he died at home.[243] His funeral was at the 8th Street Baptist Church and he was buried in Greenwood Cemetery in St. Louis County.[244] Surviving Greenwood Cemetery records do not include burials for that year, so his exact burial location is unknown.

With Joshua and Joshua W. Madison established as name variations for Wilson, more information emerges for his widow, Eliza. The year after Wilson's death the city directory listed an Elizabeth Madison as the widow of Joshua W. Madison and showed her residence rather vaguely as "alley, 7th near Pine." That is an approximate description of the address where Wilson Madison died in 1881 at "rear of 615 Pine."[245]

Elizabeth Madison's 1881 city directory listing her as a widow was her only entry after Wilson's death. What happened to her after that? Again, records work together to tell her story.

The St. Louis Death Register lists an Elizabeth Madison, "colored" thirty-nine years of age, and a widow, who died in St. Louis on 13 July 1882. Her place of death was the "alley between 7th and 8th, Olive and Pine." Because that address was also the place of residence that year for Elizabeth Madison, widow of Joshua W. Madison, this suggests that this 1882 death record is for Eliza, Wilson's widow and that she also died at home.[246] As it was for her mother and her husband, Eliza's funeral was also at the 8th Street Baptist Church.[247] She was buried in Greenwood Cemetery.[248]

The Legacy Passes to the Next Generation

Although a later 1886 *St. Louis Globe-Democrat* article about the Dred and Harriet Scott family said Wilson Madison and his wife had seven children, neither family oral tradition nor public records have confirmed that. What is known is that the deaths of Eliza and Wilson left their two surviving children, Harry and John Madison, as orphans. In spite of the high infant mortality in that time period, these two young boys survived to carry on Dred and Harriet's legacy.

<table>
<tr><th colspan="3">1876–1883 REFERENCES FOR WILSON AND ELIZA (SCOTT) MADISON</th></tr>
<tr><th>Year</th><th>Information</th><th>Source</th></tr>
<tr><td>1876</td><td>Madison, Wilson, cook. r. 6 Hicks al.</td><td>St. Louis City Directory</td></tr>
<tr><td>1877</td><td>Madison, Joshua W., cook, r. 6 Hicks al.</td><td>St. Louis City Directory</td></tr>
<tr><td>1879</td><td>Madison, Joshua W., cook, r. 7 Hicks</td><td>St. Louis City Directory</td></tr>
<tr><td rowspan="2">1881</td><td>Madison, Joshua, cook, r. al. rear 615 Pine</td><td>St. Louis City Directory</td></tr>
<tr><td>Madison, Wilson, cook, died May 18, 1881, at the rear of 615 Pine St.</td><td>St. Louis Death Registry</td></tr>
<tr><td rowspan="2">1882</td><td>Madison, Elizabeth, wid. Joshua W., r. al. 7th near Pine</td><td>St. Louis City Directory</td></tr>
<tr><td>Madison, Elizabeth, died July 13, 1882, at alley between 7th & 8th, Olive & Pine</td><td>St. Louis Death Registry</td></tr>
<tr><td>1883</td><td>No listing for Elizabeth Madison</td><td>St. Louis City Directory</td></tr>
</table>

REGISTER OF DEATHS IN THE

No.	Date of Death	Date of Certificate	Names	Sex / Condition	Age	Nativity	Place of Death
4422	July 15	Sept 16	Lydia H. Cordry	1	43		Good Samaritan Hospital
4423	" 15	" "	Martha A. Thompson	1	5 3	St. Louis	1242 Carondelet av
4424	" 15	" "	Mary E. McKennie	1	3	"	2513 Cass av
4425	" 13	" "	Elizabeth Madison	1	39	"	Alley bet 7 & 8 Olive & Pine
4426	" 15	" "	Philomena Vannto	1	19	"	413 S. 4th St
4427	" 15	" "	Sophia Kahne	1	6	"	1027 N. 8th St
4428	" 15	" "	Willie Monroe	1	73	"	2801 Wash St

Courtesy of St. Louis County Library, Special Collections

CITY OF ST. LOUIS, July 1882 51

Ward	Occupation	Disease	White / Colored	Attending Physician	Name of Cemetery	Name of Undertaker
20		Uterine Cancer	1	Jno. Harris	~~Calvary~~ Bellefontaine	A. Kron
3		Gastro Enteritis	1	A. Luloff	Holy Ghost	H. Hohmann
12		Septicaemia	1	A. A. Rowland	Holy Trinity	Lammer & Spelbrink
2		Phthisis Pulmonalis	1	Fr. O. Drake	Greenwood	J. T. Murrell
1		Cholera Infantum	1	W. C. Richardson	Calvary	B. Brockmann
4		Icterus neonatorum	1	C. G. Rohlfing	Calvary	Jno Arnold Jr.
20		Tabes Mesenterica	1	Fr. O. Drake	Bellefontaine	Smithers & Wagoner

Left side (top) and right side (bottom) of Elizabeth (Scott) Madison's 1882 St. Louis City death register listing.

WILSON & ELIZA (SCOTT) MADISON'S POSSIBLE, PROBABLE, AND DEFINITE CHILDREN		
According to the 10 January 1886 *St. Louis Globe-Democrat* article, Eliza and Wilson Madison had seven children. Previously, the only known children were Harry and John A. Madison. Listed here are names and known dates of birth and death for Harry and John along with children who might be, or probably were, children of Eliza and Wilson.		
Name	Dates	Evidence
1. Lates/Seales W. Madison	b: 29 January 1862 d: 2 August 1863	• His burial was in the same grave with Dred Scott.
2. Catherine Madison	b: 7 February 1867 d: 26 December 1867	• Her last name, race, and place of birth (921 B Franklin Avenue and Wash Street) make her a possibility.
3 Wilson Madison	b: 30 September 1868 d: 30 June 1870	• He resided in the household of Eliza and Wilson Madison and shared the first name of Wilson
4. unnamed male Madison [birth record] — was probably Harry Madison, the eldest of of Eliza and Wilson's two surviving sons	b: 30 November 1870 [birth record] d: unknown	• Birth record for unnamed son born to Elizabeth and Wilson Madison on 30 November 1870. • The mother's maiden name was Scott, and he was her sixth child.
5. Unnamed male Madison [birth record] — was probably John A. Madison, the younger of Eliza and Wilson's two surviving sons	b. 2 May 1873 [birth record] [John listed 1 May 1880 as his birth date in later years, but that does not agree with the age implied by his portrait in the 1886 *Globe-Democrat* article, nor with the age he listed on his marriage license application] d: 6 May 1931	• Birth record for unnamed son born to Elizabeth and Wilson Madison on 2 May 1873. • The 1886 *Globe-Democrat* article on Dred Scott listed John as his twelve-year-old grandson and included his picture.
6. Edw. Madison	b: 12 October 1876 d: 14 October 1876	• Edw was buried in same grave with Harriet Scott.

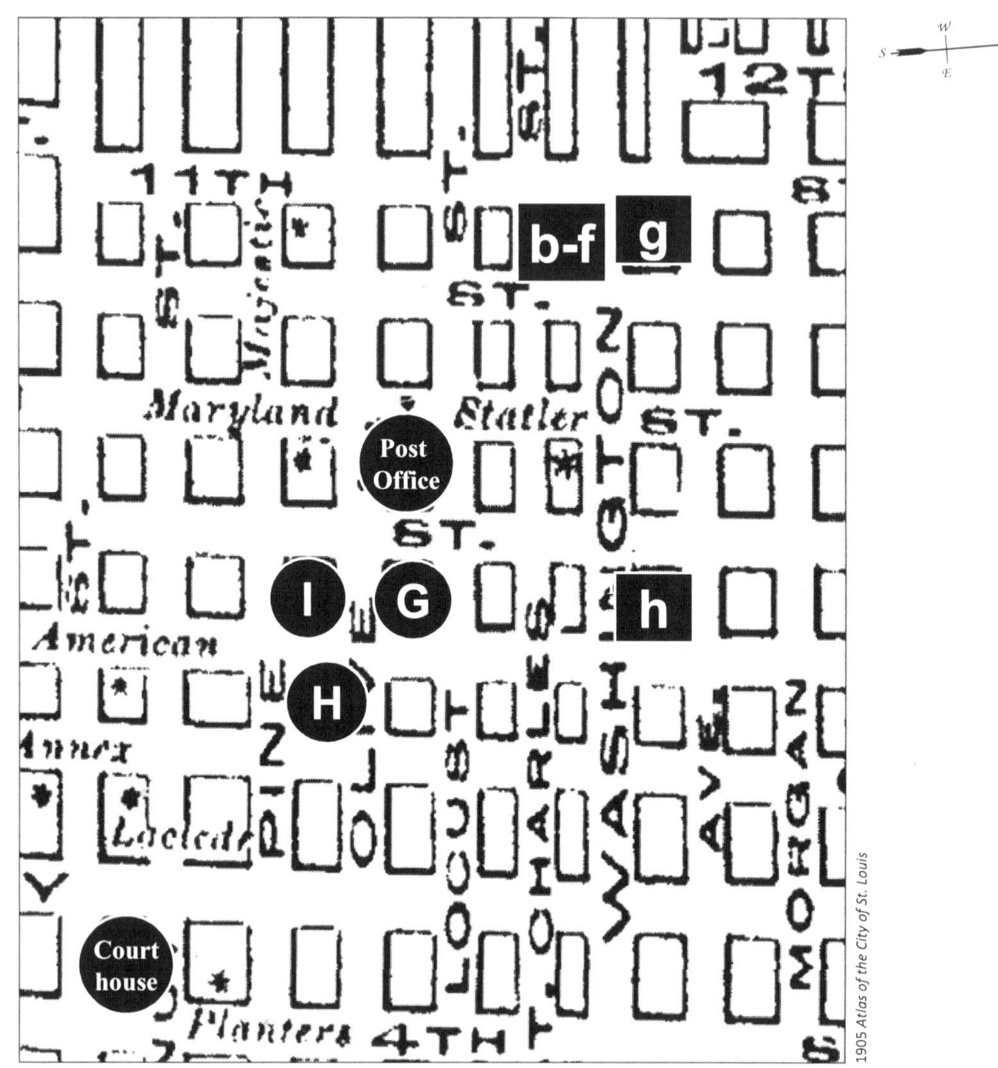

1905 *Atlas of the City of St. Louis*

Places of residence for Eliza and Wilson Madison (1879–1882)
and Lizzie/Eliza Scott (1879–1888)
Addresses were often vague, so locations are approximate

Eliza & Wilson Madison

G. 1879
H. 1881: Wilson died
I. 1882: Eliza died

Lizzie/Eliza Scott

b. 1879
c. 1880
d. 1881
e. 1882
f. 1883–84
g. 1886–87
h. 1887–88

LIZZIE AND HER NEPHEWS
1882–1912

By 1882, Lizzie had lost her parents, her sister, and her brother-in-law. After Eliza and Wilson died, Lizzie took her nephews in and raised them.[249] Harry and John were now her only family.

The boys brought with them a large charcoal portrait of Dred and Harriet, shown here. It measures about two feet by three feet and is a treasured family heirloom. The artist and date of the portrait are unknown. Unlike the individual daguerreotypes at Fitzgibbons Gallery, in this portrait Dred and Harriet are sitting side by side and they are wearing different clothes.

Although in her later life Lizzie would never admit who she was, she did acknowledge giving Harry and John a home after their parents died. Her story was that one day Harry and John were sitting on the curb holding this large charcoal portrait of Dred and Harriet and other family things. Lizzie saw them and decided to give them a home. While no one in the family believed that somewhat improbable story, no one was willing to question Lizzie about it either.[250]

Courtesy of the John A. Madison Jr. Family

The portrait of Dred and Harriet which Harry and John brought with them after their parents died.

Where Did Lizzie Live?

City directories and census data provide clues about Lizzie's residence before, at the time of, and after Wilson and Eliza's deaths. As previously mentioned, a laundress listed in records as "Eliza" or "Lizzie" Scott resided at 1010 Washington Avenue in St. Louis from 1879 to 1883.[251] In the 1884 and 1885 city directories, she is no longer at that address, but the 1886 directory lists a Lizzie Scott who does laundry work living at 614 North 11th Street.[252] This is just one block away from 1010 Washington.

The next year the 1887–1888 directory omits Lizzie at 614 North 11th Street but includes Lizzie Scott, a "colored" washerwoman at 719 Washington, four blocks farther east.[253] Fifteen years earlier, in 1872, the directory listed a "colored washerwoman" named Lizzie Scott residing at the same address.[254]

The combined city directory entries show common information for the women listed. They share the same

- name (Eliza or Lizzie Scott)
- race ("colored" or black when listed)
- marital status (single when listed)
- occupation (laundress)
- neighborhood

It is likely, therefore, that these listings are for the same person living at different addresses. That person is quite possibly Dred and Harriet's younger daughter, Lizzie, who gave her nephews, Harry and John, a home after their parents died.

1886 St. Louis Globe-Democrat Article

The *St. Louis Globe-Democrat* published an extensive article about Dred Scott and his family on 10 January 1886. It included wood-cut prints from pictures of Dred, Harriet, their daughter Eliza, and their grandson, John Madison. The article indicated that Harry and John Madison's parents had died and that they were the surviving grandsons of Dred and Harriet Scott.[255]

> "Harry, who is 14 years old and of a wild disposition, not long since left his guardian. Johnny, on the other hand, is a docile lad, and is regarded by many as an intellectual prodigy. He is a close student, though but 12 years of age, and has determined to become a lawyer. He was born "with a veil over his face" which is looked upon by negroes as a sure sign that the boy is destined to become a great man, and keep the name of Dred Scott, his famous grandfather, fresh in the minds of his people."[256]

St. Louis City Directories, 1872–1888, and Census Listings for Eliza and Lizzie Scott Who Could be the Youngest Daughter of Dred and Harriet Scott.

Year	Information	Source
1872–1873	Scott, Lizzie, (col'd) washerwoman, rear 719 Washington av	St. Louis City Directory
1874	no listing	St. Louis City Directory
1875	no listing	St. Louis City Directory
1876	Scott, Lizzie, resides 614 N. 11th (year Harreit died)	St. Louis City Directory
1877	no listing	St. Louis City Directory
1878	no listing	St. Louis City Directory
1879	Scott, Eliza, resides 1010 Washington av	St. Louis City Directory
1880	Scott, Eliza, resides 1010 Washington av	St. Louis City Directory
1880	Scott, Eliza, 30 years, black, single, washerwoman, 1010 Washington (June 1880)	U.S Census — 1st St. Louis enumeration
	Scott, Lizzie, 25 years, black, single, laundress, 1010 Washington (November 1880)	U.S Census — 2nd St. Louis enumeration
1881	Scott, Eliza N. laundress, r. 1010 Washington av	St. Louis City Directory
1882	Scott, Lizzie laundry, 1010 Washington av	St. Louis City Directory
1883–1884	Scott, Lizzie, laundress, 1010 Washington av	St. Louis City Directory
1884–1885	no listing	St. Louis City Directory
1885–1886	no listing	St. Louis City Directory
1886–1887	Scott, Lizzie, laundry, rear 614 N. 11th	St. Louis City Directory
1887–1888	Scott, Lizzie, (col'd) washerwoman, r. 719 Washington av	St. Louis City Directory

Some children are born with a veil or "caul,"—actually the amniotic membrane—still over the face.[257] It is not a common occurrence and children born with it were thought to have special gifts and abilities.[258]

The photo of John Madison appeared in that article. It challenges previously accepted fact about his birth date. John's death certificate and Madison family records say he was born on 1 May 1880.[259] There is no reason to question that until one views this portrait. Based on a birth date in 1880, John would have been five and a half years old at most in January of 1886.

However, John's portrait is not of a five-and-a-half-year-old child. It appears to be that of a teenager and shows convincingly that he must have been born before 1880.

If this 1886 *St. Louis Globe-Democrat* article was correct and Harry was fourteen, and John was twelve when it was written, that would place Harry's birth somewhere between early 1871 and early 1872 and John's birth between early 1873 and early 1874.[260] Were the birth records for the sons born to Eliza and Wilson on 30 November 1870 and on 2 May 1873, which did not include the infants' first names, perhaps for Harry and John? If this picture accurately represents John's age, that is probably the case.

Henry Sanders

The lengthy 1886 *St. Louis Globe-Democrat* article also said Harry and John's father left an annuity to provide for his family after his death. It further stated that Harry and John's mother, prior to her death in 1882, left them in the care of Henry Sanders at 1403 North 11th Street.[261]

This newspaper article contains at least some incorrect information. For example, it incorrectly

- identified John and Harry's father as Henry Madison instead of Wilson Madison
- listed Wilson's wife as Lizzie, the younger of Dred and Harriet's daughters
- said that Harriet died a few years after Dred
- stated that "... Eliza, the eldest child, followed her parents to the grave, at the early age of 25" [which would place her death about 1863]
- said that Dred's remains were lost when Wesleyan Cemetery was abandoned.[262]

Whether Henry Sanders had a role in caring for Harry and John is uncertain. Probate and guardianship records showed no entries for Wilson Madison or for the care of his sons, although that item may not have become a matter of public record. Henry Sanders, a porter, died on 25 November 1887, so any connection he had to the boys ended less than two years after the publication of the newspaper article. His St. Louis death register entry shows he was fifty-six years old, married, "colored," born in Virginia, and buried in St. Peter's Cemetery.[263]

Courtesy of Missouri History Museum, St. Louis, MO

John Madison, Surviving Grandson. St. Louis Globe-Democrat *newspaper article, 10 January 1886 on Dred Scott's family.*

In 1888, the city directory listed a Mattie Sanders, widow of Henry, living where the death register said Henry Sanders died.[264] How Henry knew Wilson and Eliza Madison, and how he and his wife may have helped care for the orphaned boys remains a mystery.

Wilson Madison

Another person, Wilson Madison, may have played a role in the lives of Harry and John. Listed in the 1888 city directory at 1616 South 3rd Street, with the same name as their deceased father, he may have been a relative.[265] The directory listing—so far the only St. Louis record found for Wilson—provided no age, race, or occupation for Wilson.

No evidence connects this Wilson Madison to Harry and John's father. His presence in St. Louis, however, raises the question of whether other Madison relatives lived in the city and might have been part of Harry and John's lives. Other African-American families named Madison lived in St. Louis, but so far no evidence has surfaced of their connection to Wilson Madison, Eliza's husband.[266]

1890–1912

The family's story after 1889, when the laundress living at or in the neighborhood of 1010 Washington disappears from the city directory, through 1912 is uncertain. During those years, St. Louis city directories usually listed at least two women as Elizabeth, Eliza, or Lizzie Scott. However, none appears a good fit for Lizzie, daughter of Dred and Harriet.[267]

By 1890, a Harry Madison and more than one John Madison appear in the city directories and continue through 1912 when John married. However, the listings provide no age or race. Porter and laborer are the most common occupations given. Two entries of interest are in the 1894–1895 directory showing Harry H. Madison and John Madison, both porters, living at 1206 Wash.[268] The information is insufficient though to determine which, if either, might be a grandson of Dred and Harriet.

Oral tradition in the Madison family said Harry died as a teenager.[269] Research on the Madison family has uncovered no additional information for him.

1890 CENSUS

If the 1890 census population schedule still existed, it might provide insight about Lizzie, John, and Harry. However, on 10 January 1921, a fire broke out in the basement of the Commerce Building in Washington, D.C. where the only copy of the 1890 census was stored. Seventy-five percent of the schedules were either destroyed by fire or damaged by water, smoke, and fire. The schedules surviving the fire were stored for another ten years, but were destroyed in the mid-1930s when the Librarian of Congress failed to identify them as being of permanent historical interest.

— Kellee Blake, "First in the Path of the Firemen: The Fate of the 1890 Population Census, Part 1," *Prologue*, 28 (1996): online *National Archives* (http://www.archives.gov/publications/prologue/1996/spring/1890-census-1.html).

Who Was Dred Scott?

One of the most celebrated cases in all American history is the Dred Scott Case, studied in school histories and yet so little understood. St. Louis was the scene and home of Dred Scott and his family. For nine years, from 1848 to 1857, legal and political turmoil centered around the medium-tall black man. The writers of the time of the famous trials (there was more than one trial), paid little attention to Dred Scott as a man and pictured him as a puppet, as a simpleton and a tool. Dred Scott was no shining hero, nor an intellectual—how many slaves were, and if they were how much written credit was given them? As a slave Fred Douglass had a brilliant mind, although he had no formal training; yet to the white writers of those days Fred Douglass was a "runaway buck," and no Negro was any more than another slave. So when the writers of the pre-civil war period state that Dred Scott was an "illiterate," a "simple-minded Negro who did not understand what his case was about," allowance for the times and closeness to the scene can be now weighed in. Dred Scott as a man was not the concern of the writers of that day—no one Negro was! In order to give a fairer idea of the famous case and the man whose name it bears, the following data is presented:

Descendants of Dred Scott

Here are four of the six living great-grandchildren of Dred Scott, with the wife of the grandson, John Madison, who died a few years ago. John Madison was the son of Eliza Scott, daughter of Dred, who married a man named Wilson Madison. In the picture are Alexander, Mrs. Grace Madison, Pauline; (standing) Rose and Joseph Henry. Dred and Bernice are not in the picture.

Dred Scott was brought to St. Louis by the Blow family in 1831 from Southampton County, Virginia (the same county and the same year that a slave named Nat Turner raised his insurrection—and they called Nat "crazy" and an "idiot", too!

The Blows were not plantation type of slave owners and likely would not have had the simpleton type of slave in their household. They had raised Dred from a boy and there were the Blow boys, one of whom played such an important part later in Dred's troublesome life.

Dred Scott was sold to an army surgeon stationed at Jefferson Barracks, a Dr. Emerson. An army officer who was a northerner would not want a dumb Negro slave as his personal servant. And it was with Dr. Emerson that Dred made his famous trips into free territories, up to Davenport and into Illinois, and again up to Fort Snelling in Minnesota territory. It was these trips that gave rise to the claim that Dred had become a free man on the great English theory that "once free always free."

But Dred's travels did not stop with his journey from Virginia, his trips up the Mis-

(Continued on page 44)

This photo of Grace Madison and four of her children appeared in Nathan B. Young's Your St. Louis and Mine, *published in 1937, photographer unknown.*

Front left to right: John A. Jr., Mrs. Grace (Cross) Madison, and Alma.
Standing left to right: Rosie and Harry.
[Correct names provided by Alma (Madison) Miller.]

JOHN AND HIS FAMILY
1912–1931

John Madison met Grace Cross in East St. Louis, Illinois, when he went to eat at her cousin's diner, where Grace was "helping out."[270] East St. Louis is on the east bank of the Mississippi River across from St. Louis, Missouri, on the west bank. By 1912, train travel between the two cities was easy via the Eads Bridge.

Grace was born to Charles A. and Belle (Chandler) Cross, in September 1891 in Villa Ridge, Pulaski County, Illinois.[271] Her great-grandfather, Christopher Cross, was a blacksmith born in Virginia. Her grandfather, Alexander Cross, was a brick mason born in Allensville, Todd County, Kentucky. Christopher and Alexander brought their families from Kentucky to the Villa Ridge area after the Civil War.[272] Grace graduated from Southern Illinois University, Carbondale, and earned her Illinois teaching certificate in 1907.[273]

Grace and John married in East St. Louis on 28 August 1912, with justice of the peace J. C. Brady officiating. It was the first marriage for both of them. Each listed East St. Louis as their residence on their marriage license application.[274] Grace signed her name to the application; John signed with his mark.

On their marriage application John said he was twenty-seven years old, born in Pittsburgh, Pennsylvania, and a porter by occupation. John gave his father's name as W. Madison. However, it was his father, Wilson, who was born in Pennsylvania, so there was some confusion over his birthplace. John did not list his mother's first name or maiden name.

Grace listed that she was twenty-one years old and born in Villa Ridge, Illinois. She recorded Chas. Cross as her father, but gave no first name or maiden name for her mother. The application did not ask the bride's occupation.

No. E 1117

MARRIAGE LICENSE

Adult.

Mr. John A. Madison

AND

Miss Grace Cross.

Issued August 28th 1912

Married August 28th 1912

Returned .... 19....

Filed OCT 2 1912

FILED

.... Clerk.

By ....

Deputy.

Registered .... 19....

on page 178 of Marriage Record 8

STATE BOARD OF HEALTH REGISTER.

.... Page............

ILLINOIS PRINTING CO., DANVILLE, ILL.

☞ This Return is to be carefully filled out and returned with the Marriage License. This return does not take the place of the Certificate which comes attached to the License, but is IN ADDITION THERETO.

ILLINOIS STATE BOARD OF HEALTH.

Return of a Marriage to County Clerk.

1. Full name of Groom, Jno A Madison
2. Place of residence, E St Louis Ill
3. Occupation, Porter
4. Age next birthday, 28 years. Color, Black Race, ...
5. Place of birth, Pittsburg Pa
6. Father's name, W Madison
7. Mother's maiden name, ...
8. Number of groom's marriage, First
9. Full name of Bride, Grace Cross
   Maiden name, if a widow, ...
10. Place of residence, E St Louis Ill
11. Age next birthday, 22 years. Color, Black Race, ...
12. Place of birth, Ellaridge Ky
13. Father's name, Thos Cross
14. Mother's maiden name, ...
15. Number of bride's marriage, First
16. Married at E St Louis in the County of St Clair and State of Illinois, the 28th day of August 1912
17. Witnesses to marriage, Rosy Metzger

N. B.—At Nos. 8 and 15 state whether 1st, 2d, 3d, 4th, &c., marriage of each. At 17 give names of subscribing witnesses to the Marriage Certificate. If no subscribing witnesses, give names of two persons who witnessed the ceremony.

August 28th 1912

We hereby certify that the information above given is correct, to the best of our knowledge and belief.

John A Madison [Groom.]

Miss Grace Cross [Bride.]

I hereby certify that the above is a correct return of a Marriage solemnized by me.

J C Brady

Justice of the Peace

Dated at E St Louis this 28th day of August 1912

Courtesy of Illinois Regional Archives Depository, Southern Illinois University, Carbondale, IL

John and Grace's 1912 marriage application.

It is obvious that John's age is not accurate on his marriage application. A person twenty-seven years old in 1912 would have been born about 1885, which would place his birth three years after the death of his mother; he probably just "revised" his age a bit for his dearly beloved. The image of John in the 1886 news article, showing him probably as a teenager, also contradicts an 1885 birth.

After their marriage, John and Grace moved across the river to St. Louis, Missouri. There they lived in the Ville neighborhood and raised their seven children: Charles, Rose, Pauline, Dred Scott, Harry, John A. Jr., and Alma.[275]

After 1912, John worked as a laborer, then as a janitor, and later as a gardener. However, his family remembered him as a cook. Alma recalled him working for the Francis family.[276] His family also remembers John as a Mason, a member of the Masonic fraternal organization.[277]

From 1913, the year after John and Grace married, until 1915, Elizabeth Scott, a laundress and listed as the widow of Walter, appears in the city directories living at 2240 Gratiot Street.[278] Was this Lizzie Scott? Her appearance, right after John's 1912 marriage, is of interest, and claiming the status of widow may have been Lizzie's effort to disguise herself. In 1913, a widow garnered more respect in the community than an "old maid."

Lizzie visited John, Grace, and their growing family. Alma remembers her mother saying when Lizzie came to visit, John wanted to give her money to return home by streetcar. She told him "I don't need your money," and then walked the three miles to her home on Gratiot Street.[279]

John A. Madison Sr. died on 6 May 1931 and was buried in Washington Park Cemetery in St. Louis County.[280] He left his widow Grace to raise their seven children, ages two through seventeen, during the Great Depression.

2240 Gratiot

2140 Gratiot

"Elizabeth" Scott lived at 2240 Gratiot from 1913–1915;
Lizzie Marshall lived at 2140 Gratiot from 1923–1945
as shown on the 1897 Whipple Fire Insurance *map.*

LIZZIE'S ASSISTANCE
1931–1945

By 1923 Lizzie Scott used the name of Lizzie Marshall. She lived at 2140 Gratiot Street, on the south side of the railroad tracks about a block from St. Louis Union Station.[281] John Madison Sr. knew her real name, but Alma and her siblings knew her only as Lizzie Marshall who lived at 2140 Gratiot until her death in 1945.[282]

During her years at that address, the city directories recorded Lizzie Marshall as either a widow or simply as Mrs. Eliz Marshall. Listings sometimes showed her as widow of Richard, although once it was of Henry, and once it was of Freeman.[283] Changing her name and inventing a deceased spouse may have simply been part of Lizzie's effort to hide. No marriage record for her has been found.

After John's death, Grace had to work to support her family. She held a teaching certificate in Illinois, but it was not recognized in Missouri where she resided. Instead, she went to work for the Francis family, John's former employer.[284]

Although Lizzie was eighty-five years old when John Sr. died in 1931, she again came to the aid of her family helping Grace care for the children. Lizzie went to Grace's home each day walking about three-and-a-half miles each way rather than taking the streetcar.

Lizzie's help was especially important because John and Grace's oldest child, Charles, contracted infantile paralysis, or polio, as a young child and never walked. Charles died the following year at the age of eighteen, on 9 September 1932. He was buried in Washington Park Cemetery.[285] Alma remembers wanting to get out of the car at the cemetery the day of Charles' funeral. Lizzie sitting beside her told Alma she must stay in the car.[286]

After Charles' death, Lizzie helped in a different way. At her home on Gratiot Street she cared for Alma, the youngest of the children and the only one not yet in school.

Alma Remembers

Every Sunday evening, Lizzie walked the three-and-a-half miles to Grace's to get Alma. Because of the distance and Alma's young age, they returned by streetcar to Lizzie's where Alma spent the week. On Friday evening, Lizzie took her back home for the weekend.

The sound of the trains coming and going at Union Station was always a part of staying with Lizzie. Her two-room house had only one entrance, a door opening onto the alley. Because she always kept her heavy drapes over her windows drawn shut even in the daytime, Lizzie and Alma would often eat breakfast by opening the outside door a bit. She also used a kerosene lamp as the house had no electricity. Although she was in her eighties, Lizzie still had a tremendous fear of someone finding out who she was.

From her childhood memories, Alma remembers Lizzie as tall and slender. Even into the 1940s, she wore long dark skirts, high-top shoes that laced, and a jacket over her blouse. She was a proud woman who spoke very little except for conversations with Grace. If anyone knew Lizzie's secrets, it would have been Grace. The two were close and often talked in the kitchen. Alma said that Lizzie treated Grace just like her child.

Lizzie was stern, but not unkind to her great-nieces and great-nephews. She was thoughtful of Alma, but never said much to her, or to her brothers and sisters. Three mornings a week Lizzie cleaned a boarding house and Alma went with her. On their way, they stopped to buy a small pie from a lady selling them on the street corner. Apple pie was Alma's favorite, but each time, Lizzie asked her "Which one do you want?" She then bought what Alma picked. Alma then sat on a bench in the boarding house entryway to eat her treat. Afterwards she played with her toys, but she knew that was where she was to stay![287]

In later years, John and Alma noticed that one of their great-nieces resembled Lizzie, reaffirming their childhood belief that Lizzie was their grandmother.[288] More than one man in the family looked enough like Dred to be his twin, so it was not surprising to see family resemblances between women in the family even in later generations.

	Place of Abode			Name	Relation	Home Data				Personal Description						Education		Place of Birth	
51	2140	78	122	Marshal Elizabeth	Head	R	$10.00		no	F	Neg	63	Wd	17		no	yes	Illinois	United
52			123	Grebe Elizabeth	Head-H	O	$8000		No	F	W	66	S			no	yes	Missouri	German
53				—— Chester O.V.	Brother				V	M	W	42	S			no	yes	Missouri	German
54	2136	79	124	Hamilton Sampson	Head	R	$8.50		no	M	Neg	46	M	24		no	yes	Mississippi	Mississi

Courtesy of Ancestry.com

Elizabeth (Lizzie) "Marshal," 1930 U.S. census, ward 7, Independent City of St. Louis, Missouri. [Shows her house address as 2140 and Gratiot Street is written down the side of the census page.]

The Importance of Education

Courtesy of Lincoln University Picture Collection, Inman E. Page Library, Jefferson City, MO

John A. Madison Jr. was the family historian.

When Alma entered kindergarten she no longer stayed with Lizzie. One of Alma's older sisters walked her home from school at lunch and took her to a neighbor's for the afternoon. Lizzie continued to help the family almost every day during the week as long as they needed her and she was able.

The Madison children's knowledge of their heritage came from their parents who proudly displayed the charcoal portrait of Dred and Harriet in their home. Their teachers also knew and reminded the children that they were descendants of Dred and Harriet Scott. [289]

The family was committed to education despite their economic struggles after John's death. In the late 1930s, city directories listed both Rose and Pauline as students.[290] By 1940, Dred Scott Madison began working as a clerk at the Sarah-Belle Pharmacy and by 1942, Harry and John Jr. also worked there as clerks.[291] By 1944, "D Scott" worked as a "defense worker."[292]

John Jr. continued his education at Stowe Teachers College, now Harris-Stowe State University, and graduated with a degree in education.[293] After U.S. Army service, he returned to St. Louis. John worked for the U.S. Postal Service and earned his law degree from Lincoln University Law School in 1955. He taught in the St. Louis school system for more than thirty years.[294]

PRESENTATIONS BEGIN AT THE OLD COURTHOUSE ABOUT THE DRED SCOTT DECISION

In 1942, the National Park Service acquired the "Old Courthouse" in downtown St. Louis, Missouri, which was no longer used. After significant repairs, the building opened to tourists in 1943 and "... a skeleton staff showed visitors through two exhibit rooms, gave them a slide lecture about the history of the site, presented talks about the Dred Scott Case in one of the second floor courtrooms, and gave walking tours of the future site of the Gateway Arch." They had no idea that the daughter of Dred and Harriet still lived in St. Louis, walking to reach her destinations, perhaps touring the courthouse!

— Robert J. Moore, *The Old Courthouse* (St. Louis, Missouri: Jefferson National Parks Association, 2004), 28.

Lizzie's Death

Lizzie belonged to the Order of the Eastern Star, a Masonic organization for women whose husbands or male relatives are Masons.[295] Her nephew, John A. Madison Sr., was a Mason, but was that Lizzie's basis for membership?[296] Had she possibly been married at one time to a Mason? Members of the Order of the Eastern Star's Phyllis Chapter in St. Louis have searched its archives for a record of Lizzie's membership or death, but nothing has yet been found.[297] With no information about which lodge she belonged to or when during her long life she joined, the search is massive.

On 19 December 1945, Lizzie Marshall died of pneumonia at Homer G. Philips Hospital. She was about ninety-nine years old.[298] Bessie Coleman, an English teacher at Sumner High School, made funeral arrangements through the Order of the Eastern Star.[299] J. H. Harrison Funeral Home handled Lizzie's service and she was buried in Greenwood Cemetery.[300] Alma remembers her saying that she wanted to be buried beside her son.[301] It is uncertain whether she had a child who died or if she considered Harry or John as a son.

Apparently Lizzie succeeded in living the anonymous, hidden life she wanted. If anyone realized that she was the daughter of Dred and Harriet Scott at the time of her death, they did not make it public knowledge.

Lizzie's life spanned the Civil War, the Spanish-American War, World War I, and World War II. Her life was one of commitment and sacrifice for her family. Lizzie raised nephews, John and Harry, after their parents, Wilson and Eliza Madison, died. After John's death, she helped Grace with their children.

Lizzie's entire life was both defined and overshadowed by the Dred Scott decision.

- She was born in 1846, the year her parents filed their freedom suits, which resulted in the U.S. Supreme Court decision on the Dred Scott case.
- She and Eliza went into hiding, possibly as early as 1852, because of the uncertainty of the outcome of the lawsuit. Their parents did not want them to be "sold away" before the case was decided.
- She and her family won freedom only because of extensive newspaper coverage regarding the Dred Scott decision. It sparked the exposé in the *Springfield Argus* newspaper revealing Calvin Chaffee's ownership of Dred and his family through his marriage to Irene Emerson. Chaffee subsequently arranged to emancipate the Scott family making it possible for Lizzie and Eliza to return home and be reunited with their parents.
- She lived as a recluse because of the trauma of her time in hiding as a young child (beginning when she was seven or eight years old and maybe younger), and possibly her response to the public's reaction to the Dred Scott decision. No evidence has surfaced that she married. She even hid her identity from her great-nieces and great-nephews. She feared anyone finding her or finding out who she was.

No record has yet been found documenting Lizzie Marshall as Dred and Harriet Scott's youngest daughter, Lizzie Scott. Perhaps the answer to her identity may be found by analyzing information for Elizabeth Scott, Lizzie Marshall, John Madison Sr., and his family, and when and how they interacted.

Elizabeth Scott

- 1913–1915: Elizabeth Scott, "widow of Walter," lived at 2240 Gratiot Street.

Lizzie Marshall

- 1882: Took John and Harry in after their mother, Eliza Madison, died.
- 1923–1945: Lived at 2140 Gratiot as a recluse and kept her heavy drapes closed so no one could see in and find out who she was.
- Prior to 1931: Walked to John Sr.'s home to visit. He offered her money to return home by streetcar, but she refused.
- 1931: After John's death in 1931, when Grace Madison had to work to support the family, Lizzie Marshall walked to the Madison home daily during the week to help care for the children. Their oldest son Charles, who never walked after having polio as a child, needed special care. Lizzie, then about eighty-five years old, walked approximately seven miles to and from the Madison home.
- 1932: When Charles Madison died, Lizzie Marshall rode in the family car at the funeral and at the cemetery remained in the car with Alma, the youngest child.
- 1932: After Charles' death, four-year-old Alma stayed with Lizzie Marshall Sunday evening through Friday evening of each week, while her mother worked. Lizzie, then about eighty-six years old, still cleaned a boarding house three mornings a week, taking Alma with her.
- About 1933: After Alma entered kindergarten, Lizzie Marshall continued to walk, as long as she was able to do so, to the Madison home to help Grace and the children with laundry, cooking, and cleaning.

John Madison Sr. and Family

- There was no question in the minds of John Sr.'s children that Lizzie Marshall was a relative.
- John Jr. and Alma thought that Lizzie Marshall was John Sr.'s mother and therefore, their grandmother. That belief was reinforced in later years when a female Madison descendant looked just like Lizzie.

The combined evidence supports the belief that Lizzie Marshall was Lizzie Scott, the youngest daughter of Dred and Harriet Scott. The final key element though, is human nature. Her support of John and Grace's family was opposite to her reclusive living pattern and she was in her eighties and nineties when she helped Grace with the children. For what other reason—beside being family—might Lizzie do these things?

The Legacy Passes to Another Generation

The years between Eliza's death in 1882 and Lizzie's death in 1945 brought many challenges for Lizzie and the Madison family. They met those challenges, stayed together, and passed to the next generation the knowledge of their heritage as descendants of Dred and Harriet Scott.

No. 2
-2-43
-17-39
X35697

DEPARTMENT OF COMMERCE 1945
BUREAU OF THE CENSUS
FILED DEC 28 1945

STATE BOARD OF HEALTH OF MISSOURI
STANDARD CERTIFICATE OF DEATH

39508
State File No. 11097

Registration District No. 318
Primary Registration District No. 1003
Registrar's No.

WRITE PLAINLY—USE UNFADING BLACK INK—MAKE A PERMANENT RECORD

1. PLACE OF DEATH:
(a) County
(b) City or town St. Louis (If outside city or town limits, write "RURAL" and name of township)
(c) Name of hospital or institution: Homer G Phillips Hospital 0 (If not in hospital or institution, write street number or location)
(d) Length of stay: In hospital or institution 10 days (Specify whether years, months or days)
In this community (years, months or days)

2. USUAL RESIDENCE OF DECEASED:
(a) State Missouri (b) County 000 / 17
(c) City or town St. Louis (If outside city or town limits, write "RURAL") 622
(d) Street No. 2140 Gratiot (If rural, give location) 0
(e) Citizen of foreign country? (Yes or No)
If yes, name country

3. (a) PRINT FULL NAME Lizzie Marshall
3. (b) If veteran, name war
3. (c) Social Security No.

4. Sex F 3
5. Color or race Col 2
6. (a) Single, widowed, married, divorced Widow
6. (b) Name of husband or wife
6. (c) Age of husband or wife if alive years
7. Birth date of deceased (Month) (Day) (Year)
8. AGE: Years ABt 90 Months Days If less than one day hr. min.
9. Birthplace (City, town, or county) Missouri 11 (State or foreign country)
10. Usual occupation Nil
11. Industry or business Unknown
FATHER 12. Name
13. Birthplace (City, town, or county) (State or foreign country)
MOTHER 14. Maiden name
15. Birthplace (City, town, or county) (State or foreign country)
16. (a) Informant J. H. Harrison
(b) Address 2906 Lawton
17. (a) Burial (Burial, cremation, or removal) (b) Date thereof 12-22-45 (Month) (Day) (Year)
(c) Place: burial or cremation Greenwood
18. (a) Signature of funeral director J. H. Harrison
(b) Address 2906 Lawton
19. (a) DEC 19 1945 (Date received local registrar) J. F. Bredeck (Registrar's signature)

MEDICAL CERTIFICATION

20. DATE OF DEATH: Month Dec. day 16 year 1945 hour 9 minute 58 A. M.
21. I hereby certify that I attended the deceased from 12-6 1945, to 12-16 1945; that I last saw her alive on 12-16- 1945; and that death occurred on the date and hour stated above.
Immediate cause of death Bronchopenumonia — Duration Unk
Due to
Due to 107
Other conditions (Include pregnancy within 3 months of death)
Major findings: Of operations
Of autopsy Yes

PHYSICIAN — Underline the cause to which death should be charged statistically.

22. If death was due to external causes, fill in the following:
(a) Accident, suicide, or homicide (specify)
(b) Date of occurrence
(c) Where did injury occur? (City or town) (County) (State)
(d) Did injury occur in or about home, on farm, in industrial place, in public place? (Specify type of place)
While at work? (e) Means of injury 0
23. Signature Clifton Hancock (M. D. or other)
Address 2601 N Whittier Date signed 12/18

(Licensed Embalmer's Statement on Reverse Side)

Courtesy of Missouri State Archives

Lizzie Marshall's 1945 Missouri death certificate.

Dred's monument in Calvary Cemetery, St. Louis, Missouri

Photo by Joseph T. Hager

Harriet's monument in Greenwood Cemetery, St. Louis County, Missouri

Photo by Ruth Ann (Abels) Hager

COMMEMORATIONS
1945–2009

Anniversary commemorations serve a number of purposes. They honor and pay tribute to the remembered event and the people who played key roles; they educate the public about that event and its significance; they bring together descendants of families involved.

Anniversaries of the Dred Scott decision have been occasions for publishing information, sometimes with images or photos of the family. Major commemorations have also acted as catalysts for further research about Dred and Harriet.

100th Anniversary of the Dred Scott Decision

The 100th anniversary was on 6 March 1957. To mark the occasion the Student Bar Association of the St. Louis University Law School sponsored a prayer service at Dred's grave site in Calvary Cemetery and placed a wreath on his grave.[302] At the prayer service, the Rev. Edward Dowling S.J., announced that descendants of Taylor Blow's family planned to place a marker on Dred's grave later that year.[303]

Among descendants of Dred and Harriet at the prayer service on 6 March were Grace Madison, the widow of Dred and Harriet's grandson, John A. Madison Sr., and four of their six surviving children—John A. Madison Jr., Dred Scott Madison, Alma (Madison) Miller, and Rose (Madison) Johnson.[304] Later that afternoon, descendants of the Blow family and of Roswell Field, Dred's lawyer, joined Dred and Harriet's descendants for a program at the Old Courthouse. John A. Madison Jr., the thirty-one–year-old great-grandson of Dred and Harriet, addressed the gathering.[305]

Prayer service at Dred Scott's grave in Calvary Cemetery on the 100th Anniversary of the Dred Scott Decision.

Men kneeling and children standing left to right: Dred Scott Madison, George Hrdlicka, Wendell Curtis Miller (in cap), Pamela Jean Miller (wearing glasses), and Raymond Scott Miller (in cap). Adults standing left to right: The Rev. Rudolph Beckmann, assistant director of the cemetery; The Rev. Edward Dowling, SJ, three unidentified men behind the priests, Rose (Madison) Johnson, Alma (Madison) Miller, Grace (Cross) Madison, John A. Madison Jr., and an unidentified man.

A Monument for Dred

Taylor Blow's granddaughter, Mrs. Charles C. Harrison Jr. of Villanova, Pennsylvania, donated a memorial monument for Dred's grave.[306] A dedication ceremony for the monument was held on 27 September 1957, the ninety-ninth anniversary of Dred's death. The memorial marker dedicated at the ceremony includes the inscription "Freed from slavery by his friend Taylor Blow."

Calvary Cemetery covers 477 acres and is the final resting place of many famous people.[307] Dred's grave is one of the few monuments for individuals marked on the cemetery map locator, and is one of the most frequently visited.* Visitors often leave pennies on the top of his monument. Various theories attempt to explain the tradition. Dred's great-great-granddaughter, Lynne Jackson, suggests it is because pennies bear the image of Abraham Lincoln, who freed the slaves.[308]

Grace (Cross) Madison

With help, Grace Madison kept her family together through the Great Depression. To celebrate Grace's life and devotion to her children, John A. Madison Jr., held a birthday party each year for his mother.[309] Grace's life won recognition in other ways as well.

In the 1970s, the St. Louis Association of Colored Women's Clubs awarded the Silver Plate Family Award to Grace as the mother of Dred Scott's descendants. She was also active in the Order of the Eastern Star and once held the post of Most Royal Grand Commandress of the Grand Court Order of Cyrenes.[310] Grace (Cross) Madison died 18 December 1983, and was buried in Washington Park Cemetery in St. Louis County.[311]

Cenotaph for Harriet

On 6 November 1999 the Elijah Lovejoy Society placed a cenotaph (a monument for someone buried elsewhere) for Harriet beside Dred's monument in Calvary Cemetery. The last line of the cenotaph inscription reads "In the course of our history, you belong to the ages."[312] They placed a cenotaph because Harriet's burial site was unknown in 1999. Now Harriet's burial in Greenwood Cemetery is an accepted fact.

---

* The Calvary Cemetery locator map is available in Appendix C.

Courtesy of the National Park Service, Jefferson National Expansion Memorial

Some of the descendants and friends who gathered to commorate the 150th anniversary of the Dred Scott Decision, 2 March 2007 at the Old Courthouse in St. Louis, Missouri.

Children in front left to right: Michael A. Madison and Koiana Madison. Adults standing left to right: Michael and Felicia Madison, Dred Scott Madison II, Stephanie Gathright, Brian and Lynne (Madison) Jackson, John A. Jr. and Marsulite (Charleston) Madison, Raymond and Phyllis Miller, Stephan Chambers and unidentified woman.

150th Anniversary of the Dred Scott Decision

Across the country, but especially in St. Louis, events commemorated the 150th anniversary of the Dred Scott decision. On 2 March 2007 the National Park Service unveiled a year-long exhibition at the Old Courthouse in downtown St. Louis titled "The Legacy of Courage: Dred Scott, the Quest for Freedom." Madison descendants from across the country gathered to remember. On 6 March, the anniversary day, they held a prayer service at Dred's grave in Calvary Cemetery and another one at Greenwood Cemetery for Harriet.

Although in failing health, eighty-one-year-old John A. Madison Jr., the family historian for sixty years, attended a number of the 150th anniversary ceremonies. It was a special time for him. He treasured the opportunity to participate in this historic event. John died on 26 July 2007, and as a U.S. Army veteran, he was buried in Jefferson Barracks National Cemetery.[313]

A Monument for Harriet

On 26 May 2009 the dedication of a memorial monument for Harriet in Greenwood Cemetery marked the 152nd anniversary of the emancipation of Dred, Harriet, Eliza, and Lizzie. Since the exact location of her grave in section "C" was never recorded, the monument, donated by Austin A. Layne Mortuary, was placed on the hill to the left side of the front of the cemetery, now known as "Harriet's Hill." A pavilion near her monument is also planned.**

Conclusion

The story of Dred and Harriet Scott's family is one of hope and love of family. It is also one of the deep commitment, hard work, and sacrifice often needed to hold one's family together and to give them direction. The Dred Scott decision overshadowed the lives of Dred, Harriet, Eliza and Lizzie, yet they persevered and survived. Theirs is a story of one American family's efforts to do their best under difficult and challenging circumstances.

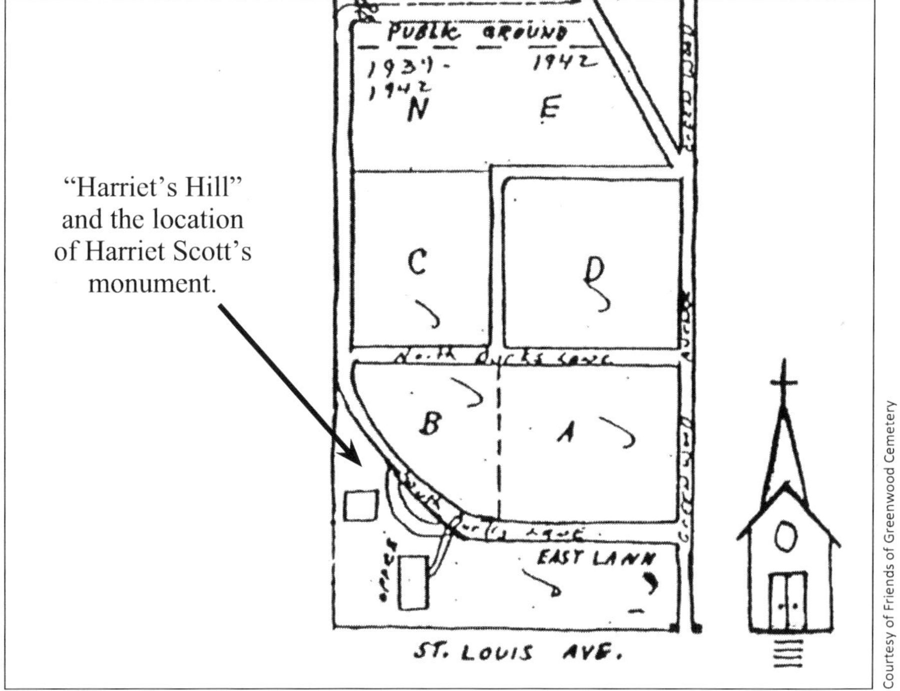

Courtesy of Friends of Greenwood Cemetery

Portion of Greenwood Cemetery map showing location of Harriet's monument.

** The Greenwood Cemetery map is available in Appendix C.

PRESERVATION OF GREENWOOD CEMETERY

In 1999 Greenwood Cemetery was neglected and overgrown with weeds and brush. On 1 March 1999, a not-for-profit organization led by Etta Daniels incorporated as The Friends of Greenwood Cemetery Association "... for the purpose of acquiring, restoring, and preserving Greenwood Cemetery ..." Ownership of the cemetery was transferred to the Friends of Greenwood Association in May 2002 and they continued their work of removing trash, clearing vegetation, and restoring the cemetery.

One of the association's goals was to nominate the cemetery for the National Register of Historic Places. While preparing that nomination in 2002, they found that Harriet Scott was one of a number of famous people buried in Greenwood. The association's focus was on the thirty-acre cemetery, and they did not publicize information about any of the individuals buried there. Greenwood Cemetery was listed on the National Register of Historic Places on 24 February 2004.

The cemetery received additional attention after Harriet Scott's death date and burial in Greenwood were discovered by this author who, with the help of Etta Daniels, provided information for a *St. Louis Post-Dispatch* article in 2006. The Friends of Greenwood Cemetery Association partnered with the Dred Scott Heritage Foundation and other community groups to continue clearing the overgrowth and restoring the cemetery. This was and continues to be an enormous task.

The ability to place a monument for Harriet in Greenwood Cemetery was the result of work by dedicated volunteers and the support of individuals, groups, institutions, and businesses in the community. The red granite monument is not only a tribute to Harriet, it is a tribute to the hundreds of dedicated people who have committed and continue to commit time, energy and money to the on-going effort to preserve Greenwood.

— Friends of Greenwood Cemetery Association, Inc. Mission Statement, photocopy received from Etta Daniels, February 2006 is in possession of the author.

— "Nomination of Greenwood Cemetery for the National Register of Historic Places, January 6, 2004," *Missouri Department of Natural Resources* (http://www.dnr.mo.gov/shpo/nps-nr/04000090.pdf), 5.

— "St. Louis County National Register Listings," *Missouri Department of Natural Resources* (http://www.dnr.mo.gov/shpo/StLouis.htm).

— "Finding a St. Louis Legend," *St. Louis Post-Dispatch*, St. Louis, Missouri, 5 March 2006, section C8, column 2.

EPILOGUE

While more is now known about the lives of Dred, Harriet, Eliza, and Lizzie, their story is not complete. It is important to continue looking for clues, which may lead to additional evidence about their lives. Although there are a number of sources that might provide information about them, two unique possibilities come to mind.

Luke Howard

The first source is Luke Howard who was also held as a slave by Peter Blow. Like Dred, Luke was born in Virginia. Entries in the 1869 Carondelet census,[314] the 1870 St. Louis U.S. census,[315] and the St. Louis death register[316] place his birth between 1791 and 1800. This would make him close in age to Dred, whose birth has been estimated between 1795 and 1809. Julia Blow, widow of Peter Blow's youngest son, William T. Blow, described Luke as "… a fellow servant of Dred …," then she went on to describe him as a "… miniter [*sic*] of Dred …"[317]

Peter Blow's monetary problems, which forced him to mortgage his slaves in Alabama, sell at least one slave there, and then sell Dred in St. Louis, make it unlikely that Peter could have purchased Luke after his departure from Virginia. Based on that, it is probable that Luke was one of the slaves who Peter brought with him from Virginia. If that is the case, then Luke and Dred would have known each other for many years. They may even have been related.

As the Blow family helped Dred, they also helped Luke. Henry T. Blow sold a parcel of land for one dollar to the trustees of the African Methodist Episcopal Church of Carondelet, Missouri. One of those trustees was Luke Howard.[318] The church was completed in 1869 with Moses Dickson, a well known St. Louis African-American minister, as first pastor. However, fire destroyed the church on 4 October 1869, just a month after its completion.[319]

The 1869 Carondelet census, taken the year before that city was incorporated into the City of St. Louis in 1870, shows Luke living in block forty-four of "Eiler's Survey." Listed with him in the household were thirty-five year-old Isabella Howard, sixteen-year-old James Howard, and six-year-old Henry F. Howard. Each was indicated as "colored."[320] That census did not record how people were related to each other so that information is lacking. They may have been family members, or they may have known each other from slave times.

Just one year later, when the 1870 federal census was taken for St. Louis, Luke was the only person in his household, and he was listed as disabled.[321] He died on 27 November 1871, in Carondelet and was buried in Sigerson Farm Cemetery in St. Louis County.[322] If Luke shared his stories and memories of Dred with relatives or friends, it is possible that those memories are now someone's family stories.

Girls In Hiding

A less likely source of information might be records or stories from those who hid Eliza and Lizzie while awaiting the outcome of Dred's U.S. Supreme Court appeal. However, since the act of hiding the girls anywhere in the United States was illegal, it is unlikely that any written record was made at the time of the event. Under the Fugitive Slave Law of 1850, anyone who "... shall harbor or conceal such fugitive, so as to prevent the discovery and arrest of such person ..." was subject to a fine of up to $1,000 and imprisonment for as long as six months.[323]

Also, because of the risk involved, it seems quite possible that few people involved with hiding them even knew their true names, much less that they were the daughters of Dred and Harriet Scott. The fewer people who knew their secret meant less chance of someone accidentally revealing their secret.

The Next Chapter

There are puzzle pieces of Dred and Harriet's family story still missing. If the sources containing those puzzle pieces still exist, someone may find them. While new information will expand the body of knowledge about the Scott family, it may also challenge or contradict existing information and beliefs. That, however, is part of the research process.

APPENDIX A

— KEY EVENTS —

Events shown in bold indicate a change of slave owner.

1795–1809	Dred Scott is born a slave in Virginia.
1818	The Peter and Elizabeth (Taylor) Blow family leaves Southampton County, Virginia, and moves to what will become Madison County, Alabama. As one of their slaves, Dred goes with them.
1820	Taylor Blow is born in Madison County, Alabama, on 26 March 1820.
1820	Harriet Robinson [Scott] is born a slave about this time, possibly in Virginia or Kentucky.
1821	Peter Blow, his family, and their slaves move west to Florence, Lauderdale County, Alabama. There they operate the Peter Blow Inn.
1830	Peter Blow family and slaves move to St. Louis, and operate the Jefferson Hotel, a boarding house.
1831–1832	**Peter Blow sells Dred to Dr. John Emerson, an Army surgeon.**
1832	Peter Blow dies on 23 June 1832 in St. Louis.
1833	Dr. Emerson takes Dred with him as his personal servant when he is assigned to Fort Armstrong, located at Rock Island, Illinois.
Before 1836	Major Lawrence Taliaferro brings Harriet to Fort Snelling as one of his slaves.
1836	Dr. Emerson moves to Fort Snelling in Wisconsin Territory and takes Dred with him.
1836–1837	Dred and Harriet meet and later marry in a civil ceremony conducted by Taliaferro, Harriet's owner and a justice of the peace. **Harriet becomes the slave of Dr. Emerson.**
1838	Dr. Emerson marries Eliza Irene Sanford on 6 February 1838, and sends for Harriet and Dred to come to Fort Jesup.
1838	Eliza Scott is born in October 1838 aboard the steamboat *Gypsy* as Harriet and Dred return to Fort Snelling with Dr. and Irene Emerson.

1840 Dr. Emerson is sent to Florida for the Seminole War. Irene moves from Fort Snelling to live with her father, Alexander Sanford, in St. Louis County, Missouri. She takes Harriet and Dred with her.

1843 Dr. Emerson and Irene move to Davenport, Iowa, where slavery is prohibited.

1843 Dr. Emerson dies in Davenport, Iowa; Irene inherits ownership of the Scott family. Irene and her infant daughter, Henrietta, once again move to St. Louis County to live with Alexander Sanford, her father.

1845 Dred goes to Texas with Captain Bainbridge, but returns to St. Louis by March 1846.

1846–1847 Harriet gives birth to their daughter, Lizzie Scott.

1846 Dred and Harriet sue for freedom in the St. Louis Circuit Court based on their years in free territory.

1847 Dred and Harriet lose their case on a technicality, but file for and are granted a new trial.

1848 Irene's father, Alexander Sanford, dies.

1848 Dred and Harriet are placed in the custody of the St. Louis County Sheriff.

1848 Irene Emerson and daughter, Henrietta, move to Springfield, Massachusetts.

1850 Dred and Harriet win their second trial. They are free.

1850 Irene Emerson's lawyers appeal her case to the Missouri Supreme Court.

1850 Court combines the two suits and only Dred's continues. Results for his verdict will apply to the family.

1850 Irene (Sanford) Emerson marries Dr. Calvin Chaffee in Springfield, Massachusetts.

1853 Missouri Supreme Court rules in favor of Irene Emerson. The Scott family are slaves.

1853 Dred's lawyer brings suit against Irene Emerson's brother, John Sanford, in federal court in St. Louis. Dred loses the case but appeals to the U.S. Supreme Court.

1857 U.S. Supreme Court denies freedom in *Scott v. Sandford*, known as the Dred Scott decision.

1857 *Springfield Argus* exposé reveals the owner of the Scott family is Massachusetts Congressman Dr. Calvin Chaffee, through his marriage to Irene (Sanford) Emerson.

1857 Dr. Calvin Chaffee arranges for transfer of "possible" ownership of Dred, Harriet, and their daughters to Taylor Blow for the sole purpose of emancipating the Scott family.

1857 John F. A. Sanford, defendant in *Scott v. Sandford*, dies in New York.

1857 Taylor Blow emancipates the Scott family in St. Louis.

1858 Dred dies in St. Louis and is buried in Wesleyan Cemetery.

1863 Lates/Seales W. Madison, an eighteen-month-old, dies and is buried in Dred's grave.

1867 Taylor Blow moves Dred's remains from Wesleyan Cemetery to Calvary Cemetery.

1870 Wilson Madison, son of Wilson and Eliza (Scott) Madison, dies with burial in Wesleyan Cemetery.

1876 Harriet Scott dies in St. Louis and is buried in Greenwood Cemetery.

1876 Edw. Madison, a two day-old infant, dies and Harriet's grave is reopened for his burial.

1881 Wilson Madison, son-in-law of Dred and Harriet, dies and is buried in Greenwood Cemetery.

1882 Eliza (Scott) Madison, oldest Scott daughter, dies with burial in Greenwood Cemetery.

1931 John A. Madison Sr. dies in St. Louis and is buried in Washington Park Cemetery.

1945 Lizzie Marshall, Dred and Harriet's youngest daughter, dies and is buried in Greenwood Cemetery.

1957 The Rev. Edward Dowling S.J., finds and confirms the location of Dred Scott's grave in Calvary Cemetery. Taylor Blow descendant, Mrs. Charles C. Harrison Jr. of Villanova, Pennsylvania, donates and places a monument on Dred's grave later that year.

2006 Ruth Ann Hager finds the date and place of death and burial for Harriet Scott and the evidence to support that the information is for Harriet, widow of Dred Scott. Then-Missouri State Archivist, Ken Winn, Ph.D., examines the evidence and adds the new information to the Missouri State Archives' web page about Dred Scott.

2007 Sesquicentennial Commemoration of the 150th anniversary of the Dred Scott decision.

2009 Dedication of "Harriet's Hill" and placement of a monument for Harriet Scott, donated by Austin A. Layne Mortuary, in Greenwood Cemetery commemorates her burial there.

APPENDIX B

— CENSUS —

1860

- "Harriotte" and Elizabeth Scott
- Wilson and Elizabeth "Maddison"

1870

- Harriet Scott in William Werden household

1880

- Eliza Scott, 1st enumeration, June 1880

1920

- John and Grace Madison family

1930

- John and Grace Madison family
- Lizzie "Marshal"

Page No. 110

SCHEDULE 1.—Free Inhabitants in 7th Ward St Louis City in the County of St Louis State of Missouri enumerated by me, on the twenty-eighth day of June 1860. John P. Gerety Ass't Marshal

Post Office St Louis

	Dwelling-houses—numbered in the order of visitation.	Families numbered in the order of visitation.	The name of every person whose usual place of abode on the first day of June, 1860, was in this family.	Description: Age.	Description: Sex.	Description: Color, {White, black, or mulatto.	Profession, Occupation, or Trade of each person, male and female, over 15 years of age.	Value of Estate Owned: Value of Real Estate.	Value of Estate Owned: Value of Personal Estate.	Place of Birth, Naming the State, Territory, or Country.	Married within the year.	Attended School within the year.	Persons over 20 y'rs of age who cannot read & write.	Whether deaf and dumb, blind, insane, idiotic, pauper, or convict.	
	1	2	3	4	5	6	7	8	9	10	11	12	13	14	
1		711	Joseph Dempsey	38	M		Laborer			Ireland					1
2			Bridget do	34	F					do					2
3			Mary do	9	"					Mo					3
4			[illegible] do	1	M					do					4
5		712	Mary Stoney	36	F		Laundress			Ireland					5
6		713	Christopher Gallagher	41	M		Porter			do					6
7			Margaret do	39	F					do					7
8			Mary A do	5	"					Mo					8
9			Ellen do	2	"					do					9
10	396	714	Richard Madden	50	M		Laborer	2000		Ireland					10
11			Margaret do	50	F					do					11
12			John do	5	M					Mo					12
13			Patk do	3	"					do					13
14			Johanna do	1/12	F					do					14
15		715	John Dillon	31	M		Laborer			Ireland					15
24			Catharine do	5	"					Mo					24
25			Bridget do	4	"					do					25
26			Nathan do	3	M					do					26
27			Michael do	1	"					do					27
28			Danl do	1/12	"					do					28
29			Dennis Fanning	40	"		Wagon Driver		400	Ireland					29
30		717	Harriotte Scott	40	F	B	Laundress			do					30
31			Elizabeth do	15	"	"	do			Mo					31
32			Ellen Henry	50	"	M	do			S.C					32
33	397	718	Bernard Gillen	40	M		Riverman			Ireland					33
34			Bridget do	35	F					do					34
35			Sarah do	10	"					Mo		1			35
36			Mary do	8	"					do		1			36
37			Catharine do	6						do					37
38		719	Edward Kelley	31	M		Porter			Ireland					38
39			Bridget do	28	F					do					39
40	398	720	Margaret Weber	60	F					Bavaria					40
	3		No. white males, ___ No. white females, ___	No. colored males, ___ No. colored females, ___			No. foreign born, ___ No. deaf and dumb, ___ No. blind, ___ No. insane, ___	4000	750	No. idiotic, ___ No. paupers, ___				No. convicts, ___	

Courtesy of Ancestry.com

"Harriotte" and Elizabeth Scott living in dwelling 396 (see circled number) 1860 U.S. census, ward 7, City of St. Louis, St. Louis County, Missouri.

Page No. 113

SCHEDULE 1.—Free Inhabitants in 7th Ward St. Louis City in the County of St. Louis State of Missouri enumerated by me, on the Twenty[illegible] day of June 1860. [illegible] Ass't Marshal

Post Office St. Louis

	Dwelling-houses numbered in the order of visitation.	Families numbered in the order of visitation.	The name of every person whose usual place of abode on the first day of June, 1860, was in this family	Age.	Sex.	Color, White, black, or mulatto.	Profession, Occupation, or Trade of each person, male and female, over 15 years of age.	Value of Real Estate.	Value of Personal Estate.	Place of Birth, Naming the State, Territory, or Country.	Married within the year.	Attended School within the year.	Persons over 20 y'rs of age who cannot read & write.	Whether deaf and dumb, blind, insane, idiotic, pauper, or convict.	
	1	2	3	4	5	6	7	8	9	10	11	12	13	14	
1			Bridget Fox	20	F					Ireland					1
2			Pat Condy	25	M		Laborer			do					2
3			Michael Fleming	27	"		do			do					3
4			John Condy	27	"		do			do					4
5			Martin Fitzgerald	27	"		do			do					5
6			John Welsh	36	"		do			Canada					6
7			Pat Coughlin	17	"		do			Ireland					7
8			Michael Welsh	27	"		do			do					8
9			Catherine Dougherty	31	F		Cook			do					9
10	407	728	John Jones	35	M	Mu	White Washer		50	Ohio					10
11			Julia do	28	F	B				Va					11
12	408	729	John Thomas	29	M	Mu	Riverman			Pa					12
13			Louisa do	27	F	"				do					13
14			Henry do	13	M	"				do					14
15			Mary Smith	8	F	"				Mo					15
16			Robert do	6	"	"				do					16
17		730	Wilson Maddison	30	M	B	Cook			Pa	1				17
18			Elizabeth	21	F	"				Va	1				18
19	409	731	Wm J Detrick	45	M	Mu	[illegible]	11000	1500	Hanover					19
20			Johanna do	45	F					Prussia					20
21			Chas W do	20	M		Clerk			Pa					21
22			Jno H do	16	"					Mo		1			22
23			Helena do	12	F					do		1			23
24			John F do	9	M					do		1			24
25	410	732	Michael Jugler	49	"		Grocer		3500	France					25
26			Mary do	39	F					do					26
27			Caroline do	14	"					Mo		1			27
28			Louisa do	12	"					do		1			28
29			Catharine do	10	"					do		1			29
30			Chas do	6	M					do		1			30
31			Louis do	4	"					do					31
32			Josephine do	1	F					do					32
33		733	Christian Snider	35	M		Clerk		100	Bavaria					33
34			Emma do	30	F					Prussia					34
35			Albert do	1	M					Mo					35

Near "Harriotte" and Elizabeth Scott,
Wilson and Elizabeth "Maddison" lived in dwelling 408 (see circled number).
1860 U.S. census, ward 7, City of St. Louis, St. Louis County, Missouri.

Page No. 115. Inquiries numbered 7, 16, and 17 are not to be asked in respect to infants. Inquiries numbered 11, 12, 15, 16, 17, 19, and 20 are to be answered (if at all) merely by an affirmative mark, as /.

SCHEDULE 1.—Inhabitants in Subdivision No 73, in the County of St Louis State of Missouri, enumerated by me on the 1st day of August, 1870. 58

Post Office: St Louis Mo. C. W. Fritch, Ass't Marshal.

Line	Dwelling-houses, numbered in the order of visitation (1)	Families, numbered in the order of visitation (2)	The name of every person whose place of abode on the first day of June, 1870, was in this family (3)	Age at last birthday (4)	Sex (5)	Color (6)	Profession, Occupation, or Trade of each person, male or female (7)	Value of Real Estate (8)	Value of Personal Estate (9)	Place of Birth, naming State or Territory of U. S.; or the Country, if of foreign birth (10)	Father of foreign birth (11)	Mother of foreign birth (12)	If born within the year, state month (13)	If married within the year, state month (14)	Attended school within the year (15)	Cannot read (16)	Cannot write (17)	Whether deaf and dumb, blind, insane, or idiotic (18)	Male Citizens of U. S. of 21 years of age and upwards (19)	Male Citizens of U. S. of 21 years of age and upwards, whose right to vote is denied or abridged on other grounds than rebellion or other crime (20)
1			Rippey Louisa	4	F	W				Missouri										
2			— Ida	2	F	W				Do										
3			Lanagan Bridget	23	F	W	Domestic Servant			Ireland	1	1				1				
4	623	906	Fogerty James	46	M	W	Contractor	$20000	$1500	Do	1	1							1	
5			— Margaret	35	F	W	Keeps house			Do	1	1								
6			— Edward	3	M	W				Missouri	1	1								
7			— Katie	12	F	W				Do	1	1	Mar							
8			[illegible]	[illegible]	[illegible]	W	[illegible]			Do						1	1			
16	625	908	Chandler John	33	M	W	Lawyer	$4000	$6000	Ohio									1	
17			— Emiline	27	F	W	Keeps house			Do										
18			— Mary	1	F	W				Missouri										
19			Ryan Mary	34	F	W	Domestic Servant			Ireland	1	1								
20			— Johanna	2	F	W				Missouri	1	1								
21	626	909	Cleary Redmond	39	M	W	Com Merchant	$40000	$20000	Ireland	1	1							1	
22			— Julia	30	F	W	Keeps house			Do	1	1								
23			— Timothy	3	M	W				Missouri	1	1								
24			— Mary	1	F	W				Do	1	1								
25			— Mary	75	F	W				Ireland	1	1								
26			Daly Mary	25	F	W	Domestic Servant			Do	1	1								
27			Rynes Mary	11	F	W	School			Missouri	1	1			1					
28	627	910	Werden William	49	M	W	Civil Engineer	$8000	$1000	Ohio									1	
29			— Sarah	38	F	W	Keeps house			Kentucky										
30			— Millie	14	F	W	School			Ohio					1					
31			— Bettie	12	F	W	"			Missouri					1					
32			— Reed	11	M	W	"			Do					1					
33			— Perry	9	M	W				Do					1					
34			— Annie	5	F	W				Do										
35			Smith Sarah	58	F	W			$5000	Delaware										
36			Scott Harriet	60	F	B	Domestic Servant			Kentucky										
37	628	911	Taylor Oliver	36	M	W	Dry Goods Merc	$12000	$15000	Pennsylvania									1	
38			— Mary	26	F	W	Keeps house			Missouri										
39			— David	2	M	W				Do										
40			O'Hern Mary	14	F	W	Domestic Servant			Do	1	1				1	1			

No. of dwellings, 6; No. of white females, 25; No. of males, foreign born, 2; No. of families, 6; No. of colored males, 0; No. of females, foreign born, 7; No. of white males, 14; No. of colored females, 1; No. of blind, —; No. of insane, —; 9; 11 11 1; 6 2 3; 7

Courtesy of Mid-Continent Public Library, Independence, MO

Harriet Scott, a domestic servant in the household of William Werden, 1870 U.S. census, ward 5, City of St. Louis, St. Louis County, Missouri.

Note A.—The Census Year begins June 1, 1879, and ends May 31, 1880.
Note B.—All persons will be included in the Enumeration who were living on the 1st day of June, 1880. No others will. Children BORN SINCE June 1, 1880, will be OMITTED. Members of Families who have DIED SINCE June 1, 1880, will be INCLUDED.
Note C.—Questions Nos. 13, 14, 22 and 23 are not to be asked in respect to persons under 10 years of age.

Page No. 2 · Supervisor's Dist. No. · Enumeration Dist. No. 11

August 1880 · A · 193

SCHEDULE 1.—Inhabitants in the City of St Louis, State of Missouri, enumerated by me on the 2nd day of June, 1880. James R. Cameron, Enumerator.

FIRST ENUMERATION — REJECTED

House	Dwelling	Family	Name	Color	Sex	Age	Relationship	Single	Married	Occupation	Health	Birthplace	Father's birthplace	Mother's birthplace
1020	48	59	[illegible] Patk	W	m	34			1	Tailor		Ireland	Ireland	Ireland
			— Ellen	W	f	35	wife		1	At Home		Ireland	Ireland	Ireland
1022	49	60	[illegible]	W	f	33			1	Dress Maker	Chronic dropsy	England	England	England
			— Caroline	W	f	31	wife		1	At Home		Pennsylvania	Penn[a]	Penn[a]
			— Jas H.	W	m	7/12 Nov	Adopted Son					Missouri	Penn[d]	Penn[d]
		61	Walters Augusta	W	f	25	Servant			Servant		Prussia	Prussia	Prussia
1016	51	65	O'Day Margaret	W	f	26	Roomer	1		Keeps Laundry		Illinois	Ireland	Ireland
			Collins Margaret	W	f	26	Roomer	1		Keeps Laundry		Ireland	Ireland	Ireland
1014	52	66	Roby Isaac	W	m	30			1	Tinner		Illinois	Illinois	Illinois
			— Candace	W	f	28	wife		1	At Home		Pennsylvania	Penn[a]	Penn[a]
			— Amos	W	m	26			1	Laborer		Illinois	England	England
			— Flora	W	f	19	Wife		1	At Home		Illinois	England	Canada
			Young Annie	W	f	17	Boarder	1		Dress Maker		Missouri		
			Geisler Katie	W	f	32	Boarder	1		Dress Maker		Missouri	Hess Cassel	H. Cassel
1014	53	67	Blackburn Susan	W	f	45	Roomer		1	Dress Maker		England	England	England
		68	Flesher Henry	W	m	46			1	no regular occupation		Virginia	Va	Va
			— Jennie	W	f	44	wife		1	At Home		Illinois	Virginia	Virginia
			Ward Belle	W	f	50	Boarder	1		Dress Maker		Virginia	Virginia	Virginia
1010	54	69	Wilkinson Joel	W	m	55	Roomer		1	Tailor		England	England	England
			Starkey S. G.	W	m	55	Roomer		1	Dyeing		New York	N York	Penn[d]
			Scott Eliza	B	f	30	Roomer	1		Washerwoman		Kentucky	Ky.	Ky
			Scott Charles	B	m	23			1	Cook on Steam Boat		Tennessee	Tenn	Tenn
			— Polly	B	f	22	wife		1	Char woman		Missouri	Missouri	Missouri
1008	55	70	Sullivan Ed. O.	W	m	47	Roomer		1	Keeps Cigar Store		Massachusetts	Ireland	Ireland
			— John T.	W	m	12	Son	1		Attends School		Missouri	Mass.	Ireland
			Le Brun Margt	W	f	38	Roomer		D	Ladies Nurse		Missouri	Missouri	Missouri
1006	56	71	Sheppard Jas A	W	m	33	Roomer	1		Carpenter		Missouri	Mo.	Maryland
			West C. W.	W	m	37	Roomer	1		Carpenter		Missouri	Mo.	Maryland
1004	57	72	Holmes Eliza	B	f	37			1	Washerwoman		Indiana	Ind[a]	Ind[a]
			— Mollie	B	f	18	daughter	1		Washerwoman		Indiana	Indiana	Ind[a]
			Oulman Chas	W	m	50	Roomer	1		Barber		Switzerland	Germany	

Eliza Scott, 1010 Washington Avenue, 1880 U.S. census, 1st enumeration (rejected), ward 2, Independent City of St. Louis, Missouri.

DEPARTMENT OF COMMERCE—BUREAU OF THE CENSUS

FOURTEENTH CENSUS OF THE UNITED STATES: 1920—POPULATION

John and Grace Madison family, 1920 U.S. census, ward 26, Independent City of St. Louis, Missouri.

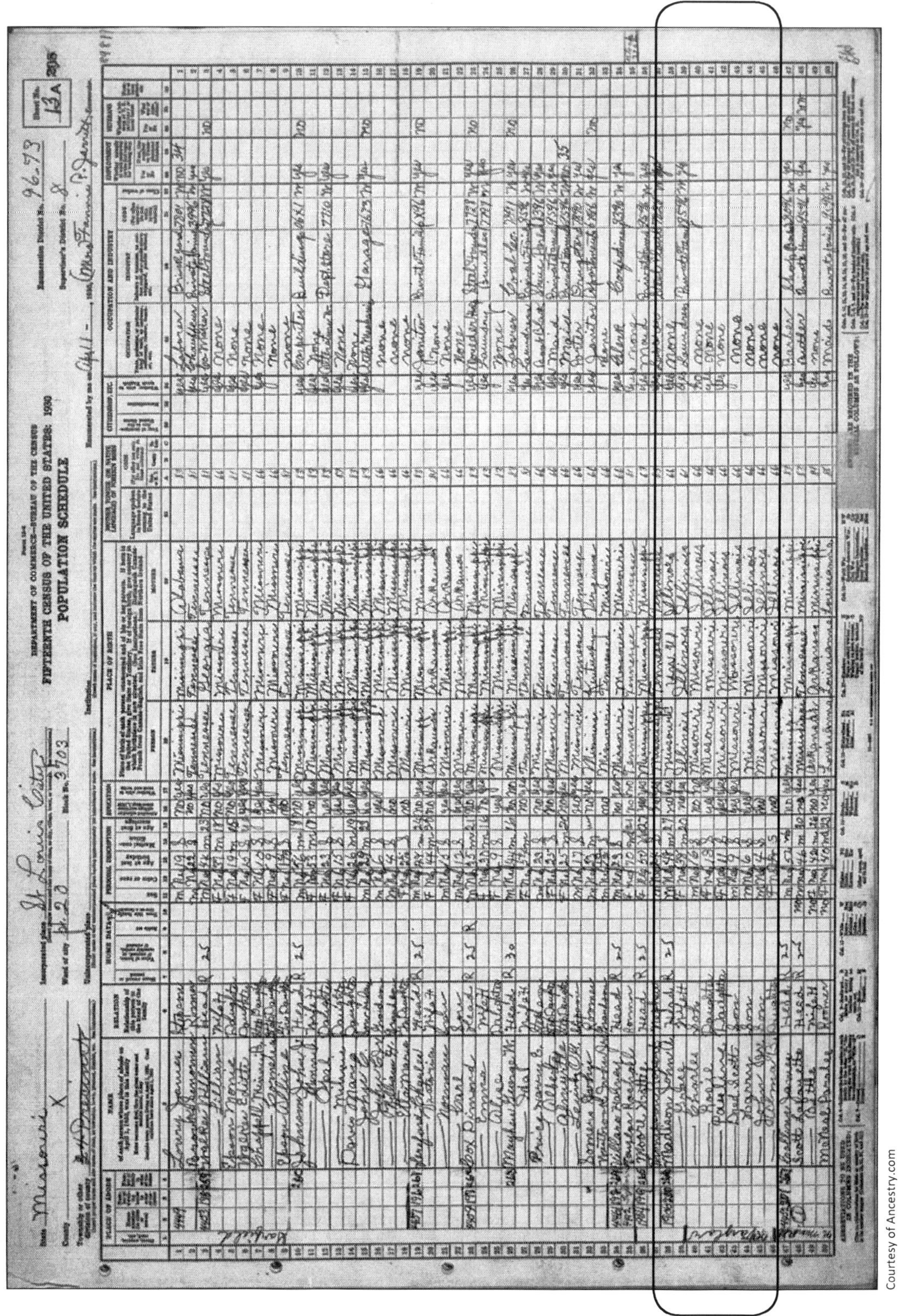
DEPARTMENT OF COMMERCE—BUREAU OF THE CENSUS
FIFTEENTH CENSUS OF THE UNITED STATES: 1930
POPULATION SCHEDULE

Courtesy of Ancestry.com

John and Grace Madison family, 1930 U.S. census, ward 20, Independent City of St. Louis, Missouri.

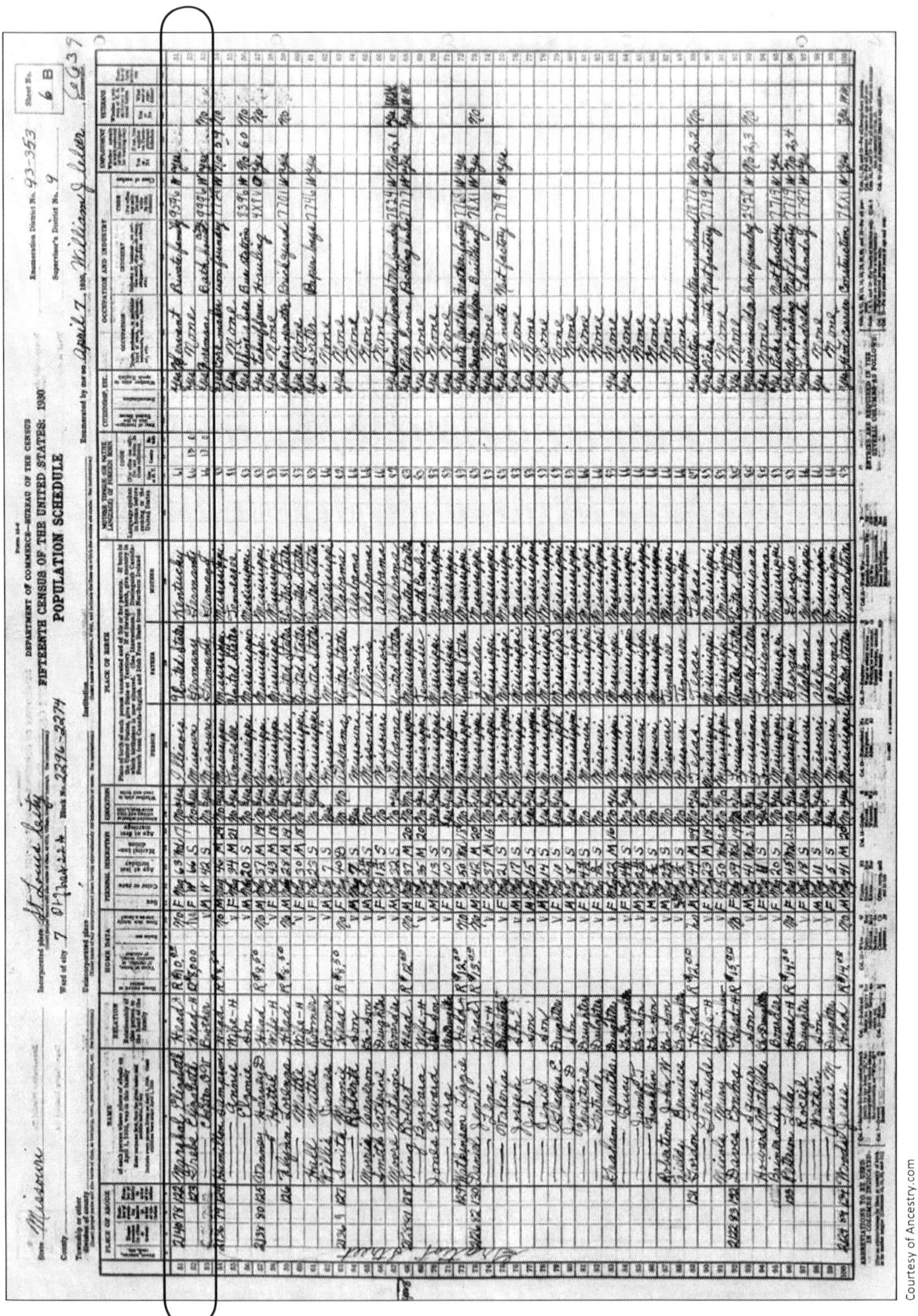

Courtesy of Ancestry.com

Elizabeth [Lizzie] "Marshal" living at 2140 Gratiot Street.
1930 U.S. census, ward 7, Independent City of St. Louis, Missouri.

APPENDIX C

— MAPS —

MAPS

- Calvary Cemetery map showing location of Dred Scott's grave.
- Greenwood Cemetery map showing location of Harriet Scott's monument.

Courtesy of The Catholic Cemeteries of the Archdiocese of St. Louis

Dred Scott's burial location in Calvary Cemetery, St. Louis, Missouri, is marked as number 19.

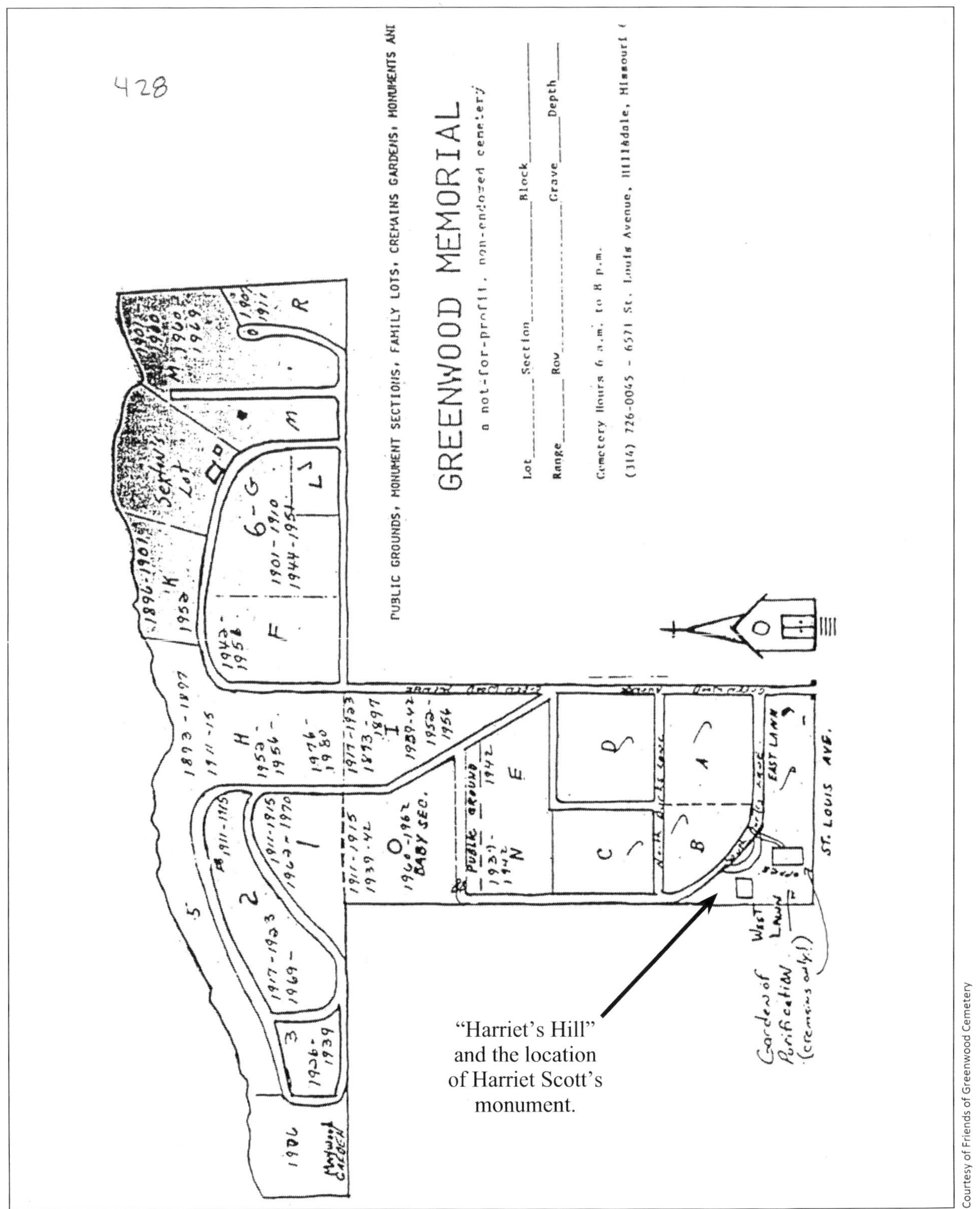

Courtesy of Friends of Greenwood Cemetery

The location of Harriet Scott's monument in Greenwood Cemetery, St. Louis, Missouri.

APPENDIX D

— LETTERS —

- Background of Chaffee / Blair letters
- C. C. Chaffee to Hon. M. Blair, 1 April 1857, with forwarding note on back from M. Blair to [Rosewell] Field, 3 April.
- C. C. Chafee to Hon. M. Blair, 11 April 1857, with forwarding note from M. Blair to [Roswell] Field, 13 April 1857 and an undated notation by R. M. Field on the back of the letter.
- C. C. Chaffee to "My dear Judge," 6 May 1857.
- C. C. Chaffee to Hon. Montgomery Blair, 14 May 1857.

History Preserved and Shared

Less than a month after the Dred Scott decision of 6 March 1857, Calvin Chaffee, the husband of Irene (Sanford) Emerson Chaffee who held the Scott family in slavery, began making arrangements for the emancipation of Dred, Harriet, and their daughters. Chaffee wrote to Montgomery Blair seeking his help to free the Scott family. Those letters were passed down through generations of Blair descendants.

In July of 2000, Richard C. Hollyday III and his sister, Edith Hollyday, great-grandchildren of Montgomery Blair, donated Blair family letters to the Library of Congress—including these from Chaffee to Blair. Their donation is now part of the Blair Family Papers in the Manuscript Division at the Library of Congress.

Calvin C. Chaffee wrote the four letters presented in this appendix in April and May of 1857. With two of those letters, Blair wrote a note to Roswell Field on the back of Chaffee's correspondence before sending it to Field in St. Louis.

The four Chaffee/Blair letters appear in this appendix, courtesy of the Library of Congress Manuscript Division. Beside each page of a letter is a transcription including misspellings and punctuation, or the lack of it, just as Chaffee wrote it.

The story of how the Chaffee/Blair letters came to be in this book is one of support and cooperation within the research community.

- Bob Moore, National Park Service Historian at the Old Courthouse in St. Louis, Missouri, found a reference in a manuscript collection at the Library of Congress to letters between Roswell Field and Montgomery Blair regarding the Dred Scott case. He told Wendy Dyer, at that time the Acting Director of the Eugene Field House in St. Louis. His information included the locator number for the records.
- Wendy forwarded the information to Tom Campbell Farnam, a long time trustee of the Eugene Field House. While his principal law office is in St. Louis, he lives in Alexandria, Virginia, which is in commuting distance to Washington, D.C., and the Library of Congress. She asked if he could possibly go to the Library of Congress and take a look at the letters.
- On 26 December 2006, Tom and his sister-in-law, Ruth Behling, a Ph.D. candidate in history, went to the Library of Congress to examine the documents. When the box that matched the locator number did not contain the desired letters, consultation with the librarian pinpointed another box. The only problem was that it was stored off-site and would take two days to retrieve it for their use. Could they come back in two days?

- Tom and Ruth went back to the Library of Congress on 29 December. This time the requested box contained the desired letters. Tom received permission to photograph the letters without using a flash.
- In 2007, during the 150th anniversary commemoration of the Dred Scott Decision, Tom, on behalf of himself and the Eugene Field House, presented Lynne Jackson, great-great-granddaughter of Dred and Harriet Scott, with a book of photo prints of the letters relating to her ancestors.
- This author was told about and saw the letters during a Friends of Dred Scott committee meeting held at the Eugene Field House. Lacking available time to work with the letters during the Eugene Field House business hours, Lynne Jackson offered the use of the copy Tom had given her.
- After transcribing the Chaffee letters, this author worked with Bruce Kirby, Manuscript Reference Librarian at the Library of Congress, to obtain photocopies of the Chaffee/Blair letters for inclusion in this book.
- Joyce Loving, Manager of St. Louis County Library's Special Collections Department, found an online article in the Library of Congress' October 2000, *Informational Bulletin* telling about the Hollyday donation and shared it with the author.
- Correspondence with Barbara Bair, a manuscript specialist at the Library of Congress, confirmed that the Chaffee letters were part of the Hollyday donation.

A special note of thanks to Barbara Bair of the Library of Congress for confirming that these letters were part of the Hollyday donation and to Thomas Campbell Farnam for sharing the story of finding the letters.

April 1, 1857

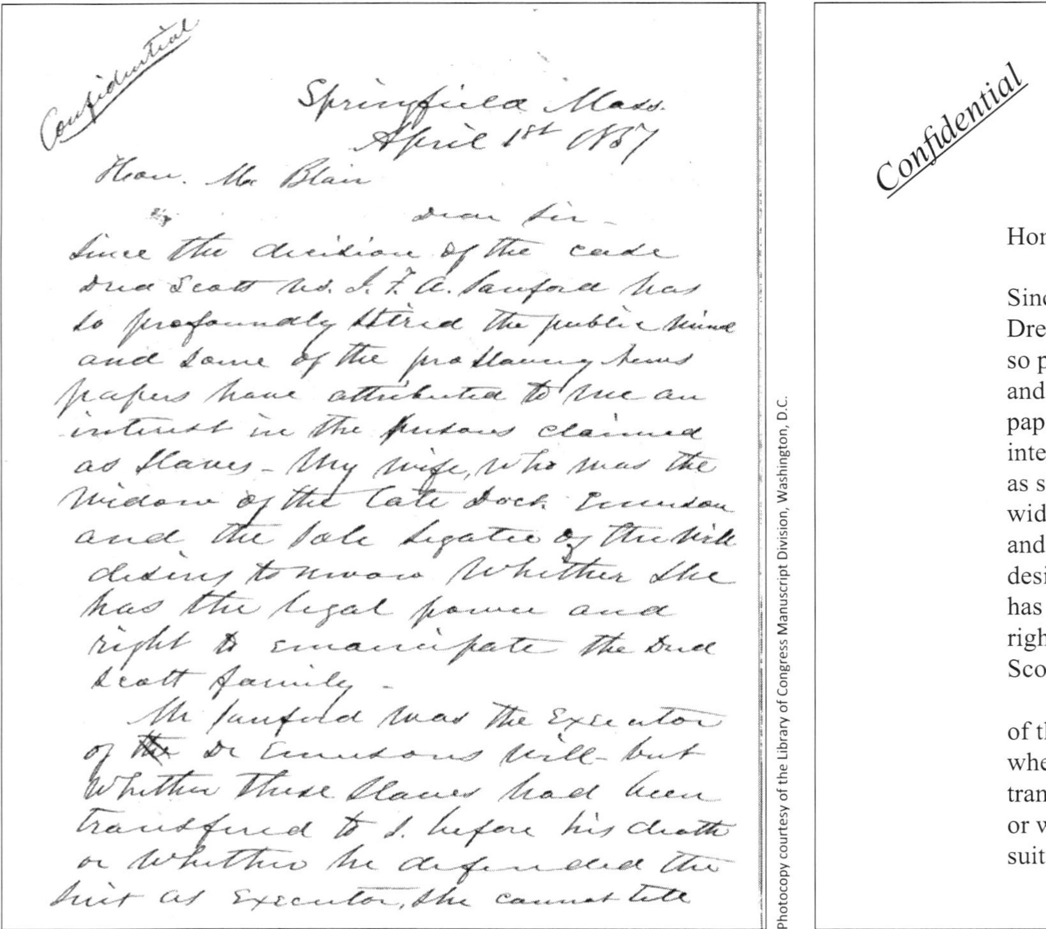

Sheet 1 of 3

Photocopy courtesy of the Library of Congress Manuscript Division, Washington, D.C.

Confidential

Springfield Mass.
April 1st 1857

Hon. M. Blair

Dear Sir –

Since the decision of the case
Dred Scott vs. J.F.A. Sanford has
so profoundly stired the public mind
and some of the proslavery news
papers have attributed to me an
interest in the persons claimed
as slaves – My wife, who was the
widow of the late Doct. Emerson
and the sole Legatee of the will
desires to know whether she
has the legal power and
right to emancipate the Dred
Scott family –

Mr Sanford was the Executor
of the Dr Emersons will – but
whether these slaves had been
transferred to J. before his death
or whether he defended the
suit as executor, she cannot tell

(Continued on page 121)

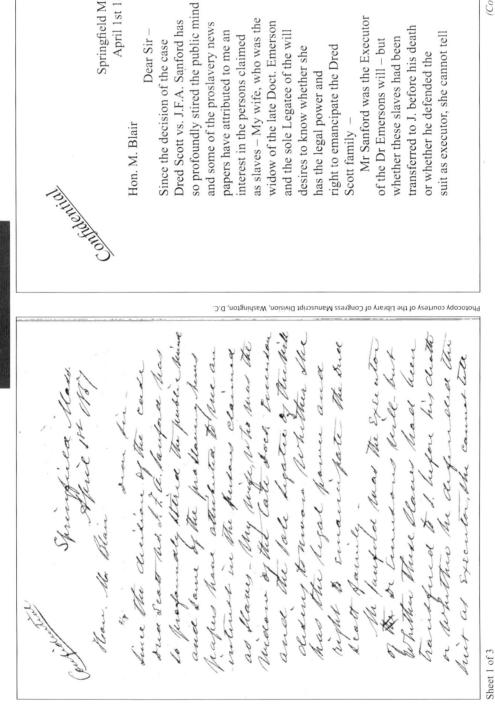

The original of this letter from C. C. Chaffee to Hon. M. Blair, dated April 1, 1857, is in the Blair Family Papers in the Maunuscript Division at the Library of Congress.

April 1, 1857 (cont)

Mr Sanfords Mental condition
is such that he can give no infor
-mation on the subject, and she
is desirous, if within her power
of washing her hands of all partici
pancy in the matter –

If she has this right and
power if you would forward
the necessary papers, she will
cheerfully execute them –

May I not hope to hear from
you at an early day?

Very respectfully
Your Obt Servt
C. C. Chaffee

Sheet 2 of 3

(Continued on page 122)

April 1, 1857 (cont)

(Continued from page 121)

Sheet 3 of 3

Dear Field,

(smudged) Will you ascertain how
the title in Dred stands whether
in Sandford in his own right or
as a Rep of Emerson – It is un
doubtedly much after Mrs Ca?
of him in Sandford –

By the way it has been very extensively
calculated in the East that the
case was got up fictitiously – & the
fact that I am in office gives color
to the story – I wish you have it con
tradicted in the Democrat.

Yrs truly
M Blair

Washington Apl 3

April 11, 1857

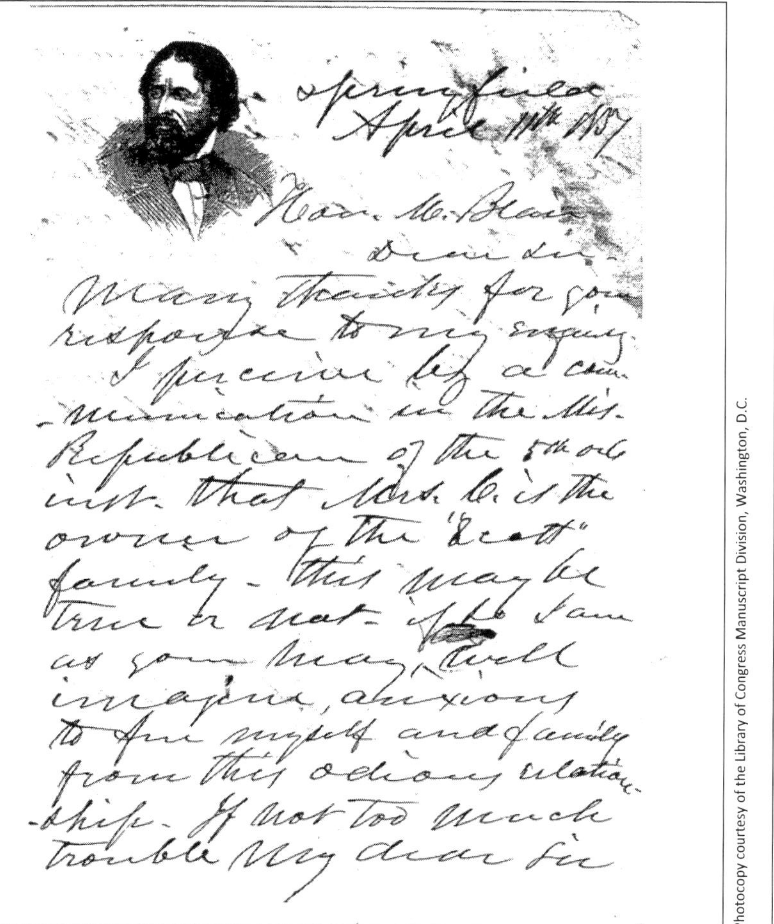

Sheet 1 of 3

Springfield
April 11th 1857

Hon. M. Blair
Dear Sir –
Many thanks for your
response to my enquiry.
I perceive by a com
-munication in the Mis-
Republican of the 5th or 6
inst. that Mrs. C. is the
owner of the "Scott"
family – this may be
true or not – if so I am
as you may well
imagine anxious
to free myself and family
from this odious relation
-ship. If not too much
trouble My dear Sir

(Continued on page 124)

The original of this letter from C. C. Chaffee to Hon. M. Blair, dated April 11, 1857, is in the Blair Family Papers in the Maunuscript Division at the Library of Congress.

April 11, 1857 (cont)

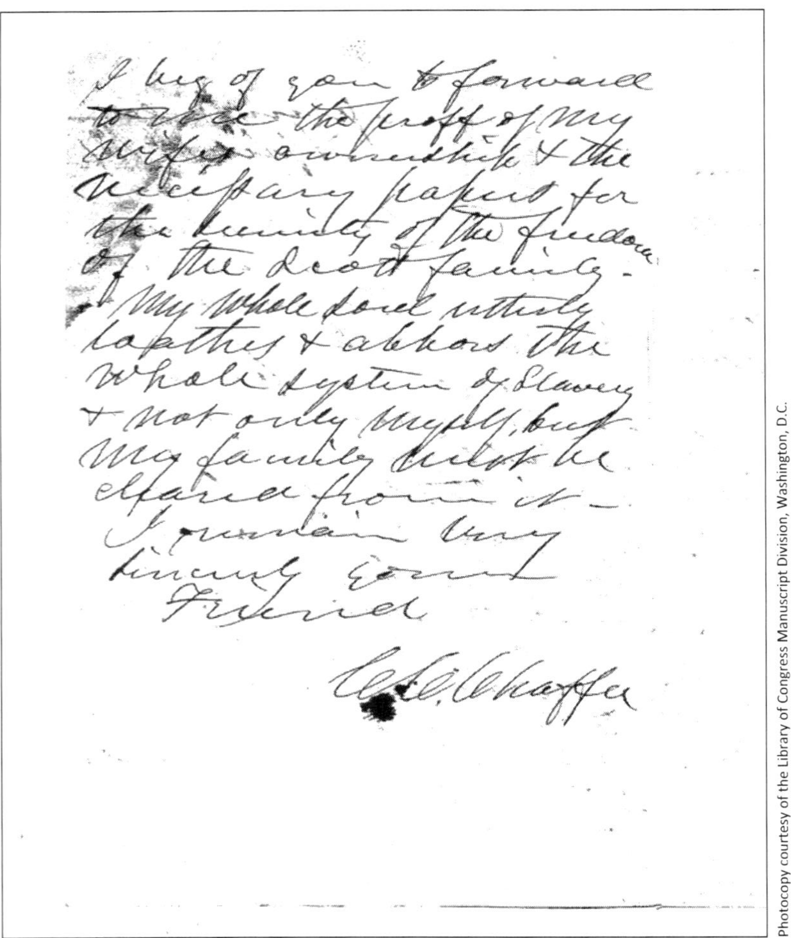

Sheet 2 of 3

I beg of you to forward
to me the proff of my
wifes ownership & the
necessary papers for
the security of the freedom
of the Scott family –
My whole soul utterly
loathes & abhors the
whole system of slavery
& not only myself, but
my family must be
cleared from it–
I remain very
Sincerely Your
Friend

C. C. Chaffee

(Continued on page 125)

April 11, 1857 (cont)

(Continued from page 124)

Sheet 3 of 3

Dear Field
I think as you have
interested yourself sufficiently
in Dred Scotts affairs then
[something marked out] for you will not object to see
him through & therefore
I send you this letter. We
will I hope get Dred free after
all tho he lost his case
in the Courts. You will be
better able to prepare the
papers etc. than I am & I
Commit it to you. *[next words are smeared or partially erased]*

Yours truly
M Blair
Washington. 13 Apl '57

Let Dred select the person
to whom the transfer
shall be made etc.

[the next is in different handwriting]

R M Field Esq
St Louis Missouri

It may be necessary to transfer Dred & family to some one in St Louis that the deed can say that it is done to emancipate them legally or

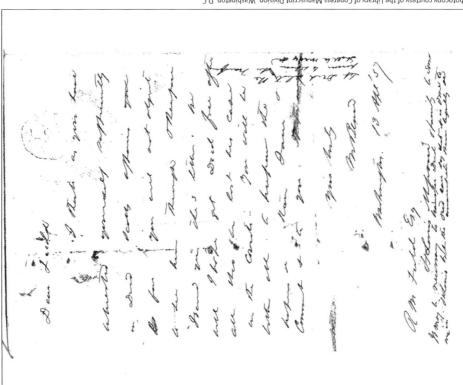

May 6, 1857

Springfield Mass.
May 6th 1857
My dear Judge
Ten thousand
thanks for your kindness and
interest in my affairs – I will try
to act worthy of them –
My wife is now in N.Y. being
summoned by the fatal illness of
her Br. J. F. A. Sanford the Deft. *[defendant]* of the
suit which has made humanity grieve
and all true Americans blush –
Mr. Sanford died yesterday at
12. M. I suppose of congestion of the
brain. My wife will remain there till
Saturday & I hope next week to get
the papers executed – of which I will
apprise you – Ever faithfully
Your obt srvt
C. C. Chaffee

Sheet 1 of 1

The original of this letter from C. C. Chaffee to "My Dear Judge" [M. Blair], dated May 6, 1857, is in the Blair Family Papers in the Maunuscript Division at the Library of Congress.

May 14, 1857

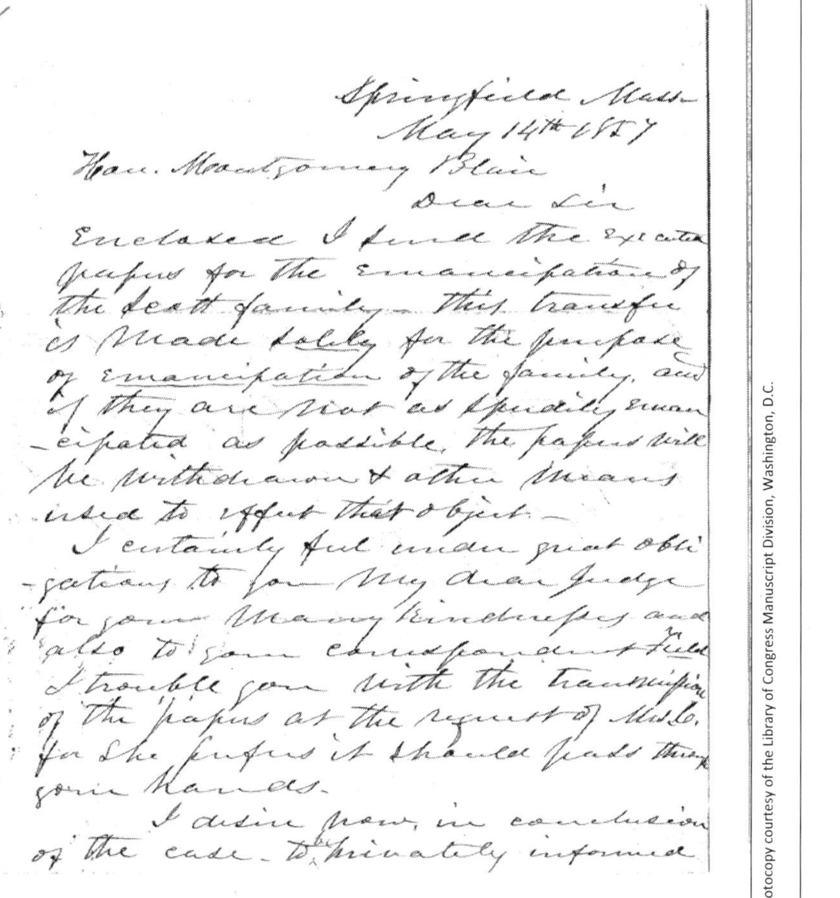

Sheet 1 of 2

Springfield Mass.
May 14th 1857
Hon. Montgomery Blair
Dear Sir
Enclosed I send the executed
papers for the Emancipation of
the Scott family – this transfer
is made solely for the purpose
of Emancipation of the family, and
if they are not as speedily Eman
-cipated as possible, the papers will
be withdrawn & other means
used to effect that object–
I certainly feel under great obli
-gations to you my dear Judge
for your many kindnesses and
also to your correspondent Field
I trouble you with the transmission
of the papers at the request of Mrs. C.
for she prefers it should pass through
your hands.
I desire now, in conclusion
of the case – to be privately informed

(Continued on page 128)

The original of this letter from C. C. Chaffee to Hon. Montgomery Blair, dated May 14, 1857, is in the Blair Family Papers in the Maunuscript Division at the Library of Congress

May 14, 1857 (cont)

of act of emancipation, but [that] there
should be no publicity given, the
subject, beyond <u>strict</u> <u>legal</u> <u>necessity</u>
This is all the boon I ask in the
premises, & I trust I may be grat
-ified.

I have made such a form
of conveyance as was least
objectionable to myself, but I
believe it accomplishes all that
is desired –

I return all the papers sought
& have retained no copies – only
two points I make in the matter
speedy action and entirely private.

I remain my dear Judge
very sincerely your friend
& obt Servt
C. C. Chaffee

P.S. I saw your Brother F. P. in N.Y.
last week & like him hugely!
C.

Sheet 2 of 2

(Continued from page 127)

APPENDIX E

— BLOW & SANFORD FAMILIES —

BLOW FAMILY

Support for Dred and Harriet's quest for freedom came from the children of Peter and Elizabeth Blow, Dred's original owner. It is important to know something about their lives in order to better understand the roles they played in Dred and Harriet's story.

The powerful and committed support of the Blow family, which centered around their blood relations and connections by marriage, was exceptional. After all, it was approximately fourteen years after Peter Blow sold Dred that his children came to Dred's aid when he and Harriet filed their freedom suits in 1846.

SANFORD FAMILY

Irene (Sanford) Emerson may have held the Scott family as her slaves, but more than half of the Sanford family—and sometimes their spouses and in-laws—also interacted with, influenced, or controlled Dred and Harriet's lives.

Regardless of the personal motivation of the individuals in the Sanford families, their actions affected the lives of the Scott family and the course of American history.

The Blow Family

Peter Blow
b: 1777, Va.
m: 1800, Va.
d: 1832, Mo.
Elizabeth (Taylor) Blow
b: 1785, Va.
d: 1831, Mo.

Mary Ann Blow
b: 1802, Va.
m: John Key in 1819, Ala.
d: 1826, Ala.

Thomas Vaughn Blow
b: 1804, Va.
d: 1812. Va.

Elizabeth Rebecca Blow
b: 1806, Va.
d: 1862. Mo.

Richard Benjamin Blow (twin)
b: 1808, Va.
d: 1813. Va.

male Blow (twin)
b: 1808, Va.
d: in infancy, Va.

Charlotte Taylor Blow
b: 1810, Va.
m: Joseph Charless, Jr. in 1831, Mo.
d: 1905, La.

Martha Ella Blow
b: 1812, Va.
m: Charles D. Drake in 1835, Mo.
d: 1841, Mo.

Peter Etheldred Taylor Blow
b: 1814, Va.
m 1: Eugenia LaBeaume in 1838, Mo
m 2: Sarah Tunstall in 1848, Mo.
d: 1866, Mo.

Henry Taylor Blow
b: 1817, Va.
m: Minerva Grimsley in 1840, Mo.
d: 1875, N.Y.

Taylor Francis Blow
b: 1820, Ala.
m: Eliza Wahrendoff in 1844, Mo.
d: 1869, Mo.

William Thomas Blow
b: 1822, Ala.
m: Julia Webster in 1853, Mo.
d: 1877, Mo.

THE BLOW SIBLINGS IN ST. LOUIS

ELIZABETH REBECCA BLOW

Born on 7 May 1806 in Virginia, Elizabeth never married. She helped care for the children of her deceased sister, Martha Blow Drake. Elizabeth died on 17 October 1862 in St. Louis.[324]

CHARLOTTE TAYLOR BLOW

Born on 9 May 1810 in Virginia,[325] Charlotte married Joseph Charless Jr. on 8 November 1831 in St. Louis.[326] Charlotte's father-in-law, Joseph Charless Sr., founded the *Missouri Gazette* in 1808, "... the first newspaper west of the Mississippi and one that advocated the abolition of slavery in the territory [Missouri] ..."[327] She died on 1 February 1905 in Covington, Louisiana, at the home of her daughter and son-in-law.[328]

MARTHA ELLA BLOW

Born on 21 May 1812 in Virginia,[329] Martha married Charles D. Drake, a lawyer, on 8 September 1835 in St. Louis.[330] Martha died on 17 January 1841 in St. Louis, just six years after their marriage.[331] Her death left Charles with two small children. Her sister Elizabeth helped Charles look after the children and that contact resulted in his continued closeness to the Blow family.[332]

PETER ETHELDRED TAYLOR BLOW

Born on 18 October 1814 in Virginia,[333] Peter married Eugenia LaBeaume on 27 December 1838 in St. Louis.[334] She died in 1847 and he married Sarah Tunstall in 1848. He started out in the dry goods business, and later went into lead mining in Washington County, Missouri.[335] One of Peter's brother-in-laws, Louis Alexander LaBeaume, was a wealthy St. Louis businessman. Another, Louis T. LaBeaume, was the St. Louis County Sheriff when Dred and Harriet were placed in the custody of the county sheriff.[336] A third, Charles Edmund LaBeaume, was a prosperous St. Louis lawyer. Peter died on 21 July 1866 in St. Louis.[337]

HENRY TAYLOR BLOW

Born on 15 July 1817[338] in Southampton County, Virginia,[339] Henry T. married Minerva Grimsley on 14 July 1840 in St. Louis.[340] He was at one time a partner with his brother-in-law, Joseph Charless Jr. Later, his successful business ventures included organizing with his brother, Peter, the Granby Mining and Smelting Company, and serving as president of the Iron Mountain Railroad.[341] Henry served in the Missouri State Senate (1854–1858), supported the Union during the Civil War, was U.S. Minister to Venezuela (1861–1862), represented his district in the U.S. House of Representatives (1863–1867), and served as minister to Brazil (1869–1871).[342] He was also the father of Susan Blow who established the "... first continuous public school kindergarten" in the U.S.[343] Henry died on 11 September 1875 in Saratoga Springs, New York.[344]

TAYLOR FRANCIS BLOW

Born on 26 March 1820 near Huntsville, Alabama,[345] Taylor married Eliza Wahrendoff on 8 October 1844 in St. Louis.[346] He became a partner with his brother-in-law, Joseph Charless Jr., in the wholesale drug and paint store, Charless, Blow & Company.[347] Taylor was about twelve in the summer of 1831 when his mother, Elizabeth, died. His father died in the summer of 1832. Some time between those two events, Dred was sold to Dr. Emerson.[348] In 1857, Taylor played a key role in emancipating the Scott family and in 1867, he moved Dred's remains from Wesleyan Cemetery to Calvary Cemetery. For the somewhat conflicting information about Taylor's actions during the Civil War, see the chapter, "The Civil War and Its Aftermath." He died on 20 August 1869 in St. Louis.[349]

WILLIAM THOMAS BLOW

Born on 8 May 1822 in Alabama,[350] William married Julia Webster on 12 July 1853 in St. Louis.[351] William had a home and mining operation in Mineral Point, Washington County, Missouri. His mine shipped white lead north on the St. Louis–Iron Mountain Railroad.[352] He died on 8 July 1877 in Washington County, Missouri.[353]

The Sanford Family

Alexander Sanford
b: abt 1788
d: 1848, Mo.

John F. A. Sanford
b: 1806, Va.
m 1: Emilie Chouteau in 1832, Mo.
m 2: Isabella Davis in 1852
d: 1857, N.Y.

Charlotte Sanford
b: 1811, Va.
m: James Barnes in 1832, Md.

Henrietta Sanford
b: 1812, Va.
m: John B. Clark in 1829, Mo.

Irene Sanford
b: 1815, Va.
m 1: Dr. John Emerson in 1836, La.
m 2: Dr. Calvin Chaffee in 1850, Mass.
d: 1903, Mass.

Mary Sanford
b: 1817, Va.
m 1: Henry Bainbridge in 1834, Fort Towson, West Choctaw Nation [Okla.]
m 2: Henry S. Humphrey in 1866, Mass
d: 1887, Mass.

Joseph Perry Sanford
b: 1818, Va.
m: Lydia Ransom in 1846, N.Y.
d: 1901, Conn.

Virginia Sanford
b: 1828, Md.
m: Samuel H. Ransom in 1846
d: 1891

Who was Alexander Sanford's wife or wives?
Two documents listed the name of Alexander Sanford's wife. A deed in Shenandoah County, Virginia, dated 24 April 1815, listed "Alexander Sanford and Mary his wife..." selling property. Then Mary (Sanford) Bainbridge listed her parents as Alexander and Mary Sanford on her 1866 marriage record to Henry S. Humphrey. However, with five years between the births of John and his sister, Charlotte, and only one to three years between the births of Charlotte through Joseph, it is possible that the Sanford siblings did not all have the same mother.

The Sanford Family

Alexander Sanford

Born about 1788, Alexander was a slave owner and strong supporter of slavery. He lived in Virginia before moving to St. Louis, Missouri, where he died in 1848.[354]

John F. A. Sanford

Born about 1806 in Winchester, Virginia,[355] John entered West Point Military Academy in 1821, but did not graduate.[356] He married Emilie Chouteau on 22 November 1832 in St. Louis,[357] and served as a sub-agent for the Indians of the upper Missouri. He lived part of the year among the tribes with whom he worked and part of the year in St. Louis. In 1834 he resigned and joined his father-in-law, Pierre Chouteau Jr. as his business partner. After the death of Emilie in 1836, Sanford moved to New York to represent his company's interest. He let Emilie's parents, Pierre and Emilie (Gratiot) Chouteau, raise his son, Benjamin Chouteau Sanford.[358]

John married his second wife, Isabella Davis, in 1852.[359] From 1851 until his death in 1857, which includes the life-span of *Scott v. Sandford*, he and later his wife and children, lived at a very prestigious address, 138 Fifth Avenue, in New York City.[360] John made his fortune in the fur trade, mining, and railroad businesses.[361] He died 5 May 1857 in an insane asylum after a mental breakdown.[362]

Charlotte Sanford

Born about 1811 in Virginia,[363] Charlotte married Lieutenant James Barnes on 16 February 1832 in Baltimore, Maryland.[364] James graduated from West Point Military Academy in the class of 1829 along with Robert E. Lee.[365] James left the military in 1836 and as a civil engineer made his fortune in railroads. He rejoined the Union Army at the outbreak of the Civil War and rose to the rank of Brigadier General.[366]

Henrietta Sanford

Born about 1812 in Virginia,[367] Henrietta married Captain John B. Clark on 2 December 1829 at St. Louis, Missouri.[368] He held the rank of Major when he died on 23 August 1847 as a casualty in the Mexican War.[369] At the time of the 1850 census. Henrietta, widowed with three children, lived in Springfield, Massachusetts.[370]

Irene Sanford

Born in September 1815 in the Shenandoah Valley of Virginia,[371] Irene married Dr. John Emerson on 6 February 1838 at Natchitoches, Louisiana.[372] When he died in 1843, she inherited ownership of Dred and his family. She married Dr. Calvin Chaffee in Springfield, Massachusetts, on 21 November 1850.[373] Irene died on 11 February 1903 in Springfield, Massachusetts.[374]

Mary Sanford

Born about 1817 in Virginia,[375] Mary married Captain Henry Bainbridge on 20 February 1834 at Fort Towson, West Choctaw Nation.[376] Henry, a graduate of West Point Military Academy in the class of 1821,[377] was a Lieutenant Colonel when he died 1 June 1857 in the steamer Louisiana fire in Galveston Bay.[378] Mary lived in Springfield, Massachusetts, with her sister and brother-in-law, Charlotte and James Barnes, when the 1860 census was taken.[379] She married Henry S. Humphrey on 2 October 1866[380] and died on 23 April 1887 at Springfield, Massachusetts.[381]

Joseph Perry Sanford

Born on 13 September 1818 in Winchester, Virginia, Joseph became a naval captain. He married Lydia Ransom on 7 January 1846 near Albany, New York. He died on 5 December 1901 at Stanford, Connecticut, and was buried in Springfield, Massachusetts.[382]

Virginia Sanford

Born on 7 January 1828 in Maryland, married Samuel Henry Ransom on 11 December 1846.[383] Virginia's husband, S. H. Ransom, was a wealthy merchant in Albany, New York.[384] She died on 13 January 1891.[385]

REFERENCE NOTES

The following acronyms are used in this list:

FHL—Family History Library
SLCL—St. Louis County Library
NARA—National Archives & Records Administration

Dred and Harriet, pages 1–16

1. Walter Ehrlich, *They Have No Rights: Dred Scott's Struggle for Freedom* (1979; reprint, Bedford, Massachusetts: Applewood Books, 2007), 9.
2. Joseph M. Menius, *Susan Blow—Gateway to Education* (St. Clair, Missouri: Page One Publishing, 1993), 5–6.
3. Walter Garland Duke, *Henry Duke, Councilor and His Descendants and Connections* (Richmond, Virginia: Dietz Press, 1949), 77; digital images, *HeritageQuest Online* (http://www.heritagequestonline.com). Also, Menius, *Susan Blow*, 9, 16.
4. Ehrlich, *They Have No Rights*, 9.
5. John A. Bryan, "The Blow Family and Their Slave Dred Scott: Part I," *Missouri Historical Society Bulletin*, 4 (1948): 223–224.
6. Menius, *Susan Blow*, 9. Also, Bryan, "The Blow Family and Their Slave Dred Scott: Part I," 224.
7. "Dred and Harriet Scott's Application for License as Free Negroes," volume 11, book 9, page 9. St. Louis County, Missouri, County Court Proceedings; Missouri Historical Society, St Louis, Missouri.
8. "Visit to Dred Scott—His Family—Incidents of His Life—Decision of the Supreme Court," *Frank Leslie's Illustrated Newspaper*, New York, 27 June 1857, reissue, page 1 and 50.
9. Menius, *Susan Blow*, 10.
10. St. Francis Xavier Catholic [College] Church (St. Louis City, Missouri) Baptisms, 1864–1886, page 34, Baptism of Taylor Francis Blow, 7 April 1865; FHL microfilm 1,871,244, available at SLCL as SLAPR–62, St. Louis, Missouri. [Historians have consistently noted that, unlike his brothers and sisters, Taylor Blow had no middle name. However, as an adult he was baptized a Catholic in 1865 and his baptismal record states "... Taylor Francis Blow (a Convert from [blot] presbeterianism) son of Peter Blow and Elizabeth Rebecca Taylor, born March 26, 1820." Although he may have never used his middle name or initial, this one document, for which he personally provided the information, proves that Francis was his middle name.] Also, Bryan, "The Blow Family and Their Slave Dred Scott: Part I," 224.

11. Gwenyth Swain, *Dred and Harriet Scott: A Family's Struggle for Freedom* (St. Paul, Minnesota: Borealis Books, 2004), 13–14.
12. Swain, *Dred and Harriet Scott*, 14.
13. "The Original Dred Scott as Resident of St. Louis—Sketch of His History," *St. Louis Daily Evening News*, 3 April 1857, St. Louis, Missouri, page 2, column 1.
14. Swain, *Dred and Harriet Scott*, 14.
15. Swain, *Dred and Harriet Scott*, 16.
16. Bryan, "The Blow Family and Their Slave Dred Scott: Part I," 224.
17. Joseph M. Menius, "Blow's Brought about Change" (St. Louis: J. M. Menius, no date), sheet A, Blow Family History File, Carondelet Historical Society.
18. Charlotte Taylor Blow Charless, *A Biographical Sketch of the Life and Character of Joseph Charless in a Series of Letters to His Grandchildren* (1869), 7; digital images, *Project Gutenberg* (http://www.gutenberg.org/wiki).
19. Bryan, "The Blow Family and Their Slave Dred Scott: Part I," 224. Also, Menius, *Susan Blow*, 11. Also, Swain, *Dred and Harriet Scott*, 18.
20. Charless, *A Biographical Sketch of the Life and Character of Joseph Charless*, 9.
21. Gary V. Sluyter, *St. Louis' Hidden Treasure: A History of the Charless Home 1853–2003* (St. Louis, Missouri: The Senior Circuit, 2003), 17, 20.
22. Charless, *A Biographical Sketch of the Life and Character of Joseph Charless*, 9.
23. Ehrlich, *They Have No Rights*, 11.
24. Sluyter, *St. Louis' Hidden Treasure: A History of the Charless Home 1853–2003*, 22.
25. "Missouri's Dred Scott Case, 1846–1857," *Missouri State Archives* (http://www.sos.mo.gov/achives/resources/africanamerican/scott/scott.asp).
26. William A. Meese, *Early Rock Island* (Moline, Illinois: Press of Desaulniers & Company, 1905), 82; digital images, *HeritageQuest Online* (http://www.heritagequestonline.com). Also, *Past and Present of Rock Island County, Ill.* (Chicago: H. F. Kett & Company, 1877), 118; digital images, *HeritageQuest Online* (http://www.heritagequestonline.com).
27. Ehrlich, *They Have No Rights*, 17.
28. "Missouri's Dred Scott Case, 1846–1857," *Missouri State Archives.* Also, "The Slavery Question in Illinois," *Illinois State Historical Library* (http://www.state.il.us/HPA/lovejoy/illinois.htm).
29. Ehrlich, *They Have No Rights*, 19.
30. Don E. Fehrenbacher, *The Dred Scott Case: Its Significance in American Law and Politics* (New York: Oxford University Press, 1978), 244.
31 Robert B. Roberts, *Encyclopedia of Historic Forts* (New York: Macmillan Publishing Co., 1988), 438.
32. "Missouri's Dred Scott Case, 1846–1857," *Missouri State Archives.* Also, Ehrlich, *They Have No Rights*, 19.
33. Colonel John H. Bliss, "Reminiscences of Fort Snelling," *Collections of the Minnesota Historical Society*, 6 (1894): 336. Also, Jeffrey A. Hess, "Dred Scott from Fort Snelling to Freedom," *Historic Fort Snelling Chronicles*, 2 (1975), not paginated.
34. Ehrlich, *They Have No Rights*, 20. Also, "Missouri's Dred Scott Case, 1846–1857," *Missouri State Archives.*
35. Lawrence Taliaferro, "Auto-biography of Maj. Lawrence Taliaferro," *Collections of the Minnesota Historical Society*, 6 (1894): 190, 235
36. 1860 U.S. census, St. Louis County, Missouri, population schedule, City of St. Louis, ward 7, page 110, dwelling 396, family 707, Harriet Scott; digital image, *HeritageQuest Online* (http://www.heritagequestonline.com); citing NARA publication M653, roll 653.

37. Ehrlich, *They Have No Rights,* 199, note 16.
38. Ehrlich, *They Have No Rights*, 21.
39. Ehrlich, *They Have No Rights*, 21.
40. Fehrenbacher, *The Dred Scott Case*, 244.
41. Fehrenbacher, *The Dred Scott Case*, 244–245.
42. Ehrlich, *They Have No Rights*, 22.
43. Natchitoches Parish, Louisiana, Conveyances, book 24, page 302, no. 1775, Dr. John Emerson and Eliza Irene Sanford, Celebration of Marriage, 1838; Parish Clerk of Court's office, Natchitoches.
44. Ehrlich, *They Have No Rights*, 22.
45. Ehrlich, *They Have No Rights*, 23.
46. Fehrenbacher, *The Dred Scott Case*, 246.
47. The 1870 birth record for her son listed Eliza Madison as "Elizabeth" (St. Louis City, Missouri, St. Louis Register of Births, volume 68b: 142, unnamed Madison infant; SLCL microfilm RBSL–2), and her 1882 St. Louis Death Register entry also listed her as Elizabeth (St. Louis City, Missouri, St. Louis Register of Deaths, volume 13: 51, Elizabeth Madison, 1882; SLCL microfilm RDSL–22); Eliza's 1870 federal census record listed her as "Lizzie Madison." 1870 U.S. census, St. Louis County, Missouri, population schedule, City of St. Louis, ward 8, page 87 (penned), dwelling 811, family 1622, Lizzie Madison; digital images, *HeritageQuest Online* (http://heritagequestonline.com); citing NARA publication M593, roll 818.
48. Ehrlich, *They Have No Rights*, 25.
49. Ehrlich, *They Have No Rights*, 189.
50. Fehrenbacher, *The Dred Scott Case*, 247.
51. Ehrlich, *They Have No Rights*, 26.
52. Robert E. Parkin, *Overland Trails and Trials and Community Today* (Overland, Missouri: Krawll Printing Company, 1956), 11. Also, William Hyde and Howard L. Conard, editors, *Encyclopedia of the History of St. Louis, a Compendium of History and Biography for Ready Reference*, 4 volumes (New York: Southern History Co., 1899), 3: 1688.
53. Kenneth C. Kaufman, *Dred Scott's Advocate: A Biography of Roswell M. Field* (Columbia, Missouri: University of Missouri Press, 1996), 145.
54. Kaufman, *Dred Scott's Advocate*, 118.
55. Kaufman, *Dred Scott's Advocate*, 144.
56. Ehrlich, *They Have No Rights*, 27.
57. Fehrenbacher, *The Dred Scott Case*, 247–248.
58. Charles E. Snyder, "John Emerson, Owner of Dred Scott," *Annals of Iowa*, 21 (1938): 452–453; digital images, *Internet Archive* (http://www.archive.org/details/johnemersonowner00snyd).
59. Benjamin F. Shambaugh, *History of the Constitutions of Iowa* (Des Moines, Iowa: Historical Department of Iowa, 1902), 120: digital images, *HeritageQuest Online* (http://heritagequestonline.com).
60. Robert R. Dykstra, *Bright Radical Star: Black Freedom and White Supremacy on the Hawkeye Frontier* (Cambridge, Massachusetts: Harvard University Press, 1993), 9. Also, "Iowa Judicial Branch: Early Civil Rights Cases." *Iowa Courts* (http://www.iowacourts.gov/Public_Information/Iowa_Courts_History/Civil_Rights).
61. Ehrlich, *They Have No Rights*, 28.
62. St. Louis County, Missouri, John Emerson probate case file, no. 1914, 1844, collection 4, images 2–3; digital images, "Missouri's Judicial Records," *Missouri State Archives* (http://www.sos.mo.gov/archives/stlprobate). Also, Ehrlich, *They Have No Rights*, 28.

63. Ehrlich, *They Have No Rights*, 29.
64. Fehrenbacher, *The Dred Scott Case*, 249.
65. Ehrlich, *They Have No Rights*, 29.
66. Marc E. Kollbaum, *Gateway to the West: The History of Jefferson Barracks from 1826–1894,* volume 1 (St. Louis: Friends of Jefferson Barracks, no date), 9. Also, "Jefferson Barracks," *St. Louis County* (http://www.co.st-louis.mo.us/parks/j-b.html).
67. Fehrenbacher, *The Dred Scott Case*, 249.
68. "Visit to Dred Scott …," *Frank Leslie's Illustrated Newspaper*, 27 June 1857.
69. "Visit to Dred Scott …," *Frank Leslie's Illustrated Newspaper*, 27 June 1857.
70. Fehrenbacher, *The Dred Scott Case*, 249.
71. Fehrenbacher, *The Dred Scott Case*, 656, note 30. [This is a good description of evidence regarding Dred and Harriet's time with the Bainbridge family.]
72. Ehrlich, *They Have No Rights*, 189.
73. 1860 U.S. census, St. Louis County, Missouri, population schedule, City of St. Louis, ward 7, page 110 (penned), dwelling, 396, family 707, Harriotte and Elizabeth Scott. [This census entry shows fifteen-year-old Elizabeth Scott in the household with forty-year-old Harriotte Scott.] Also, 1880 U.S. census, St. Louis County, Missouri, population schedule, City of St. Louis, (first enumeration), ward 2, enumeration district (ED) 11, page 193 (stamped), dwelling 54, family 69, Eliza Scott; digital image, *HeritageQuest Online* (http://heritagequestonline .com); citing NARA publication, T9, roll 717. [This entry lists "Eliza Scott" as black, 30 years of age, a roomer (boarder), single, and a washerwoman.]
74. Fehrenbacher, The Dred Scott Case, 249.
75. "Visit to Dred Scott …," *Frank Leslie's Illustrated Newspaper*, 27 June 1857.
76. Fehrenbacher, *The Dred Scott Case*, 250.
77. "Visit to Dred Scott …," *Frank Leslie's Illustrated Newspaper*, 27 June 1857.
78. Kaufman, *Dred Scott's Advocate*, 141.
79. Ehrlich, *They Have No Rights*, 41.

Suing for Freedom, pages 17–24

80. Fehrenbacher, *The Dred Scott Case*, 250. Also, "Freedom Suits Case Files, 1814–1860," *St. Louis Circuit Court Historical Records Project* (http://stlcourtrecords.wustl.edu). [Select the search feature, then enter the key word "Dred Scott" or "Harriet Scott." Select "view case" to see an image of the original petition where Dred and Harriet signed own petitions with an "X" indicating they could not write their names.]
81. Ehrlich, *They Have No Rights*, 36.
82. "Missouri's Dred Scott Case, 1846–1857," *Missouri State Archives.*
83. Fehrenbacher, *The Dred Scott Case*, 85.
84. Fehrenbacher, *The Dred Scott Case*, 79.
85. "Missouri's Dred Scott Case, 1846–1857," *Missouri State Archives.*
86. Robert Moore Jr., "A Ray of Hope, Extinguished: St. Louis Slave Suits for Freedom," *Gateway Heritage*, 14 (1993–1994): 5.
87. Ehrlich, *They Have No Rights*, 36.
88. Ehrlich, *They Have No Rights*, 38.

89. Ehrlich, *They Have No Rights*, 38–39.
90. Ehrlich, *They Have No Rights*, 47.
91. The Christ Church Cemetery burial register recorded the burial of sixty-year-old "A. Sanford" on 14 February 1848 with the added notation "from Owens Station." [A. Sanford, Register of Christ Church Cemetery, 1840–1856, Archives of the Episcopal Diocese of Missouri; digital image, courtesy of Sue Rehkopf, Archivist, for lot number nine in Christ Church Cemetery in St. Louis. Also, St. Louis County, Missouri, Alexander Sanford probate case file, no. 2486, 1848, collection 3, page 5; digital images, "Missouri's Judicial Records," *Missouri State Archives* (http://www.sos.mo.gov/archives/stlprobate).] The only other person buried in lot nine, which Sanford owned, was a J. B. Clark who died in Mexico. Sanford's son-in-law, Major John B. Clark, died as a casualty in the Mexican War, on 23 August 1847. [U.S. Congress, Henrietta S. Clark, 35th Congress, 1st session, House Report 82, Serial Set volume no. 964, (1858), page 1; digital images, *LexisNexis* (http://www.lexisnexis.com), LexisNexis Congressional Publications.] The date listed on his burial record was 15 April 1848, which would not be an unrealistic time delay for the return of his body to St. Louis during war time. [J. B. Clark, Register of Christ Church Cemetery, 1840–1856.]
92. St. Louis County, Missouri, Land Records, book Z4: 414–416, Recorder of Deeds, City of Saint Louis, Missouri; FHL microfilm 531,584. [John F. A. Sanford sold the farm "California" to James H. Lucas.]
93. Kaufman, *Dred Scott's Advocate*, 170.
94. "City Directories for New York, New York," 1848, 357; digital images, *Footnote.com* (http://www.footnote.com). Also, Leroy R. Hafen, editor, *Mountain Men and Fur Traders of the Far West* (Lincoln, Nebraska: University of Nebraska Press: 1982), 47.
95. Ehrlich, *They Have No Rights*, 55.
96. "Motion," Revised Dred Scott Collection, *Washington University Digital Gateway* (http://digital.wustl.edu/d/dre/newtrial.html). [The first "Motion" hyperlink leads to the database record and the document's transcription and image for Dred. The second "Motion" hyperlink leads to the database record and the document's transcription and image for Harriet.] Also, Ehrlich, *They Have No Rights*, 49, and Fehrenbacher, *The Dred Scott Case*, 255.
97. Ehrlich, *They Have No Rights*, 49.
98. *The Revised Statutes of the State of Missouri, Revised and Digested by the Thirteenth General Assembly, Begun and Held during the Years One Thousand Eight-hundred and Forty-four and One Thousand Eight Hundred and Forty-five* (St. Louis: Chambers & Knapp, 1845), 283–284, Freedom, "An Act to Enable Persons Held in Slavery to Sue for their Freedom." [Section sixteen of "Freedom" explains how a county sheriff, if he hired out a slave suing for freedom, should handle the wages earned including returning them after the case ended to whichever party won the suit.]
99. Moore, "A Ray of Hope, Extinguished: St. Louis Slave Suits for Freedom," 5.
100. Ehrlich, *They Have No Rights*, 47.
101. Ehrlich, *They Have No Rights*, 51. Also, "Local Events of 1849," James Green, *The Saint Louis Business Directory for the Year of Our Lord 1850*; microfilm reprint, *United States City Directories through 1860, St. Louis, Missouri*, fiche 1339, *1850* (No place: no publisher, no date), 38.
102. Ehrlich, *They Have No Rights*, 51.
103. St. Louis County, Missouri, "Probate Files," David N. Hall, case 3424, Louis LaBeaume sworn statement, 6 December 1851; St. Louis County Library microfilm CIPR–171. [Kris Zapalac, Ph.D. discovered this unpaid bill for Dred's hiring fees in David N. Hall's probate packet and shared it with this author.]
104. J(oseph) H. Sloss, *The St. Louis Directory for 1848*, microfilm reprint, *United States City Directories through 1860, St. Louis, Missouri*, fiche 1338, *1848* (No place: no publisher, no date), 85, 104.
105. Fehrenbacher, *The Dred Scott Case*, 256.
106. Ehrlich, *They Have No Rights*, 53. Also, "Missouri's Dred Scott Case, 1846–1857," *Missouri State Archives*.

107. St. Louis County, Missouri, Circuit Court Execution Record Book 7, page 395. Abstract courtesy of the Missouri State Archives—St. Louis.

108. Lawrence O. Christensen, *et al.*, editors, "John F. A. Sanford," *Dictionary of Missouri Biography* (Columbia, Missouri: University of Missouri Press, 1999), 665. [John Sanford married his first wife, Emilie Chouteau, the daughter of Pierre Chouteau Jr., on 22 November 1832 in St. Louis. Emilie died four years later, on 23 April 1836, after giving birth to their only son, Benjamin Chouteau Sanford. John Sanford remained partners with Pierre Chouteau Jr. until Sanford died in 1857.]

109. Kaufman, *Dred Scott's Advocate*, 166.

110. Fehrenbacher, *The Dred Scott Case*, 257.

111. "Petition for Leave to Sue for Freedom," The Revised Dred Scott Case Collection, *Washington University Digital Gateway* (http://digital.wustl.edu/d/dre/circuit1.html).

112. Hampden County, Massachusetts, Marriages 1850–1862, City of Springfield, 5: 6, Calvin C. Chaffee and Irene Emerson, 1850; FHL microfilm 185,416.

113. C. C. Chaffee to Hon. M. Blair, letter, 11 April 1857; photocopy of original housed at the Library of Congress in the Blair Family papers. Also, "Letter from Dr. Chaffee—The Dred Scott Case," *The Springfield Daily Republican,* Springfield, Massachusetts, 16 March 1857, page 2; photocopy courtesy of the Museum of Springfield History, Springfield, Massachusetts.

114. Ehrlich, *They Have No Rights*, 66.

115. "Missouri's Dred Scott Case, 1846–1857," *Missouri State Archives*. Also, Ehrlich, *They Have No Rights*, 67.

116. Fehrenbacher, *The Dred Scott Case,* 267.

Protecting their Daughters, pages 25–28

117. "The Dred Scott Case, Whose Slave Is He?" *St. Louis Republican,* 3 April 1857, page 2, column 2; photocopy courtesy of Missouri History Museum, St. Louis, Missouri.

118. "Visit to Dred Scott …," *Frank Leslie's Illustrated Newspaper*, 27 June 1857.

119. "The Original Dred Scott as Resident of St. Louis —Sketch of His History," *St. Louis Daily Evening News*, 3 April 1857. Five newspapers duplicating the story of Eliza and Lizzie disappearing, or a variation of it, were the *Daily Atlas* (Boston, Massachusetts) on 11 April 1857, the *National Era* (Washington, D.C.) on 16 April 1857, the *Syracuse Daily Courier* (Syracuse, New York) on 18 April 1857, *The Athens Messenger and Hocking Valley Gazette* (Athens, Ohio) on 1 May 1857, and *Frank Leslie's Illustrated Newspaper* (New York) on 27 June 1857.

120. "Missouri's Dred Scott Case, 1846–1857," *Missouri State Archives.*

121. "Dred Scott Free at Last—Himself and His Family Emancipated," *St. Louis Daily Evening News*, 26 April 1857, St. Louis, Missouri, page 2, column 1. This article was repeated, with minor variations, in "Dred Scott Free at Last—Himself and His Family Emancipated." *Ohio State Journal.* Columbus, Ohio, 10 June 1857, page 1; digital images, *America's GenealogyBank* (http://www.genealogybank.com). The well known article in *Frank Leslie's Illustrated Newspaper* (New York), 27 June 1857 included the content of both the 3 April and 26 April *St. Louis Daily Evening News* articles.

A NEW SUIT IN FEDERAL COURT, PAGES 29–32

122. "Missouri's Dred Scott Case, 1846–1857," *Missouri State Archives.*
123. Ehrlich, *They Have No Rights,* 36.
124. "Missouri's Dred Scott Case, 1846–1857," *Missouri State Archives*.
125. Ehrlich, *They Have No Rights*, 83.
126. Ehrlich, *They Have No Rights*, 82.
127. Ehrlich, *They Have No Rights*, 86.
128. "Missouri's Dred Scott Case, 1846–1857," *Missouri State Archives.*
129. "Petition to sue for freedom, Harriet Scott, filed 6 April 1846," "Dred Scott Collection," *Washington University Digital Gateway* (http://library.wustl.edu/vlib/dredscott/new_exhibits/ds01.html#02). [The digital image of Harriet's original petition to sue begins "To the Hon. John M. Krum, Judge of the St. Louis Circuit Court. The petition of Harriet, a woman of color, states …"] Also, Kaufman, *Dred Scott's Advocate*, 185.
130. Kaufman, *Dred Scott's Advocate*, 185.
131. Roswell Field to Montgomery Blair, letter, 24 December 1854; photograph of original housed at the Library of Congress in the Blair Family papers. [photo courtesy of Thomas Campbell Farnam]. Also, Hyde and Conard, *Encyclopedia of the History of St. Louis …*, 1: 174.
132. Fehrenbacher, *The Dred Scott Case*, 281.
133. "Missouri's Dred Scott Case, 1846–1857," *Missouri State Archives.*
134. Ehrlich, *They Have No Rights*, 96–97.
135. "Missouri's Dred Scott Case, 1846–1857," *Missouri State Archives.*

EMANCIPATION, PAGES 33–44

136. William H. Chaffee, *The Chaffee Genealogy: Embracing the Chafe, Chafy, Chafie, Chafey, Chafee, Chaphe, Chaffy, Chaffie, Chaffey, Chaffe, Chaffee Descendants of Thomas Chaffe, of Hingham, Hull, Rehoboth and Swansea, Massachusetts: Also Certain Lineages from Families in the United States, Canada, and England, Not Descended from Thomas Chaffe, 1635–1909* (New York: Grafton Press, 1909), 305. Also, Springfield, Hampden County, Massachusetts, Marriages 1850–1862, 5: 6, Calvin Chaffee and Irene Emerson, 1850, FHL microfilm 185,416.
137. "Letter from Dr. Chaffee—The Dred Scott Case," *The Springfield Daily Republican*, 16 March 1857.
138. Kaufman, *Dred Scot's Advocate*, 167.
139. Chaffee, *Chaffee Genealogy*, 303.
140. "Calvin Clifford Chaffee, (1811–1896)," *Biographical Directory of the United States Congress, 1774–Present* (http://bioguide.congress.gov).
141. Ehrlich, *They Have No Rights*, 75–76. Also, Fehrenbacher, *The Dred Scott Case*, 272.
142. Fehrenbacher, *The Dred Scott Case*, 420.
143. *The Liberator*, Boston, Massachusetts, 20 March 1857, page 47, issue 12, column D; digital images, *GaleCengage Learning* (http://www.gale.cengage.com), 19th Century Newspapers Online.

144. "Dred Scott," *Bangor Daily Whig and Courier*, Bangor, Maine, 18 March 1857, page 2; digital images, *Access Newspaper Archive* (http://access.newspaperarchive.com).
145. "Dred Scott's Owner," *Union and Advertiser*, Nunda, New York, 27 March 1857, page 2, column 3; photocopy courtesy Monroe County Library System, Rochester, New York.
146. "Letter from Dr. Chaffee—The Dred Scott Case," *The Springfield Daily Republican*, 16 March 1857.
147. C. C. Chaffee to Hon. M. Blair, letter, 1 April 1857, Blair Family papers.
148. Ehrlich, *They Have No Rights*, 180.
149. C. C. Chaffee to Hon. M. Blair, 11 April 1857, Blair Family papers.
150. C. C. Chaffee to "My Dear Judge" [Montgomery Blair], letter, 6 May 1857; photocopy of original housed at the Library of Congress in the Blair Family papers.
151. *The Revised Statutes of the State of Missouri, Revised and Digested by the Eighteenth General Assembly, during the Session of One Thousand Eight Hundred and Fifty-four and One Thousand Eight Hundred and Fifty-five* ..., 2 volumes (City of Jefferson, Missouri: James Lusk, 1856), 2: 1478–79, chapter 150, "An Act Concerning Slaves."
152. Harrison Anthony Trexler, "Slavery in Missouri 1804–1865," *John Hopkins University Studies in Historical and Political Science* (Baltimore: John Hopkins Press, 1914), 209. Also, Ernst C. Krohn, "Slavery in St. Louis 1804–1860," *Missouri Historical Society Bulletin*, 30 (1974): 255.
153. The *Syracuse Daily Courier*, Syracuse, New York, 18 April 1857, page 2, and the *Athens Messenger* and *Hocking Valley Gazette*, Athens, Ohio, 1 May 1857, page 1, said the girls' whereabouts remained a mystery.
154. "The Dred Scott Case, Whose Slave Is He?" *St. Louis Republican*, St. Louis, Missouri, 3 April 1857.
155. Le Roy Hafen and Scott Eckberg, *Fur Traders, Trappers, and Mountain Men of the Upper Missouri* (Lincoln, Nebraska: University of Nebraska Press, 1995), 59.
156. Notation by R. M. Field, Esq. immediately following the notation of M. Blair, both written on the back of the letter of Calvin Chaffee to Montgomery Blair, 11 April 1857; photocopy of original housed at the Library of Congress in the Blair Family Papers.
157. St. Louis County, Missouri, Land Records, book 186, page 199, quit claim deed from C. Chaffee to T. Blow, City of St. Louis Archives, St. Louis, Missouri.
158. C. C. Chaffee to Hon. Montgomery Blair, letter, 14 May 1857; photocopy of original housed at the Library of Congress in the Blair Family Papers.
159. C. C. Chaffee to Hon. Montgomery Blair, letter, 14 May 1857, Blair Family Papers.
160. St. Louis County, Missouri, Land Records, book 186: 199.
161. St. Louis County, Missouri, Circuit Court Records, volume 26, page 263, Writ of Emancipation by Taylor Blow for Dred, Harriet, Eliza, and Lizzie Scott: digital images, "The Revised Dred Scot Case Collection," *Washington University Digital Gateway* (http://digital.wustl.edu/d/dre). [search terms "Taylor Blow" and "emancipation"]
162. The *Daily Ohio Statesman*, 18 June 1857, Columbus, Ohio, page 3; digital images, *America's GenealogyBank* (http://www.genealogybank.com).
163. "Missouri's Dred Scott Case, 1846–1857," *Missouri State Archives*.
164. Kaufman, *Dred Scott's Advocate*, 226.
165. Kaufman, *Dred Scott's Advocate*, 226, footnote 66.
166. "Dred Scott and His 'Republican' Owner," *Syracuse Daily Courier*, Syracuse, New York, 30 May 1857, page 2, column 5; digital images, *Access Newspaper Archive* (http://access.newspaperarchive.com).
167. "Calvin Clifford Chaffee," *Biographical Directory of the United States Congress, 1774–Present*.

168. "Massachusetts. Congressional Nominations," *New York Times*, 2 October 1858, New York, page 2; digital images, *ProQuest Historical New York Times, 1851–2005* (http://proquest.umi.com).

169. "Calvin Clifford Chaffee," *Biographical Directory of the United States Congress, 1774–Present.*

170. Chaffee, *Chaffee Genealogy,* 305. Also, George Washington Cullum and Wirt Robinson, *Biographical Register of the Officers and Graduates of the U.S. Military Academy at West Point, New York, from Its Establishment, in 1802, to 1890* (Boston: Houghton, Mifflin and Co., 1891), 851; digital images, *Google Books* (http://books.google.com).

171. "Death of an Army Officer," *New York Times*, 9 July 1867, New York, page 1; digital images, *ProQuest Historical New York Times, 1851–2005* (http://proquest.umi.com).

172. Chaffee, *Chaffee Genealogy*, 303.

173. "Visit to Dred Scott ...," *Frank Leslie's Illustrated Newspaper*, 27 June 1857.

Together as a Family, pages 45–52

174. "Visit to Dred Scott ...," *Frank Leslie's Illustrated Newspaper*, 27 June 1857.

175. *Kennedy's 1859 St. Louis City Directory* (page 423), lists Harriet as a widow living in the alleyway near Carr between 6th and 7th. The author of the *Frank Leslie's Illustrated Newspaper* article said he had difficulty finding Dred and Harriet's home. The picture of the city block bordered by Carr, Wash, 6th, and 7th, appearing in Compton and Dry's *1875 Pictorial St. Louis, the Great Metropolis of the Mississippi Valley: A Topographical Survey Drawn in Perspective, A.D. 1875* (1875; reprint, No place: ImagineInk Publishing, 2004), plate 22, shows many dwellings in the internal alley area of that block. This may have been where the Scott family lived in 1857 at the time of their emancipation.

176. "America's First Look into the Camera," *Library of Congress* (http://lcweb2.loc.gov/ammem/daghtml).

177. "Visit to Dred Scott ...," *Frank Leslie's Illustrated Newspaper*, 27 June 1857.

178. "Visit to Dred Scott ...," *Frank Leslie's Illustrated Newspaper*, 27 June 1857.

179. Kaufman, *Dred Scott's Advocate*, 227.

180. "Visit to Dred Scott ...," *Frank Leslie's Illustrated Newspaper,* 27 June 1857.

181. "Visit to Dred Scott ...," *Frank Leslie's Illustrated Newspaper*, 27 June 1857.

182. "Free Negro bond for Dred Scott.," and "Free Negro bond for Harriet Scott.," Dexter P. Tiffany Collection; Missouri History Museum, St. Louis, Missouri.

183. "Dred and Harriet Scott's Application for License as Free Negroes." volume 11, book 9, page 9; St. Louis County, Missouri, County Court Proceedings.

184. *The Revised Statutes of the State of Missouri ... One Thousand Eight Hundred and Fifty-five*, 2: 1096, chapter 114, "An Act Concerning Free Negroes and Mulattoes."

185. "Dred Scott. Life of the Famous Fugitive and Missouri Slave Litigant," *St. Louis Daily Globe*, St. Louis, Missouri, 10 January 1886, Dred Scott Collection; Missouri History Museum, St. Louis, Missouri.

186. *Gould's St. Louis City Directory for 1882*, microfilm reprint, *United States City Directories, 1882–1901, St. Louis, Missouri,* roll 1, *1882* (New Haven, Connecticut: Research Publications, no date), 757, Elizabeth Madison.

187. 1860 U.S. census, St. Louis County, Missouri, population schedule, ward 7, City of St. Louis, page 113 (penned), dwelling 408, family 730, Wilson and Elizabeth Maddison. Also, St. Louis City, Missouri, St. Louis Register of Deaths, 11: 171, Wilson Madison, 1881; SLCL microfilm RDSL–20. [To calculate his birth date, subtract his age at death, forty-three years, seven months, and twenty-three days from his date of death, 18 May 1881.]

188. *Edwards' Annual Director* [sic] *to the Inhabitants, Institutions & Incorporated Companies, Manufacturing Establishments, Business, Business Firms &c., in the City of St. Louis for 1864*, microfilm reprint, *United States City Directories, 1861–1881, St. Louis, Missouri*, roll 2, *1864* (New Haven, Connecticut: Research Publications, no date), 378, Wilson Madison. Also, *Gould & Aldrich's Annual Directory of the City of St. Louis, for 1872, Embracing a General Directory of the Citizens, a Business Directory, and a Street Directory from Official Surveys*, microfilm reprint, *United States City Directories, 1861–1881*, St. Louis, *Missouri*, roll 6, *1872* (New Haven, Connecticut: Research Publications, no date), 496, Wilson Madison.

189. 1860 U.S. census, St. Louis County, Missouri, population schedule, page 113 (penned), dwelling 408, family 730, Wilson and Elizabeth Maddison. Also, 1870 U.S. census, St. Louis County, Missouri, population schedule, City of St. Louis, ward 8, page 87 (penned), dwelling 811, family 1622, Wilson and Lizzie Madison household.

190. 1860 U.S. census, St. Louis County, Missouri, population schedule, page 110 (penned), dwelling 396, family 707, Harriotte Scott.

191. 1860 U.S. census, St. Louis County, Missouri, population schedule, page 113 (penned), dwelling 408, family 730, Wilson and Elizabeth Maddison.

Civil War and its Aftermath, pages 53–60

192. Ehrlich, *They Have No Rights*, 240, footnote 17. Also, Fehrenbacher, *The Dred Scott Case*, 569. Also, Kaufman, *Dred Scott's Advocate*, 228. [Each of these historian refers to the 10 January 1886, *St. Louis Globe-Democrat* article, "Dred Scott, Life of the Famous Fugitive and Missouri Slave Litigant," which stated that "Harriet, his wife, died a few years later, and not long after Eliza, the eldest child, followed her parents to the grave, at the early age of 25."]

193. Allen E. Wagner, *Good Order and Safety: A History of the St. Louis Metropolitan Police Department 1861–1906* (St. Louis: Missouri History Museum, 2008), 23.

194. Wagner, *Good Order and Safety*, 23.

195 *The Revised Statutes of the State of Missouri ... One Thousand Eight Hundred and Fifty-five*, 2: 1101, chapter 114, "An Act Respecting Slaves, Free Negroes and Mulattoes."

196. St. Louis County, Missouri, Records, County Court, 10: 324, 23 April 1861, Elizabeth Scott; microfilm of typed transcription of original records, SLCL microfilm SLCCR–3. [Applications for Free Negro Licenses]

197. "Free Negro bond of Elizabeth Scott, 23 April 1861," Dexter P. Tiffany Collection; Missouri History Museum, St. Louis, Missouri.

198. Wagner, *Good Order and Safety*, 31. Also, William C. Winter, *The Civil War in St. Louis: A Guided Tour* (St. Louis, Missouri: Missouri Historical Society Press, 1994), 49–53.

199. *The War of the Rebellion: A Compilation of the Official Records of the Union and Confederate Armies, 1881* (1881; reprint, National Historical Society, 1971), series 1, volume 3, 442. Also, Winter, T*he Civil War in St. Louis: A Guided Tour*, 72.

200. *The War of the Rebellion*, series 1, volume 3, 466–467.

201. *Union Provost Marshals' File of Papers Relating to Individual Civilians*, microfilm publication M345, 300 rolls (Washington, D.C.: National Archives and Records, 1967), roll 28, St. Louis, Missouri, 11 July 1862, Oath of Taylor Blow. Also, *Union Provost Marshals' File of Papers Relating to Individual Civilian*s, roll 28, Testimony of N. H. Clark, 14 October 1863. [Taylor Blow's documents, filmed out of alphabetical order, were located via the Missouri State Archives index of the Missouri files in this film set (http://www.sos.mo.gov/archives/provost) and the assistance of their staff as being situated between John Blodan and Charly Bloom. Taylor was charged with disloyalty on 14 October 1863 because of remarks made one night while out drinking. At first he vowed his absolute loyalty to the Union. According to the testimony of his drinking companion, N. Clark, he then said he

was "for the Union without regard to the abolitionist or secessionists." Taylor then protested "... that they had negroes in front of his property on Market Street [soldiers in the U.S. Colored Troops]." Clark reported Taylor cursed "any man that would put arms into the hands of negroes to fight white men ..." and "... Congress for making such a law." Clark and another witness who gave evidence both included in their statements that Taylor was drunk at the time. Charges were dropped two days later after as it was decided that "... his remarks were the effects of intoxicating drink & not from any disloyalty."]

202. St. Louis City, Missouri, St. Louis Register of Deaths, volume K: 175, Lates Madison, 1863; SLCL microfilm RDSL–7. [Lates' age, calculated by subtracting his age at the time of his death, shown on his death register entry as one year, six months, and four days, from his date of death, 1 August 1863, results in his birth date of 29 January 1862.]

203. List of Colored Persons, Wesleyan Cemetery Record Book, unpaginated, burial of Dred Scott, 18 September, 1857, with notation added for burial of Lates W. Madison on 2 August 1863; Centenary Methodist Church Archives, currently being processed by St. Louis County Library in conjunction with Centenary Methodist Church.

204. St. Louis City, Missouri, St. Louis Register of Deaths, volume K: 175, Lates Madison, 1863.

205. List of Colored Persons, Wesleyan Cemetery Record book, burial of Dred Scott and Lates W. Madison. [Gloria Dettleff found Dred's Wesleyan burial record, along with that of the baby Lates W. Madison, while searching for, but not finding, one of her own ancestors. Knowing Dred was also buried in Wesleyan, she searched the microfilm, found his entry, and graciously shared the record with this author.]

206. Gloria Dettleff, compiler, *"List of Colored Persons" in Wesleyan Cemetery St. Louis, Missouri, 1847–1868*, (2008); digital images, *St. Louis County Library* (http://www.slcl.org/sc/pdfs/Wesleyan_cemetery_colored_persons.pdf). [Dettleff's compilation shows numerous entries where a child was buried in the same grave with another person.]

207. Calvary Cemetery Office (St. Louis, Missouri), Calvary Cemetery Association deed to Taylor Blow for purchase of lot 177 in section 1, containing 100 square feet, dated 26 October 1867; photocopy courtesy of the Archdiocese of St. Louis Catholic Cemeteries, Calvary Cemetery.

208. Calvary Cemetery Office (St. Louis, Missouri) lot owner card, lot 177, section 1, owned by Taylor Blow showing Dred Scott as the only burial in that lot; photocopy courtesy of the Archdiocese of St. Louis Catholic Cemeteries, Calvary Cemetery.

209. St. Louis County, Missouri, Will Books, 1: 124–125, Taylor Blow; FHL microfilm 1,405,570. Also, will, Taylor Blow probate case file, no. 08906, collection 1, page 3; digital images, "Missouri's Judicial Records," *Missouri State Archives* (http://www.sos.mo.gov/archives/mojudicial).

210. Ehrlich, *They Have No Rights*, 183. Also, Kaufman, *Dred Scott's Advocate*, 238.

211. *Laws of the State of Missouri Passed at the Regular Session of the XXVIIth General Assembly, Begun and Held at the City of Jefferson, Wednesday, January 1, 1873* (Jefferson City, Missouri: Regan and Carter, 1873), 208. Also, *"Minutes of Special Meeting of the Board of Trustees of the Wesleyan Cemetery Association," May 2, 1921,* Centenary Methodist Church Archives, and *Mr. and Mrs. Francis Emmett Williams, Centenary Methodist Church of St. Louis the First Hundred Years 1839–1939* (St. Louis, Missouri: Mound City Press, 1939), 65.

212. *Laws of the State of Missouri ... Acts of 1874*, 208.

213. The "new" Wesleyan Cemetery was located at Olive Boulevard and Hanley Road, outside the St. Louis city limits.

214. Alma (Madison) Miller, interview by Ruth Ann (Abels) Hager, 26 January 2009; audio recording and transcript privately held by Ruth Ann (Abels) Hager, 2009.

215 Harriet's absence from the city directories for 1868–1873 erroneously supported the belief that she had died during the Civil War. Wilson and Eliza's absence for 1866–1871 makes them more difficult to research.

216. St. Louis City, Missouri, St. Louis Register of Deaths, volume 2: 38, Cath Madison, 1867; SLCL microfilm RDSL–10. Also, Gloria Dettleff, *"List of Colored Persons" in Wesleyan Cemetery St. Louis, Missouri, 1847–1868*, 47.

217. Wilson's birth date of 30 September 1868 was calculated by subtracting his exact age at death, one year, nine months, from his date of death, 20 June 1870.

218. St. Louis City, Missouri, St. Louis Register of Deaths, volume 3: 283, Wilson Madison, 1870; SLCL micro-film RDSL–11.

HARRIET'S LAST YEARS, PAGES 61–68

219. *200 Years of U.S. Census Taking, Population and Housing Questions, 1790–1990* (Washington, D.C.: Bureau of the Census, 1989), 26.

220. 1870 U.S. census, St. Louis County, Missouri, population schedule, City of St. Louis, ward 5, page 58 (stamped), dwelling 627, family 911, William Werden household; digital images, *HeritageQuest Online* (http://www.heritagequestonline.com); citing NARA publication M593, roll 815.

221. *Edward's St. Louis Directory 1870*, microfilm reprint, *United States City Directories, 1861–1881, St. Louis, Missouri*, roll 5, *1870* (New Haven, Connecticut: Research Publications, no date), 911, William Werden.

222. *Edward's St. Louis Directory, 1870,* 180 [Henry Brookings at 2221 Scott], 214 [John Chandler at 2227 Scott], and 222 [Redman Cleary at 2225 Scott].

223. St. Louis City, Missouri, Records of Births, 1870–1873, 1870: 192, Unnamed male Madison; St. Louis County Library microfilm RBSL–2.

224. St. Louis City, Missouri, Records of Births, 1870–1873, 1873: 142, Unnamed male Madison; St. Louis County Library microfilm RBSL–2.

225. *Gould's St. Louis Directory, for 1874*, microfilm reprint, *United States City Directories, 1861–1881, St. Louis, Missouri*, roll 7, *1874* (New Haven, Connecticut: Research Publications, no date), 806, Harriet Scott.

226 *Gould's St. Louis Directory, for 1875*, microfilm reprint, *United States City Directories, 1861–1881, St. Louis, Missouri*, roll 8, *1875* (New Haven, Connecticut: Research Publications, no date), 826, Harriet Scott.

227. *Gould's St. Louis Directory, for 1876, Being a Complete Index to the Residents of the Entire City, and a Classified Business Directory to Which is Added an Appendix Containing Useful Information of the Churches, Banks, Insurance Companies, City, State, and Other Miscellaneous Matters; Also a Street Directory, 1876,* microfilm reprint, *United States City Directories, 1861–1881, St. Louis, Missouri*, roll 9, *1876* (New Haven, Connecticut: Research Publications, no date), 582, Wilson Madison.

228. St. Louis City, Missouri, St. Louis Register of Deaths, volume 7: 131, Harriet Scott, 1876; SLCL microfilm RDSL–16.

229. *Gould's St. Louis Directory, for 1876*, 60. [location of Hicks Alley]

230. Geo. E. Stevens, *History of Central Baptist Church* (St. Louis, Missouri: King Publishing, 1927), 39.

231. Greenwood Cemetery Records, Record of the Greenwood Cemetery from 1 January 1874 to 31 December 1883, Harriet Scott, 1876, 58–59; photocopies of original records held by Etta Daniels, cemetery historian, photographed by Ruth Ann (Abels) Hager, 13 February 2008. Also, "Finding a St. Louis Legend," *St. Louis Post-Dispatch*, St. Louis, Missouri, 5 March 2006, page C8, column 4; original newspaper held by Ruth Ann (Abels) Hager.

232. 'The Late Henry T. Blow," *New York Times*, New York, New York, 13 September 1875, page 4; digital images, *ProQuest* (http://proquest.umi.com) *ProQuest Historical Newspapers New York Times* (1851–2005). Also, St. Louis City, Missouri, St. Louis Register of Deaths, volume 3: 111, Taylor Blow, 1869; SLCL microfilm RDSL–11.

233. Conversation with Etta Daniels, Greenwood Cemetery historian, 13 February 2008.

234. St. Louis City, Missouri, St. Louis Register of Deaths, volume 7: 216, Edw. Madison, 1876; SLCL microfilm RDSL–16.

235. Greenwood Cemetery Records, Record … from 1 January 1874 to 31 December 1883, Harriet Scott, 1876, 58–59 and Edw. Madison, 1876, 66–67. [Etta Daniels, historian for Friends of Greenwood Cemetery, discovered that Edw. Madison was buried in the same grave with Harriet Scott and shared the imformation with the author.]

236. *Gould's St. Louis Directory, for 1876*, [Page 61 of the street directory section lists New St. Charles Road followed by Nineteenth Street with no listing for "Nick Street." However, page 60 lists Hicks Alley.]

ELIZA AND LIZZIE, PAGES 69–74

237. Gould & Aldrich's *Annual Directory of the City of St. Louis, for 1872*, 682, Lizzie Scott. Also, *Gould's St. Louis Directory for 1879, United States City Directories, 1861–1881, St. Louis, Missouri*, roll 12, *1879* (New Haven, Connecticut: Research Publications, no date), 880, Eliza); subsequent years by the same title: *1880* (933, Eliza), *1881* (1011, Eliza), *1882* (1039, Lizzie), *1883* (993, Lizzie).

238. 1880 U.S. census, City of St. Louis, Missouri, population schedule, (1st enumeration), enumeration district (ED) 11, page 193A (stamped), dwelling 54, family 69, Eliza Scott. Also, 1880 U.S. census, City of St. Louis, Missouri, population schedule (2nd enumeration), enumeration district (ED) 37, page 288B (stamped), dwelling 101, family 154, Lizzie Scott; digital images, *Ancestry Library Edition* (http://ancestry.libraryedition.com); citing NARA microfilm publication T9, roll 727.

239. *Gould's St. Louis City Directory for 1879*, 646, Joshua W. Madison; also subsequent years by the same title: (1881) 736, Joshua Madison; (1882), 757, Elizabeth, widow of Joshua W. Madison. [Joshua W. Madison (Wilson and Eliza) lived at 7 Hicks Alley in 1879; Joshua Madison's residence was listed as "alley rear of 615 Pine" in 1881; by 1882, the residence of Elizabeth, widow of Joshua W., was listed as "alley, 7th near Pine."]

240. 1880 U.S. City of St. Louis, Missouri, population schedule, (2nd enumeration), enumeration district (ED) 37, page 288B (stamped), dwelling 100, family 153, Charles Scott.

241. *Gould's St. Louis Directory, for 1876*, 582, Wilson Madison. Also, *Gould's St. Louis Directory for 1877,* microfilm reprint, *United States City Directories, 1861–1881*, St. Louis, Missouri, roll 10, *1877* (New Haven, Connecticut: Research Publications, no date), 621, Wilson Madison.

242. St. Louis City, Missouri, St. Louis Register of Deaths, volume 11: 171, Wilson Madison, 1881; SLCL microfilm 239. RDSL–20. Also, *Gould's St. Louis City Directory for 1881*, 736.

243. St. Louis City, Missouri, St. Louis Register of Deaths, volume 11: 171, Wilson Madison, 1881; SLCL microfilm RDSL–20. Also, *Gould's St. Louis Directory for 1881,* 736, Joshua Madison.

244. Stevens, *History of Central Baptist Church*, 39. [Although this history records that Wilson died after his wife, rather than before, it does record his burial was from their church.] Also, St. Louis Register of Deaths, volume 11: 171, Wilson Madison, 1881.

245. *Gould's St. Louis Directory, for 1881*, 736, Joshua Madison. Also, St. Louis Register of Deaths, volume 11: 171, Wilson Madison, 1881.

246. St. Louis Register of Deaths, 13: 51, Elizabeth Madison, 1882; SLCL microfilm RDSL–22. Also, *Gould's St. Louis City Directory for 1882*, 757, Elizabeth Madison.

247. Stevens, *History of Central Baptist Church*, 39. [Like other sources, this history has confusion over the names of Dred and Harriet's daughters, recording them as Lizzie and Jane, and says that Lizzie was the wife of Wilson.]

248. St. Louis Register of Deaths, 13: 51, Elizabeth Madison, 1882. Also, Greenwood Cemetery Records, Record … from 1 January 1874 to 31 December 1883, Elizabeth Madison, 1882, 232–233 indicating grave 314, section C.

Lizzie and Her Nephews, pages 75–80

249. Alma (Madison) Miller, interview by Ruth Ann (Abels) Hager, 14 August 2009; audio recording and transcript privately held by Ruth Ann (Abels) Hager, 2009.
250. Alma (Madison) Miller, interview, 14 August 2009.
251. *Gould's St. Louis Directory, for 1879,* 880, Eliza Scott; also subsequent years by the same title: (1880) 933, Eliza Scott; (1881) 1011, Eliza N. Scott; (1882) 1039, Lizzie Scott; (1883) 993, Lizzie Scott.
252. *Gould's St. Louis Directory, for 1886 …*, microfilm reprint, *United States City Directories, 1882–1901, St. Louis, Missouri*, roll 5, *1886* (New Haven, Connecticut: Research Publications, no date), 1071, Lizzie Scott.
253. *Gould's St. Louis Directory, for 1887 …*, microfilm reprint, *United States City Directories, 1882–1901, St. Louis, Missouri*, roll 6, *1887* (New Haven, Connecticut: Research Publications, no date), 682, Lizzie Scott.
254. *Gould & Aldrich's Annual Directory of the City of St. Louis, for 1872*, 682, Lizzie Scott.
255. "Dred Scott," *St. Louis Globe-Democrat*, 10 January 1886, clipping, Dred Scott Collection; Missouri History Museum, St. Louis, Missouri.
256. "Dred Scott," *St. Louis Globe-Democrat*, 10 January 1886.
257. Loudell F. Snow, *Walkin' Over Medicine* (1993; reprint, Detroit, Michigan: Wayne State University Press, 1998), 60.
258. Arvilla Payne-Jackson and John Lee, *Folk Wisdom and Mother Wit: John Lee—An African American Herbal Healer* (Westport, Connecticut: Greenwood Press, 1993), 18.
259 Missouri, death certificate no. 19482, John Madison, (1931); digital images, *Missouri State Archives* (http://www.sos.mo.gov/archives/resources/deathcertificates).
260. Birth year ranges for a twelve-year-old person and a fourteen-year-old person on 10 January 1886 were based on whether the boys had just turned twelve and fourteen or whether they were ready to turn thirteen and fifteen years of age.
261. "Dred Scott," *St. Louis Globe-Democrat*, 10 January 1886.
262. "Dred Scott," *St. Louis Globe-Democrat*, 10 January 1886.
263. St. Louis City, Missouri, St. Louis Register of Deaths, volume 21: 10, Henry Sanders, 1887; St. Louis County Library microfilm RDSL–29.
264. *Gould's St. Louis Directory, for 1888*, microfilm reprint, *United States City Directories, 1882–1901, St. Louis, Missouri*, roll 7, *1888* (New Haven, Connecticut: Research Publications, no date), 1090, Mattie Sanders.
265. *Gould's St. Louis Directory, for 1888*, 827, Wilson Madison.
266. See for example the listings for the last name of Madison in St. Louis City Directories for the following years: (1870) 587, (1872) 496,·(1875) 601, and (1884) 729.
267. The occupation for one Lizzie/Elizabeth Scott was teacher when it could not be established if Dred and Harriet's daughter, Lizzie, could read or write, *St. Louis City Directory* for (1894) 1334, (1895) 1345, (1896) 1458–1459, (1897) 1532, (1898) 1510, (1900) 1659, (1901) 1746), (1903) 1711. There were other listings for Elizabeth Scott showing addresses far from Lizzie's known neighborhoods, such as 3028 Locust (1894) 1333, and 3008 N. 20th (1895) 1344.
268. *Gould's St. Louis Directory, for 1894–95*, microfilm reprint, *United States City Directories, 1882–1901, St. Louis, Missouri*, roll 13, *1894–1895* (New Haven, Connecticut: Research Publications, no date), 963, Harry H. Madison and John Madison.
269. Alma (Madison) Miller, interview, 14 August 2008.

John and His Family, pages 81–84

270. Alma (Madison) Miller, interview, 14 August 2008.

271. 1900 U.S. census, Pulaski County, Illinois, population schedule, Villa Ridge Precinct, page 313A (stamped), enumeration district (ED) 74, sheet 6A, dwelling 101/111, family 108/113 [renumbered], Grace Cross; digital image, *Ancestry Library Edition* (http://www.ancestrylibraryedition.com); citing NARA publication T623, roll 336.

272. Pulaski County, Illinois, death certificate, Charles Augustus Cross, died 4 January 1924; County Clerk's Office, Mound City, Illinois; photocopy courtesy of the Pulaski County Clerk's Office, Mound City, Illinois. Also, Shirley J. Carlson, "Black Migration to Pulaski County, Illinois, 1860–1900," *Illinois Historical Journal*, 80 (1987): 38. [Both Alexander Cross and his son, Charles Augustus Cross, were born in Allensville, Todd County, Kentucky, so that may also have been the Cross family's last place of residence in Kentucky.]

273. Obituary, "Grace Madison; Relative of Famed Slave Dred Scott," *St. Louis Post-Dispatch*, St. Louis, Missouri, 21 December 1983, page 14A; microfilm image.

274. St. Clair County, Illinois, Marriage license and application, Grace Cross and John Madison, 1912; Illinois Regional Archives Depository (IRAD), SIU–Carbondale, Illinois.

275. 1930 U.S. census, St. Louis City, [independent city], Missouri, population schedule, City of St. Louis, ward 20, page 205 (stamped), enumeration district (ED) 96–73, sheet 13A, dwelling 200, family 266, John Madison family; digital image, *Ancestry Library Edition* (http://www.ancestrylibraryedition.com); citing NARA publication T625, roll 1238.

276. Alma (Madison) Miller, interview, 14 August 2008.

277. Conversation with Lynne (Madison) Jackson, fall 2007, July 2009.

278. *Polk-Gould's St. Louis Directory, 1913*, microfilm reprint, *United States City Directories, 1902–1935, St. Louis, Missouri,* roll 12, *1913* (Woodbridge, Connecticut: Research Publications, no date), 1914, Elizabeth Scott, widow of Walter; also subsequent years by the same title: (1914) 1930, Elizabeth Scott, widow of Walter; (1915) 1901, Elizabeth Scott, widow of Walter.

279. Alma (Madison) Miller, interview, 14 August 2008.

280. Missouri, death certificate no. 19482, John Madison, (1931). Also, burial cards, Washington Park Cemetery, John Madison, section 8, grave 964; St. Louis Genealogical Society, 2007; St. Louis County Library film SLCEM-74.

Lizzie's Assistance, pages 85–92

281. *Polk-Gould St. Louis Directory, 1923,* microfilm reprint, *United States City Directories, 1902–1935, St. Louis, Missouri,* roll 22, *1923* (Woodbridge, Connecticut: Research Publications, no date), 1672, Lizzie Marshall.

282. Alma (Madison) Miller, interview, 1 August 2008.

283. *Polk-Gould's St. Louis Directory, 1923*, 1672, Lizzie Marshall (widow of Henry). Also, *Polk-Gould St. Louis Directory, 1924,* microfilm reprint, *United States City Directories, 1902–1935, St. Louis, Missouri,* roll 23, *1924* (Woodbridge, Connecticut: Research Publications, no date), 1739, Lizzie Marshall (widow of Richard). Also, *Gould's St. Louis (Missouri) City Directory, 1930*, microfilm reprint, *United States City Directories, 1902–1935, St. Louis, Missouri,* roll 29, *1930* (Woodbridge, Connecticut: Research Publications, no date), 746, Eliz Marshall (widow of Freeman).

284. Alma (Madison) Miller, interview, 14 August 2008.

285. Missouri, death certificate no. 30546, Charles Madison, (1932); digital images, *Missouri State Archives* (http://www.sos.mo.gov/archives/resources/deathcertificates). Also, burial cards, Washington Park Cemetery, Charles Madison, section 6, lot 40, grave 2.

286. Alma (Madison) Miller, interview, 14 August 2008.

287. Alma (Madison) Miller, interview, 14 August 2008.

288. Alma (Madison) Miller, interview, 14 August 2008.

289. Alma (Madison) Miller, interview, 14 August 2008.

290. *Gould's St. Louis (Missouri) City Directory, 1936* (St. Louis: Polk-Gould Directory Co., 1936) 811, Rose Madison; subsequent years with same title: (1937) 819, Rosie and Pauline Madison; and (1938) 788, Rose E. Madison.

291. *Gould's St. Louis (Missouri) City Directory, 1940* (St. Louis: Polk-Gould Directory Co., 1940) 746 Scott Madison; subsequent years by the same title: (1942) 867, Dredscott, Harry, and John Madison.

292. *Gould's St. Louis (Missouri) City Directory 1944*, microfilm reprint (St. Louis, Missouri: Polk-Gould Directory Co., 1944), 751, D. Scott Madison.

293. Mrs. John A. Madison Jr., phone conversation with Ruth Ann Hager, 16 June 2009.

294. "Teacher Dies; Was Descendant of Dred Scott, John A. Madison Jr." *St. Louis Post-Dispatch,* St. Louis, Missouri, 30 July 2007, second edition, page B1; online text, *NewsBank* (http://www.newsbank.com), America's Newspapers. Also, funeral program for Dr. John A. Madison Jr., 2 August 2007; privately held by Ruth Ann (Abels) Hager, and phone conversation with Mrs. John A. Madison Jr., 16 June 2009.

295. Alma (Madison) Miller, interview, 14 August 2008.

296. Conversation with Lynne (Madison) Jackson, fall 2007, July 2009.

297. Vicki Jennings, Past Worthy Matron, Order of the Eastern Star (OES), Kansas, and H. Lorraine Jeter, Past Grand Worthy Matron, OES, Illinois, put this author in contact with Priscilla Harris, Grand Worthy Matron, Harmony Chapter, OES, Missouri, regarding possible records Lizzie Marshall might have left as a member of their organization. Mrs. Harris and members of the Phyllis Chapter continue the search for records of her membership.

298. Missouri death certificate no. 39508 (1945) Lizzie Marshall; digital images, *Missouri State Archives* (http://www.sos.mo.gov/archives/resources/deathcertificates).

299. Alma (Madison) Miller, interview, 14 August 2008.

300. Missouri, death certificate no. 39508 (1945) Lizzie Marshall. Also, Greenwood Cemetery Records, Lizzie Marshall, [page number does not show], Greenwood Cemetery Records 1904–1996, volume 3, 1940–1996, block 180, section D, Western Historical Manuscript Collection, University of Missouri—St. Louis.

301. Alma (Madison) Miller, interview, 14 August 2008.

Commemorations, pages 93–98

302. "Wreath for Dred Scott's Grave," *St. Louis Post-Dispatch*, St. Louis, Missouri, 6 March 1957, newspaper clipping, Dred Scott Collection, Missouri History Museum, St. Louis, Missouri. Also, "Observe Anniversary of Dred Scott," *St. Louis Argus*, St. Louis, Missouri, 8 March 1957, page 1, column 2; [film from the State Historical Society of Missouri—no identification on the film leader itself.]

303. "Observe Anniversary of Dred Scott," *St. Louis Argus*, 8 March 1957.

304. "Observe Anniversary of Dred Scott," *St. Louis Argus*, 8 March 1957.

305. "Dred Scott Ceremonies Planned Today," *St. Louis Post-Dispatch*, St. Louis, Missouri, 6 March 1957, newspaper clipping, Dred Scott Collection; Missouri History Museum, St. Louis, Missouri. Also, funeral program for Dr. John A. Madison Jr., 2 August 2007.

306. "Observe Anniversary of Dred Scott," *St. Louis Argus*, 8 March 1957.

307. "Calvary Cemetery," *Catholic Cemeteries of the Archdiocese of St. Louis* (http://www.archstl.org/cemeteries) [Under the "Locations" button, click on "Calvary."]

308. Tim O'Neil, "Heirs to History Three Local Descendants of the Case's (Key Players Tell What It Means to Them," *St. Louis Post-Dispatch*, St. Louis, Missouri, 6 March 2007, third edition, page A1; online text, *NewsBank* (http://www.newsbank.com), America's Newspapers.

309. Alma (Madison) Miller, interview, 14 August 2008.

310. "Grace Madison: Relative of Famed Slave Dred Scott," 21 December 1983.

311. Burial cards, Washington Park Cemetery, Grace Mae Madison, section 8, lot 1583, grave 1; St. Louis Genealogical Society, 2007; St. Louis County Library microfilm SLCEM–74.

312. Calvary Cemetery (St. Louis, Missouri), Harriet Scott cenotaph, transcription made by Ruth Ann (Abels) Hager from photograph of cenotaph taken by Joseph T. Hager, 6 January 2008.

313. Funeral program for Dr. John A. Madison Jr., 2 August 2007.

EPILOGUE, PAGES 99–100

314. 1869 census, City of Carondelet, Missouri, Luke Howard household, unpaginated; microfilm, Missouri Historical Society, St. Louis County Library film CAR–1. [This census of the city of Carondelet was taken the year before it became part of the city of St. Louis.].

315. 1870 U.S. census, St. Louis County, Missouri, population schedule, Carondelet, page 596 (stamped), dwelling 1157, family 1339, Luke Howard; digital images, *HeritageQuest Online* (http://www.heritagequestonline.com); citing National Archives microfilm publication M593, roll 809.

316. St. Louis City, Missouri, St. Louis Register of Deaths, volume 4: 228, Luke Howard, 1871; SLCL microfilm RDSL–12.

317. "Letter from Julia (Webster) Blow to Miss Mary Louis Dalton," dated 13 March 1907, Dred Scott Collection; Missouri History Museum, St. Louis, Missouri.

318. Transcription of the "Articles of Agreement between Henry T. Blow and the trustees of the African Methodist Episcopal Church at Carondelet, Missouri," dated 27 July 1868, transcription provided by Ron Bolte, President, Carondelet Historical Society.

319. "Ruins of Freedman's Church and School, Carondelet, Mo.: Moses Dickson, Pastor," photocopy of a single printed page, including a photo by Tobias, showing the burned out church shell; photocopy provided by Ron Bolte, President, Carondelet Historical Society.

320. 1869 census, City of Carondelet, Missouri, Luke Howard household.

321. 1870 U.S. census, St. Louis County, Missouri, population schedule, Carondelet, page 596 (stamped), dwelling 1157, family 1339, Luke Howard.

322. St. Louis City, Missouri, St. Louis Register of Deaths, 4: 228, Luke Howard, 1871.

323. *United States Congress, U.S. Statutes at Large*, volume 9 (Boston: Little, Brown and Co., 1862), 464, "An Act to Amend, and Supplementary to, the Act entitled 'An Act Respecting Fugitives from Justice, and Persons Escaping from the Service of their Masters,' approved February twelfth, one thousand seven hundred and ninety-three;" digital image, A Century of Lawmaking for a New Nation: U.S. Congressional Documents and Debates, 1774–1875, *Library of Congress* (http://memory.loc.gov/ammem/amlaw/lwsllink.html).

APPENDIX E — BLOW & SANFORD FAMILIES, PAGES 129–134

324. St. Louis City, Missouri, St. Louis Register of Deaths, volume K: 52, Elizabeth B. Blow, 1862; SLCL microfilm RDSL-7.
325. Bryan, "The Blow Family and Their Slave Dred Scott: Part I," 223. Also, 1860 U.S. census, St. Louis County, Missouri, population schedule, St. Louis Township, page 969 (penned), dwelling 664, family 675, Charlotte T. Charless; digital images, *HeritageQuest Online* (http://www.heritagequestonline.com); citing NARA publication M653, roll 656.
326. St. Louis County, Missouri, Marriage Records, Recorder of Deeds, City of St. Louis, volume 1: page 180, Charlotte T. Blow and Joseph Charless, 1831; FHL microfilm 469,561, available at SLCL as ST.L.6130, St. Louis, Missouri.
327. Erhlich, *They Have No Rights*, 195, footnote 8.
328. Bryan, "The Blow Family and Their Slave Dred Scott: Part I," 223. Also, Menius, "Blows Brought about Change," sheet A.
329. Menius, *Susan Blow*, 9.
330. St. Louis County, Missouri, Marriage Records, Recorder of Deeds, City of St. Louis, volume 1: page 259, Martha Ella Taylor Blow and Charles Daniel Drake, 1835; FHL microfilm 469,561, available at SLCL as ST.L.6130, St. Louis, Missouri.
331. Bryan, "The Blow Family and Their Slave Dred Scott: Part I," 223. Also, Menius, "Blows Brought about Change," sheet A.
332. Ehrlich, *They Have No Rights*, 10.
333. Bryan, "The Blow Family and Their Slave Dred Scott: Part I," 224. Also, Menius, *Susan Blow*, 9.
334. St. Louis County, Missouri, Marriage Records, Recorder of Deeds, City of St. Louis, book 3: page 334, (Correction of the Marriage Record for Peter E. Blow and Eugenia LaBeaume, originally incorrectly recorded in book 2, page 135, as 7 December 1838, instead of 7 November 1838); FHL microfilm 469,562, available at SLCL as ST.L.6131 St. Louis, Missouri.
335. Bryan, "The Blow Family and Their Slave Dred Scott: Part I," 229.
336. "22 St. Louis Circuit Court Record 111." Revised Dred Scott Case, *Washington University Digital Gateway,* (http://digital.wustl.edu/d/dre/newtrial.html). [Select "Browse" option, then "Bond documents re: hiring out of Dred and Harriet Scott, 1848–1854."]
337. Bryan, "The Blow Family and Their Slave Dred Scott: Part I," 224. Also, Menius, *Susan Blow*, 25, and Menius, "Blows Brought about Change," sheet A.
338. Bryan, "The Blow Family and Their Slave Dred Scott: Part I," 224. Also, Menius, *Susan Blow*, 9, and Menius, "Blows Brought about Change," sheet A.
339. 'The Late Henry T. Blow," *New York Times*, 13 September 1875.
340. St. Louis County, Missouri, Marriage Records,Recorder of Deeds, City of St. Louis, book 2: page 246, Henry T. Blow and Minerva Grimsley; 1840; FHL microfilm 469,561, available at SLCL as ST.L.6130, St. Louis, Missouri.
341. Carol Ferring Shepley, *Tales from Bellefontaine Cemetery: Movers and Shakers, Scalawags and Suffragettes* (St. Louis: Missouri History Museum, 2008), 35.
342. "Henry Taylor Blow (1817–1875)," *Biographical Directory of the United States Congress, 1774–Present* (http://bioguide.congress.gov). Also, "The Late Henry T. Blow," *New York Times*, 18 September 1875.
343. "The Carondelet Historical Society and Carondelet Historic Center," *Carondelet Historical Society* (http://stlouis.missouri.org/carondelet/history/HisSoc.html).

344. Bryan, "The Blow Family and Their Slave Dred Scott: Part I," 224.

345. St. Francis Xavier Catholic [College] Church (St. Louis City, Missouri) Baptisms, 1864–1886, page 34. Also, Bryan, "The Blow Family and Their Slave Dred Scott: Part I," 224.

346. St. Louis County, Missouri, Marriage Records, Recorder of Deeds, City of St. Louis, book 3: page 111, Taylor Blow and Eliza Augusta Wahrendorff, 1844; FHL microfilm 469,562, available at SLCL as ST.L.6131, St. Louis, Missouri.

347. Bryan, "The Blow Family and Their Slave Dred Scott: Part I," 229–230.

348. Ehrlich, *They Have No Rights*, 10–11, 13.

349. Bryan, "The Blow Family and Their Slave Dred Scott: Part I," 224. Also, Menius, "Blows Brought about Change," sheet A.

350. Bryan, "The Blow Family and Their Slave Dred Scott: Part I," 224. Also, Menius, "Blows Brought about Change," sheet A.

351. St. Louis County, Missouri, Marriage Records, Recorder of Deeds, City of St. Louis, book 6: page 176, William T. Blow and Julia S. Webster, 1853; FHL microfilm 528,175, available at SLCL as ST.L.6133, St. Louis, Missouri.

352. Menius, *Susan Blow*, 20.

353. St. Louis City, Missouri, St. Louis Register of Deaths, volume 8: page 7, William Thomas Blow, 1877; SLCL microfilm RDSL-7.

354. Kaufman, *Dred Scott's Advocate*, 145. Also, A. Sanford, Register of Christ Church Cemetery, 1840–1856.

355. "Passport application for John F. A. Sanford," Passport Applications, 1795–1905, volume 30, 1845, National Archives; digital images, *Footnote* (http://www.footnote.com).

356. *Register of Graduates and Former Cadets of the United States Military Academy,* Eisenhower Centennial Edition (West Point, New York: Association of Graduates, USMA, 1990), 252.

357. Basilica of St. Louis, King of France [Old Cathedral] (St. Louis, Missouri), Marriages, 1781–1834, quarante neuvieme [page 49], marriage of John F. A. Sanford and Emily Chouteau (1832); FHL microfilm 1,902,831, Item 6, available in SLCL as SLAPR–173. [John and Emily's marriage record was recorded in English, but most of the other marriage records and the page numbering system were written in French.]

358. Hafen and Eckberg, *Fur Traders, Trappers, and Mountain Men of the Upper Missouri*, 56.

359. Hafen and Eckberg, *Fur Traders, Trappers, and Mountain Men of the Upper Missouri,* 58.

360. "City Directories for New York, New York," 1851, (John F. Trow, publisher) 468; digital images, *Footnote* (http://www.footnote.com), John F. A. Sanford; also subsequent years of New York City Directories with different publishers through *Footnote.com*: (1852, Charles R Rode, publisher) 450, John F. A. Sanford; (1853, John F. Trow, publisher) 606, John F. A. Sanford; (1854, John F. Trow, publisher) 647, John F. A. Sanford; (1855, John F. Trow, publisher), 722, John F. A. Sanford; (1856, John F. Trow, publisher) 726 John F. A. Sanford. Also, "Died," [Sanford] *New York Daily Times*, 6 May 1857, page 5; *ProQuest* (http://www.proquest.com) *ProQuest Historical Newspapers: New York Times (1851–2005*).

361. Christensen, *Dictionary of Missouri Biography*, 665. Also, "Died," *New York Daily Times*, 6 May 1857.

362. Hafen and Eckberg, *Fur Traders, Trappers, and Mountain Men of the Upper Missouri*, 59.

363. 1850 U.S. census, Hampden County, Massachusetts, population schedule, Springfield, page 104 (stamped), dwelling 1613, family 1762, Charlotte Barnes; digital images, *Ancestry Library Edition* (http://www.ancestry library.com); citing NARA publication M432, roll 319.

364. Saint Peters Protestant Episcopal Church (Baltimore, Maryland), Register, 1803–1885, page 79, marriage of Charlotte A. Sanford and James Barnes (1832); Maryland Historical Society, Baltimore, Maryland; FHL microfilm 13,703, SLCL, St. Louis, Missouri.

365. *Register of Graduates and Former Cadets of the United States Military Academy*, 255.

366. *John Sanford Barnes: A Memorial and a Tribute* (No place: privately printed, 1912), 7; digital images, *Internet Archive* (http://www.archive.org). Also, U.S. Congress, Letter from the Commissioner of Pensions, transmitting a list of all widows of officers of high rank, Army or Navy, whose pensions have been fixed, or increased by special acts of Congress, 48th Congress, 1st session, Senate Miscellaneous Document, Serial Set volume no. 2171 (1884), page 6; digital images, *LexisNexis* (http://www.lexisnexis.com), *LexisNexis Congressional Publications.*

367. 1850 U.S. census, Hampden County, Massachusetts, population schedule, Springfield, page 234 (penned), dwelling 1817, family 1986, Henrietta Clark; digital images, *Ancestry Library Edition* (http://www.ancestrylibrary.com); citing NARA publication M432, roll 319.

368. St. Louis County, Missouri, Marriage Records, Recorder of Deeds, City of St. Louis, book 4: page 170, Capt. J. B. Clarke and Henrietta Sanford, 1829; FHL microfilm 528,174 available as ST.L.6132, SLCL, St. Louis, Missouri. Also, "Married," Baltimore Patriot, Baltimore, Maryland, 29 December 1829, page 2; digital images, *America's GenealogyBank* (http://www.genealogybank.com). [Sanford–Clark]

369. U.S. Congress, Henrietta S. Clark, 1. Also, "Obituary: Mrs. H. S. Humphrey," *New York Times,* New York, New York, 27 April 1887, page 5; *ProQuest* (http://www.proquest.com) *ProQuest Historical Newspapers: New York Times (1851–2005).*

370. 1850 U.S. census, Hampden County, Massachusetts, population schedule, City of Springfield, page 234 (penned), dwelling 1817, family 1986, Henrietta Clark.

371. "The Famous Dred Scott Case," *New York Times*, New York, New York, 22 December 1895, page 26; digital images, *ProQuest* (http://proquest.umi.com) *ProQuest Historical Newspapers: New York Times (1851–2005).*

372. Natchitoches Parish, Louisiana, Conveyances, book 24, page 302, no. 1775.

373. Springfield, Massachusetts, Marriages 1850–1862, volume 5: page 6.

374. "Reminder of the Dred Scott Case," *The Landmark*, Statesville, North Carolina, 20 February 1903, page 4; digital images, *Access Newspaper Archive* (http://access.newspaperarchive.com).

375. "Obituary: Mrs. H. S. Humphrey," *New York Times*, New York, New York, 27 April 1887, page 5; digital images, *ProQuest* (http://proquest.umi.com) *ProQuest Historical Newspapers: New York Times (1851–2005).*

376. "Married," *Baltimore Patriot*, Baltimore, Maryland, 14 April 1834, page 3; digital images, *America's GenealogyBank* (http://www.genealogybank.com). [Sanford–Bainbridge]

377. *Register of Graduates and Former Cadets of the United States Military Academy*, 249.

378. U.S. Congress, Mary Bainbridge, Widow of Lieutenant Colonel Henry Bainbridge, 35th Congress, 1st session, House Report 27, Serial Set volume no. 964, (1858), page 1; digital images, *LexisNexis* (http://www.lexisnexis.com) *LexisNexis Congressional Publications.*

379. 1860 U.S. census, Hampden County, Massachusetts, population schedule, City of Springfield, page 199 (penned), dwelling 1599, family 1716, Mary Bainbridge; digital image, *HeritageQuest Online* (http://www.heritagequestonline.com); citing NARA publication M653, roll 503.

380. Springfield, Massachusetts, Marriages 1863–1869, volume 6: page 63, Mary Bainbridge and Henry S. Humphrey, 1866, FHL microfilm 185,416.

381. "Obituary: Mrs. H. S. Humphrey," *New York Times*, New York, New York, 27 April 1887, page 5; digital images, *ProQuest* (http://proquest.umi.com) *ProQuest Historical Newspapers: New York Times* (1851–2005).

382. Albert Rathbone, *Samuel Rathbone, and Lydia Sparhawk, His Wife: A Record of their Descendants and Notes Regarding their Ancestors* (No place: privately published, 1937), 52. Also, "Died [Capt. Joseph Perry Sanford]," *New York Times*, New York, New York, 6 December 1901, page 9; digital images, *ProQuest* (http://proquest.umi.com) *ProQuest Historical Newspapers: New York Times* (1851–2005).

383. Rathbone, *Samuel Rathbone, and Lydia Sparhawk, His Wife*, 49. Also, 1860 U.S. census, Albany, New York, population schedule, Albany, 9th ward, page 410 (stamped), dwelling 558, family 731, Virginia Ransom; digital images, *AncestryLibrary Edition* (http://www.ancestrylibraryedition.com); citing NARA publication M653, roll 720.

384. 1860 U.S. census, Albany, New York, population schedule, Albany, page 410 (stamped), dwelling 558, family 731, Samuel H. Ransom. [The 1860 federal census for the S. H. Ransom household lists Samuel as a merchant with $200,000 in real estate and $50,000 in personal estate.]

385. Rathbone, *Samuel Rathbone, and Lydia Sparhawk, His Wife*, 49.

SOURCE LIST

Sources for this book are divided into two groups, archival and published. Many, but not all, are referenced in endnotes.

ARCHIVAL—documents in their original format, often handwritten, or as microfilm images or digital images of the originals.

PUBLISHED—resources which were printed and published for distribution.

The following acronyms are used in this list:

CHS—Carondelet Historical Society
FHL—Family History Library
LOC—Library of Congress
MHM—Missouri History Museum
ML—Mercantile Library
MSA—Missouri State Archives
SLCL—St. Louis County Library
NARA—National Archives & Records Administration
WHMC-StL—Western Historical Manuscript Collection—St. Louis

ARCHIVAL SOURCES

Census

Massachusetts. Hampden County. 1850 U.S. census, population schedule. NARA microfilm publication and Ancestry Library Edition.

Massachusetts. Hampden County. 1860 U.S. census, population schedule. NARA microfilm publication, Ancestry Library Edition, Footnote.com, and HeritageQuest Online.

Missouri. St. Louis, City of. 1880–1920 U.S. census, population schedule. NARA microfilm publication, Ancestry Library Edition, and HeritageQuest Online.

Missouri. St. Louis, City of. 1930 U.S. census, population schedule. NARA microfilm, Ancestry Library Edition, Footnote.com, and HeritageQuest Online.

Missouri. St. Louis County. 1840 U.S. census. NARA microfilm publication and Ancestry Library Edition.

Missouri. St. Louis County. 1850 U.S. census, population schedule. NARA microfilm publication and Ancestry Library Edition.

Missouri. St. Louis County. 1860 U.S. census, population schedule. NARA microfilm publication, Ancestry Library Edition, Footnote.com, and HeritageQuest Online.

Missouri. St. Louis County. 1865 St. Louis city census, population schedule. MHS, St. Louis, Missouri. Microfilm. SLCL, St. Louis, Missouri.

Missouri. St. Louis County. 1866 St. Louis city census, population schedule. MHS, St. Louis, Missouri. Microfilm. SLCL, St. Louis, Missouri.

Missouri. St. Louis County. 1869 Carondelet census, population schedule. MHS, St. Louis, Missouri. Microfilm. SLCL, St. Louis, Missouri.

Missouri. St. Louis County. 1870 U.S. census, population schedule. NARA microfilm publication, Ancestry Library Edition, and HeritageQuest Online.

Church and Cemetery Records

Archives of the Episcopal Diocese of Missouri (St. Louis, Missouri). Register of Christ Church Cemetery, 1840–1856. Digital images provided to author. 2009.

Basilica of St. Louis, King of France [Old Cathedral] (St. Louis, Missouri). Marriages, 1781–1834. FHL microfilm 190,831, available as SLCL microfilm SLAPR–173. SLCL, St. Louis, Missouri.

Bellefontaine Cemetery Office (St. Louis, Missouri). Lot map. Photocopies provided to author. 2009.

Calvary Cemetery Office (St. Louis, Missouri). Lot card and deed. Photocopies provided to author. 2008.

Catholic Cemeteries of St. Louis. St. Louis, Missouri: Calvary Cemetery, 1988. Microfiche. SLCL, St. Louis, Missouri.

"Catholic Cemeteries of the Archdiocese of St. Louis. Archdiocese of St. Louis." *Archdiocese of St. Louis*. http://www.archstl.org/cemeteries.

Centenary Methodist Church Archives (St. Louis, Missouri). [Centenary Methodist Church Archives, which include the Wesleyan Cemetery Records, are currently being processed by SLCL in conjunction with Centenary Methodist Church.]

Greenwood Cemetery Records. Photocopied records privately held by Etta Daniels, Cemetery historian. Photographs made by author, 13 February 2008.

St. Francis Xavier Catholic (College) Church (St. Louis City, Missouri). Baptisms, 1864–1886. FHL microfilm 1,871,244, available as SLCL microfilm SLAPR–62. SLCL, St. Louis, Missouri.

Saint Peter's Protestant Episcopal Church (Baltimore, Maryland). Register, 1803–1885. Maryland Historical Society, Baltimore, Maryland. FHL microfilm 13,703. SLCL, St. Louis, Missouri.

Scott, Harriet. Cenotaph plaque inscription. Calvary Cemetery, St. Louis, Missouri.

Washington Park Cemetery (St. Louis, Missouri). Cemetery cards. St. Louis Genealogical Society microfilm, available as SLCL microfilm SLCEM–74. SLCL, St. Louis, Missouri.

Wesleyan Cemetery Records (St. Louis, Missouri). FHL microfilm 1,405,557. SLCL, St. Louis, Missouri.

Federal, State, and Local Government Records

Illinois. St. Clair County. Marriage records. Illinois Regional Archives Depository (IRAD). Southern Illinois University—Carbondale. Carbondale, Illinois. Photocopy provided to author. 2008.

Louisiana, Natchitoches Parish. Conveyances. Parish Clerk of Court's office. Natchitoches, Louisiana. Photocopy provided to author. 2008.

Massachusetts. Hampden County. City of Springfield. Marriages 1850–1869. FHL microfilm 185,416. SLCL, St. Louis, Missouri.

Missouri. St. Louis, City of. Board of Election Commissioners. *St. Louis City Ward Maps*. CD-ROM, digital images. St. Louis, Missouri: St. Louis Genealogical Society, 2005.

Missouri. St. Louis, City of. Circuit Clerk's Office. Circuit Court Case Files.

Missouri. St. Louis, City of. Recorder of Deeds Office. Marriage and Land Records. St. Louis City Hall Archives.

Missouri. St. Louis, City of. Register of Births 1850–1908. St. Louis Department of Vital Records, City of St. Louis. MSA microfilm, available as SLCL microfilm RBSL. SLCL, St. Louis, Missouri.

Missouri. St. Louis, City of. Register of Deaths 1850–1908. St. Louis Department of Vital Records, City of St. Louis. MSA microfilm, available as SLCL microfilm RDSL. SLCL, St. Louis, Missouri.

Missouri. St. Louis County. Circuit Court Case Files. Court Clerk's Office, St. Louis. Digital images. St. Louis Circuit Court and Washington University. *Dred Scott Case Collection.* http://library.wustl.edu/vlib/dredscott.

Missouri. St. Louis County. Circuit Court Case Files. Court Clerk's Office, St. Louis. Digital images. St. Louis Circuit Court and Washington University. *St. Louis Circuit Court Historical Records Project.* http://stlcourtrecords.wustl.edu.

Missouri. St. Louis County. Circuit Court Case Files. Court Clerk's Office, St. Louis. Digital images. St. Louis Circuit Court and Washington University. *The Revised Dred Scott Case Collection.* http://digital.wustl.edu/d/dre.

Missouri. St. Louis County. County Court Records. County Council/County Clerk's Office. St. Louis, Missouri: [St. Louis County Archives], no date. Available as SLCL microfilm SLCCR. SLCL, St. Louis, Missouri.

Missouri. St. Louis County. Probate Court. Will books. MSA microfilm, available as SLCL microfilm CIWI, St. Louis, Missouri.

Missouri. St. Louis County. Probate Court Case files. Probate Court Clerk's Office, St. Louis. Digitial images. St. Louis Probate Court and Missouri State Archives. *Missouri's Judicial Records.* http://www.sos.mo.gov/archives/mojudicial.

Missouri. State Archives. Digital images. *Missouri State Archives. Death Certificates, 1910–1958.* http://www.sos.mo.gov/archives/resources/deathcertificates.

"St. Louis County National Register Listings." *Missouri Department of Natural Resources.* http://www.dnr.mo.gov/shpo/StLouis.htm.

Union Provost Marshals' File of Papers Relating to Individual Civilians. NARA microfilm publication M345. Washington, D.C.: National Archives and Records, 1967.

Manuscript Collections

Blair Family Papers. LOC. Washington, D.C. Photocopies provided to author.

Blow Family History File. CHS. St. Louis, Missouri.

Blow Family Papers. MHM. St. Louis, Missouri.

County Court Proceedings, St. Louis County, Missouri. MHM. St. Louis, Missouri.

Dexter P. Tiffany Collection. MHM. St. Louis, Missouri.

Dred Scott Collection. MHM. St. Louis, Missouri.

Greenwood Cemetery Records, WHMC—StL, St. Louis, Missouri.

R. A. Hager's Manuscript Collection

Daniels, Etta. Discussion of Greenwood Cemetery records with author. 13 February 2008. Notes. Privately held by author.

Friends of Greenwood Cemetery, St. Louis, Missouri. Information packet. Photocopies received from Etta Daniels, February 2006. Privately held by author.

Funeral program for Dr. John A. Madison Jr., 2 August 2007. Privately held by author.

Madison, Mrs. John A. Jr. Phone conversation with author. 16 June 2009. Notes. Privately held by author.

Miller, Alma (Madison). Interviews by author. 2008–2009. Audiotapes, transcripts, and notes. Privately held by author.

PUBLISHED SOURCES

Articles

Arenson, Adam. "Freeing Dred Scott: Confronting an Icon in the History of Slavery, 1857–2007." *Common-place* 8 (April 2008). E-journal. http://www.common-place.org/vol-08/no-03/arenson.

Arenson, Adam. "City of Manifest Destiny: St. Louis and the Cultural Civil War, 1848–1877." Ph.D. Dissertation. 2007. Yale University.

Bliss, Colonel John H. "Reminiscences of Fort Snelling." *Collections of the Minnesota Historical Society* 6 (1894): 336.

Bryan, John A. "The Blow Family and Their Slave Dred Scott: Part I." *Missouri Historical Society Bulletin* 4 (July 1948): 223–231.

Bryan, John A. "The Blow Family and Their Slave Dred Scott: Part II Dred Scott's Suit." *Missouri Historical Society Bulletin* 5 (October 1948): 19–33.

Carlson, Shirley J. "Black Migration to Pulaski County, Illinois, 1860–1900." *Illinois Historical Journal* 80 (Spring 1987), 37–46.

"Cholera Epidemics in St. Louis." *Glimpses of the Past*. 3 (March 1936): 45–76.

Faatz, Mabel Keilbach. "Final Resting Place? Not Quite!" *St. Louis Genealogical Society Quarterly* 9 (December 1976): 85–89.

Fineberg, Gail. "Blair Family Treasures: Historic Papers Added to Library's Cache." *Library of Congress Information Bulletin* 59 (October 2000). Online archives. *Library of Congress*. http://www.loc.gov/loc/lcib/0010/blair.html : 2008.

Hess, Jeffrey A. "Dred Scott from Fort Snelling to Freedom." *Historic Fort Snelling Chronicles* 2 (1975): not paginated.

"Historical Notes and Comments." *Missouri Historical Review* 41 (October 1946–July 1947): 328–329. [Notes on Judge J. Hugo Grimm's Calvary Cemetery research regarding the burial of Dred Scott.]

Hunter, Lloyd A. "Slavery in St. Louis 1804–1860" *Missouri Historical Society Bulletin* 30 (July 1974), 233–265.

"Iowa Courts." *Iowa Judicial Branch: Early Civil Rights Cases*. http://www.iowacourts.gov/Public_Information/ Iowa_ Courts_History/Civil_Rights.

"Jefferson Barracks." *St. Louis County*. http://www.co.st-louis.mo.us/parks/j-b.html.

McKoy, Kathy. "Afro-American Cemeteries in St. Louis." *Gateway Heritage* 6 (Winter 1985–86): 30–37.

Moore, Robert, Jr. "A Ray of Hope, Extinguished: St. Louis Slave Suits for Freedom." *Gateway Heritage* 14 (Winter 1993–94): 1–15.

"Memorials: Richard C. Hollyday Jr. '50" Online archives. *Princeton Alumni Weekly*. (Jan. 28, 2004). *Princeton Alumni Weekly*. http://paw.princeton.edu/memorials/22/98/index.xml?undergraduate_class=1950.

Reichard, Maximilian. "Black and White on the Urban Frontier: The St. Louis Community in Transition, 1800–1830." *Missouri Historical Society Bulletin* 33 (October 1976): 3–17.

Snyder, Charles E. "John Emerson, Owner of Dred Scott." *Annals of Iowa* 21 (October 1938): 440–461. Online archives. *Internet Archive*. http://www.archive.org/details/johnemersonowner00snyd.

Taliaferro, Lawrence. "Auto-biography of Maj. Lawrence Taliaferro." *Collections of the Minnesota Historical Society* 6 (1894): 190.

Turner, J. Milton, and Irving Dilliard. "Dred Scott Eulogized by James Milton Turner: Historical Observance of the Turner Centenary: 1840–1940." *The Journal of Negro History* 26 (January 1941): 1–11.

VanderVelde, Lea, and Sandhya Subramanian. "Mrs. Dred Scott." *Yale Law Journal* 106 (1997): 1033–1122. Online archives. *LexisNexis Academic*. http://academic.lexisnexis.com.

Violette, E. M. "The Black Code in Missouri." Proceedings of the Mississippi Valley Historical Association for the Year 1912–1913 6 (1913), 287–316. Digital images. *Google Books*. http://books.google.com.

Woodhouse, Barbara Bennett. "Dred Scott's Daughters: Nineteenth Century Urban Girls at the Intersection of Race and Patriarchy." *Buffalo Law Review* 48 (Fall 2000): 669–702. Online archives. *Westlaw*. http://westlaw.com.

BOOKS

Atlas of the City and County of St. Louis, by Congressional Townships: Showing All the Surveys of the Public Lands and of the Confirmed French and Spanish Grants, New Madrid Locations, and Entries of Public Lands up to the 1st Day of January, 1838: With the Names of the Original Claimants and Number of Acres Claimed by Each. 1838. Reprint. Jefferson City, Missouri: Capital City Family Research, 1985.

Atlas of the City of St. Louis. No place: St. Louis Plat and Record Co., 1905.

Atlas of St. Louis County. No place: Julius Hutawa, no date.

Aubin, C. T. *Whipple's Fire Insurance Maps*. [St. Louis, Missouri: A. Whipple, 1876?]. Digital image provided to author courtesy of Washington University Library, St. Louis, Missouri.

Beckwith, Paul. *Creoles of St. Louis*. St. Louis, Missouri: Nixon-Jones Printing, 1893.

Black, Henry Campbell. *Black's Law Dictionary*. Sixth edition. St. Paul, Minnesota: West Group, 1990.

Central's Place of Worship and Parish House: History of Central Baptist Church. St. Louis, Missouri: King Publishing, 1927.

Chaffee, William H. *The Chaffee Genealogy: Embracing the Chafe, Chafy, Chafie, Chafey, Chafee, Chaphe, Chaffy, Chaffie, Chaffey, Chaffe, Chaffee Descendants of Thomas Chaffe, of Hingham, Hull, Rehoboth and Swansea, Massachusetts: Also Certain Lineages from Families in the United States, Canada, and England, Not Descended from Thomas Chaffe, 1635–1909*. New York: Grafton Press, 1909.

Charless, Charlotte Taylor Blow. *A Biographical Sketch of the Character of Joseph Charless. 1869*. Digital images. *Project Gutenberg*. http://www.gutenberg.org/wiki.

Christensen, Lawrence O., et al. *Dictionary of Missouri Biography*. Columbia, Missouri: University of Missouri Press, 1999.

Cox, James. *Old and New St. Louis: A Concise History of the Metropolis of the West and Southwest, with a Review of its Present Greatness and Immediate Prospects*. St. Louis, Missouri: Central Biographical Publishing Co., 1894.

Cunningham, Mary B., and Jeanne C. Blythe. *The Founding Family of St. Louis*. St. Louis, Missouri: Midwest Technical Publications, 1977.

Dettleff, Gloria, compiler. "List of Colored Persons" in Wesleyan Cemetery St. Louis, Missouri, 1847–1868. 2008. Digital images. *St. Louis County Library*. http://www.slcl.org/sc/pdfs/Wesleyan_cemetery_colored_persons.pdf.

Dosch, Donald F. *The Old Courthouse: Americans Build a Forum on the Frontier*. St. Louis: Jefferson National Expansion Historical Association, 1979.

Dry, Camille. *Pictorial St. Louis, the Great Metropolis of the Mississippi Valley: A Topographical Survey Drawn in Perspective A.D. 1875*. 1875. Reprint. No place: ImagineInk Publishing, 2004.

Duke, Walter Garland. *Henry Duke, Councilor and His Descendants and Connections*. Richmond, Virginia: Dietz Press, 1949. Digital images. *HeritageQuest Online*. http://www.heritagequestonline.com.

Dykstra, Robert R. *Bright Radical Star: Black Freedom and White Supremacy on the Hawkeye Frontier*. Cambridge, Massachusetts: Harvard University Press, 1993.

Eakin, Joanne Chiles, and Annette W. Curtis. *The Little Gods: Union Provost Marshals in Missouri 1861–1865*. Revised and enlarged edition. Independence, Missouri: Two Trails Publishing, 2002.

Ehrlich, Walter. *They Have No Rights: Dred Scott's Struggle for Freedom*. 1979. Reprint. Bedford, Massachusetts: Applewood Books in cooperation with Jefferson National Parks Association, [2007].

Fleming, Ann Carter. *St. Louis Family History Research Guide*. St. Louis, Missouri; Fleming Publishing, 2008.

Gerteis, Louis S. *Civil War St. Louis*. Lawrence, Kansas: University Press of Kansas, 2001.

Gilreath, Amelia C., compiler. *Shenandoah County, Virginia Deed Books Series, Volume 7: Deed Books U and V 1813–1815*. Nokesville, Virginia: A. C. Gilreath, 1993.

Fehrenbacher, Don E. *The Dred Scott Case: Its Significance in American Law and Politics*. New York: Oxford University Press, 1978.

Hafen, LeRoy R., editor. *Mountain Men and Fur Traders of the Far West*. Lincoln, Nebraska: University of Nebraska Press, 1982.

Hafen, LeRoy Reuben, and Scott Eckberg. *Fur Traders, Trappers, and Mountain Men of the Upper Missouri*. Lincoln, Nebraska: University of Nebraska Press, 1995.

Hansen, Marcus. *Old Fort Snelling, 1819–1858*. 1918. Digital images. *HeritageQuest Online*. http://heritagequestonline.com.

Harris, NiNi. *A History of Carondelet*. St. Louis, Missouri: Patrice Press, 1991.

Hyde, William, and Howard L. Conard, editors. *Encyclopedia of the History of St. Louis, a Compendium of History and Biography for Ready Reference*. 4 volumes. New York: Southern History Co., 1899.

"John Sanford Barnes: A Memorial and a Tribute. 1912." Digital images. *Internet Archive*. http://www.archive.org.

Kaufman, Kenneth C. *Dred Scott's Advocate: A Biography of Roswell M. Field*. Columbia, Missouri: University of Missouri Press, 1996.

Kollbaum, Marc E. *Gateway to the West: The History of Jefferson Barracks from 1826–1894*. Volume 1. St. Louis, Missouri: Friends of Jefferson Barrcks, no date.

Lee, George R. *Slavery North of St. Louis*. Canton, Missouri: Lewis County Historical Society, no date.

Lincoln University. *The Archives*. Jefferson City, Missouri: Lincoln University, 1955. Digital images. [Lincoln University yearbook] Lincoln University Yearbooks. *Missouri Digital Heritage*. http://cdm.sos.mo.gov/cdm4/browse.php?CISOROOT=%2Flincyrbk2 : 2009.

Litwack, Leon F. *North of Slavery: The Negro in the Free States, 1790–1860*. Chicago, University of Chicago Press, 1961.

Meese, William A. *Early Rock Island (1905). HeritageQuest Online*. http://www.heritagequestonline.com.

Menius, Joseph M. *Susan Blow—Gateway to Education*. St. Clair, Missouri: Page One Publishing, 1993.

Mobley, Jane. *Home Place: A Celebration of Life in Bridgeton, Missouri*. Bridgeton, Missouri: City of Bridgeton, 1993.

Moore, Robert J. *The Old Courthouse*. St. Louis, Missouri: Jefferson National Parks Association, 2004.

Morris, Ann. *Sacred Green Space: A Survey of Cemeteries in St. Louis County*. [St. Louis, Missouri]: A. Morris, 2000.

Old Cemeteries, St. Louis County, Missouri. 6 volumes. St. Louis, Missouri: St. Louis Genealogical Society, 1982–2003.

Parkin, Robert E. *Overland Trails and Trials and Your Community Today*. Overland, Missouri: Krawll Printing, 1956.

Past and Present of Rock Island County, Ill. (1877). HeritageQuest Online. http://www.heritagequestonline.com : 2008.

Payne-Jackson, Arvilla, and John Lee. *Folk Wisdom and Mother Wit: John Lee—An African American Herbal Healer*. Westport, Connecticut: Greenwood Press, 1993.

Pitzman, Julius. *Atlas of the City and County of Saint Louis, Missouri. 1878*. Reprint. St. Louis: St. Louis Genealogical Society, 1997. Also CD-ROM version. 1878. Reprint. St. Louis: St. Louis Genealogical Society, 2005.

Plat Book of St. Louis County, Missouri, 1909. CD-ROM. 1909. Reprint. St. Louis: St. Louis Genealogical Society, 2007.

Rathbone, Albert. *Samuel Rathbone and Lydia Sparhawk, his Wife*. No place: no publisher, 1937.

Register of Graduates and Former Cadets of the United States Military Academy. Eisenhower Centennial Edition. West Point, New York: Association of Graduates, USMA, 1990.

Roberts, Robert B. *Encyclopedia of Historic Forts*. New York: Macmillan Publications, 1988.

Rombauer, Robert J. *The Union Cause in St. Louis in 1861*. St. Louis, Missouri: Press of Nixon-Jones Printing Co., 1909.

Shambaugh, Benjamin F. *History of the Constitutions of Iowa. Des Moines, Iowa: Historical Department of Iowa, 1902*. Digital images. *HeritageQuest Online*. http://heritagequestonline.com.

Snow, Loudell F. *Walkin' Over Medicine*. 1993. Reprint. Detroit, Michigan: Wayne State University Press, 1998.

Stevens, Geo. E. *History of Central Baptist Church*. St. Louis, Missouri: King Publishing, 1927.

Stowe Teacher's College. *Les Collegiens*. St. Louis, Missouri: Stowe Teacher's College, 1945.

Stowe Teacher's College. *Les Collegiens*. St. Louis, Missouri: Stowe Teacher's College, 1947

Stroud, George M. *A Sketch of the Laws Relating to Slavery in the Several States of the United States of America with Some Alterations and Considerable Additions*. Philadelphia: No publisher, 1856. Digital images. *Google Book Search*. http://books.google.com.

Sluyter, Gary V. *St. Louis' Hidden Treasure: A History of the Charless Home 1853–2003*. St. Louis, Missouri: The Senior Circuit, 2003.

Swain, Gwenyth. *Dred and Harriet Scott: A Family's Struggle for Freedom*. St. Paul: Borelis Books, 2004.

Trexler, Harrison Anthony. *Slavery in Missouri 1804–1865. John Hopkins University Studies in Historical and Political Science*. Baltimore: John Hopkins Press, 1914.

Two Hundred Years of U.S. Census Taking: Population and Housing Questions, 1790–1990. Washington, D.C.: Bureau of the Census, 1989.

Wagner, Allen E. *Good Order and Safety: A History of the St. Louis Metropolitan Police Department 1861–1906*. St. Louis: Missouri History Museum, 2008.

Whipple, Alphonse. *Whipple's Fire Insurance Map of St. Louis, Mo. Volume 1, 1897*. [St. Louis, Missouri: A. Whipple, 1897]. Digital image provided to author courtesy of Washington University Library, St. Louis, Missouri.

Williams, Francis Emmett, and Mrs. Williams. *Centenary Methodist Church of St. Louis the First Hundred Years, 1839–1939*. St. Louis, Missouri: Mound City Press, 1939.

Winter, William C. *The Civil War in St. Louis: A Guided Tour*. St. Louis, Missouri; Missouri Historical Press, 1994.

CITY DIRECTORIES

City Directories for New York, New York. Footnote.com. http://footnote.com : 2009. 1850 (John Doggett, pub.), 1851, 1853–1857 (John F. Trow, pub.), 1852 (Charles R. Rode, pub.).

City Directories of the United States through 1860. St. Louis, Missouri. No place: no publisher, no date. (microfiche)

City Directories of the United States, 1882–1901. St. Louis, Missouri. New Haven, Connecticut: Research Publications, no date.

Polk, R. L., compiler. *St. Louis, Missouri, City Directory. St. Louis, Missouri: R. L. Polk Directory Co., 1936–1942, 1944, 1946–1947*. Microfilm of St. Louis Public Library copies. SLCL. St. Louis, Missouri.

United States City Directories, 1902–1935. St. Louis, Missouri. Woodbridge, Connecticut: Research Publications, no date.

NEWSPAPERS

19th Century U.S. Newspapers Online. Digital images. *Gale*. http://www.gale.cengage.com.

Access NewspaperArchive. Digital images. *NewspaperARCHIVE.com*. http://www.newspaperarchive.com/.

African-American Newspapers: 19th Century Pt's 1, 2, & 3. Digital images. *Accessible Archives*. http://www.accessible.com.

America's GenealogyBank. Digital images. *GenealogyBank*. http://www.genealogybank.com.

America's Historical Newspapers. Digital images. *Newsbank.com*. http://infoweb.newsbank.com.

America's Newspapers. Online text. *Newsbank.com*. http://infoweb.newsbank.com.

Massachusetts. Springfield. *The Springfield Daily Republican*. 16 March 1857. Museum of Springfield History, Springfield, Massachusetts. Photocopy provided to author.

Missouri. St. Louis. *Missouri Republican*, March–May 1857. MHM, St. Louis, Missouri.

Missouri. St. Louis. *St. Louis Argus*. 1915–1997 (incomplete run). Microfilm. SLCL, St. Louis, Missouri.

Missouri. St. Louis. *St. Louis Daily Evening News*. March–April 1857. ML, St. Louis, Missouri.

Missouri. St. Louis. *St. Louis Globe-Democrat*. 1853–1986. Microfilm. SLCL, St. Louis, Missouri.

Missouri. St. Louis. *St. Louis Post-Dispatch*. 1874 to date. Microfilm. SLCL, St. Louis, Missouri.

Missouri. St. Louis. *St. Louis Post-Dispatch*. 1988 to present. Full-text: electronic edition. *Newsbank.com*. http//:newsbank.com.

Missouri. St. Louis. *St. Louis Republican*. April 3, 1857. MHM, St. Louis, Missouri. Microfilm.

New York. New York. *Frank Leslie's Illustrated Newspaper*. 27 June 1857. Reprint.

New York. Nunda. *Union and Advertiser*. 27 March 1957. Monroe County Library System, Rochester, New York. Photocopy provided to author.

ProQuest Historical Newspapers *New York Times (1851–2005)*. Digital images. *ProQuest*. http://proquest.umi.com.

ProQuest Historical Newspapers *St. Louis Post-Dispatch* (1874–1922). Digital images. *ProQuest*. http://proquest.umi.com.

PUBLISHED GOVERNMENT DOCUMENTS

American National Biography Online. http://www.anb.org.

"America's First Look into the Camera." *Library of Congress*. http://lcweb2.loc.gov/ammem/daghtml.

"Before Dred Scott: Freedom Suits in Antebellum Missouri." *Missouri State Archives*. http://www.sos.mo.gov/archives/education/aahi/beforedredscott/rachelV.asp.

Biographical Directory of the United States Congress. http://bioguide.congress.gov.

"Dred Scott Sesquicentennial." *Jefferson National Expansion Memorial*. http://www.dredscottanniversary.org.

"Elijah Lovejoy 1802–1837: The Slavery Question in Illinois." *Illinois State Historical Library*. http://www.state.il.us/HPA/lovejoy/illinois.htm : 2009.

"Fort Jesup." *National Park Service*. http://www.nps.gov/history/nr/travel/caneriver/for.htm.

"Fort Jesup State Historic Site." *CaneRiverHeritage.org*. http://www.caneriverheritage.org/main_file.php/fortjesup.php.

"Historic Fort Snelling: A Brief History of Fort Snelling." *Minnesota Historical Society*. http://www.mnhs.org/places/sites/hfs/history.html.

Heitman, Fancis B. *Historical Register and Dictionary of the United States Army, 1789–1903*. Vol. 1. Washington, D.C.: U.S. Government Printing Office, 1903. Database. *Ancestry Library Edition*. http://www.ancestrylibrary.com.

"Lexis Nexis U.S. Serial Set Digital Collection," *Lexis Nexis*. http://lexisnexis.com.

Missouri. *Laws of the State of Missouri Passed at the Fifteenth General Assembly, Begun and Held at the City of Jefferson, on Monday, the Twenty-fifth Day of December, Eighteen Hundred and Forty-eight, and Ended on Monday the Twelfth Day of March, Eighteen Hundred and Forty-nine*. City of Jefferson, Missouri: Hampton L. Boon, 1849.

Missouri. *Laws of the State of Missouri Passed at the First Session of the Tenth General Assembly, Begun and Held at the City of Jefferson, on Monday, the Nineteenth Day of November, in the Year of Our Lord, One Thousand Eight Hundred and Thirty-eight*. City of Jefferson, Missouri: Calvin Gunn, 1838.

Missouri. *Laws of the State of Missouri Passed at the Regular Session of the XXVIIth General Assembly, Begun and Held at the City of Jefferson, Wednesday, January 1, 1873*. Jefferson City, Missouri: Regan & Carter, 1873.

Missouri. *Laws of the State of Missouri Passed by the Nineteenth General Assembly, Begun and Held at the City of Jefferson on Monday, the 29th Day of December 1856*. City of Jefferson, Missouri: James Lusk, 1857.

Missouri. *Revised Statutes of the State of Missouri, Revised and Digested by the Eighth General Assembly, During the Years One Thousand Eight Hundred and Thirty-four, and One Thousand Eight Hundred and Thirty-five, Together With the Constitutions of Missouri and of the United States*. Saint Louis, Missouri: Chambers, Knapp & Co., 1840.

Missouri. *The Revised Statutes of the State of Missouri, Revised and Digested by the Eighteenth General Assembly, during the Session of One Thousand Eight Hundred and Fifty-four and One Thousand Eight Hundred and Fifty-five; To Which are Prefixed the Constitutions of the United States and of the State of Missouri with an Appendix, Including Certain Local Acts of This State, and Laws of Congress, and Form Book*. 2 volumes. City of Jefferson, Missouri: James Lusk, 1856.

Missouri. *The Revised Statutes of the State of Missouri, Revised and Digested by the Thirteenth General Assembly, Begun and Held During the Years One Thousand Eight Hundred and Forty-four and One Thousand Eight Hundred and Forty Five; ... One Thousand Eight Hundred and Forty-five*. St. Louis: Chambers & Knapp, 1845.

"Missouri's Dred Scott Case, 1846–1857." *Missouri State Archives*. http://www.sos.mo.gov/archives/resources/africanamerican/scott/scott.asp.

Quisenberry, Anderson Chenault. *General Zachary Taylor and the Mexican War*. Frankfort, Kentucky: Kentucky State Historical Society, 1911.

"Suits for Freedom, St. Louis, 1804–1865." *National Park Service, U.S. Department of the Interior, Jefferson National Expansion Memorial*. http://www.nps.gov/jeff/historyculture/upload/Slave%20Suits%20for%20Freedom%20List.pdf.

United States. Congress. *Statutes at Large, 1789–1875*. Digital images. *Library of Congress. A Century of Lawmaking for a New Nation: Statutes at Large, 1789–1875*. http://memory.loc.gov/ammem/amlaw/lwsl.html.

The War of the Rebellion: A Compilation of the Official Records of the Union and Confederate Armies. 1881. Reprint. Harrisburg, Pennsylvania: National Historical Society, 1971.

MISCELLANEOUS

"Camp Jackson—St. Louis, Missouri: Waymark." *Waymarking.com*. http://www.waymarking.com/waymarks/WM1VJB.

"Central Baptist Church Legacy," *Central Baptist Church in St. Louis.* http://cbcstl.org

"Fort Armstrong—Rock Island, IL: Waymark." *Waymarking.com*. http://www.waymarking.com/waymarks/WM2G41.

INDEX

This index includes persons, places, subjects, and events. Women appear under both their maiden name and married names(s) with alternate surnames appearing in either parentheses (maiden) or brackets [married]. If a woman married more than once, the multiple married names appear in brackets in order of the marriages.

Forts, towns, and counties are listed both under the state in which they are currently located and by the place name. Names using St. or Saint are indexed under Saint.

—— *Unknown Surnames* ——

Aspasia, 23
Catiche, 23
Charles, 23
Isador, 23
Marguerite, 23
Marie, 23
Mary Charlotte, 23
Phillis, 7
Pierre, 23
Rachel, 19
Ralph, 13
Sally, 23
Theotiste, 23
Winny, 14

—— *Numbers* ——

8th Street Baptist Church, 66, 70–71

—— *A* ——

Abels, Ruth Ann [Hager], 103
African Methodist Episcopal Church, 99
Agreed Statement of Facts, 27
Alabama, Florence, 2, 7, 15, 101
  Huntsville, 5, 131
  Lauderdale County, 7, 15, 101
  Madison County, 2, 5, 7, 15, 101
Albany, New York, 133
Alexandria, Virginia, 118
Allensville, Kentucky, 81
American Party, 33
Anti-Abolitionist Society, 11
Aspasia (slave), 23
Atlantic [steamship], 7
Austin A. Layne Mortuary, 97, 103

—— *B* ——

Bailey, Gamaliel, 30
Bainbridge, Henry, 10–11, 13–14, 102, 132–133
  Mary (Sanford) [Humphrey], 10–11, 13–14, 132–133
Bair, Barbara, 119
Baltimore, Maryland, 133
Bangor Daily Whig & Courier, 36
Barnes, Charlotte (Sanford), 11, 19, 34, 132–133
  James, 11, 19, 34, 132–133
Barnum's Hotel, 47
Bay, Samuel Mansfield, 18–20
Beckmann, Rudolph, Rev. 94
Behling, Ruth, 118

Bellefontaine Cemetery, 58
Bettendorf, Iowa, 8–9
Black Republican, 42
Blair, Eliza (Gist), 31
    Francis Preston, 31
    M., 117, 120, 122–123, 125–126,
    Montgomery, 30–31, 36, 39, 117–118, 127
Blair Family Papers, 118, 120, 123, 126–127
Blair House, 31
Blow, Charlotte Taylor [Charless], 7–8, 130–131
    Eliza (Wahrendoff), 7, 130–131
    Elizabeth Rebecca, 7, 130–131
    Elizabeth (Taylor), 5, 7–8, 101, 129–131
    Eugenia (LaBeume), 7, 130–131
    Fannie, 57
    Henry Taylor, 7, 29, 49, 66, 99, 130–131
    Julia (Webster), 7, 99, 130–131
    Martha Ella [Drake], 7, 29, 130–131
    Mary Ann [Key], 7, 130
    Mary (Scott), 5
    Minerva (Grimsley), 7, 130–131
    Peter, 5, 7–8, 15, 49, 99, 101, 129–131
    Peter Etheldred Taylor, 5, 7, 29, 130–131
    Richard, 5
    Richard Benjamin, 130
    Sarah (Tunstall), 7, 130–131
    Susan, 66, 131
    Taylor Francis, 7, 29, 39–42, 49, 55, 57–59, 66, 93, 95, 101–103, 130–131
    Thomas Vaughn, 130
    William Thomas, 7, 99, 130–131
Brady, J. C., 81
Bridgeton, Missouri, 11–12

— C —

California (farm), 11–13, 19
Calvary Cemetery, 57–59, 92–96, 102–103, 113–114, 131
Camp Jackson, 52, 54
Camp Jackson Affair, 54–55
Campbell, William, 12
Carondelet, Missouri, 13, 99–100
Catiche (slave), 23
Cemetery, Bellefontaine, 58
    Calvary, 57–59, 92–96, 102–103, 113–114, 131
    Greenwood, 66, 70–71, 88, 92, 95–98, 103, 113, 115
    Jefferson Barracks National, 96
    Sigerson Farm, 100
    St. Peter's, 78
    Washington Park, 83, 85, 95, 103
    Wesleyan, 52, 54–59, 78, 102–103, 131
Cenotaph, 95
Chaffee, C. C., 41, 117, 120–124, 126–127
    Calvin, Dr., 11, 21, 33, 35–36, 38–39, 42–44, 88, 102, 117–118, 132–133
    Clemens, 33, 43
    Eliza Irene (Sanford) [Emerson], *see* Chaffee, Irene
    Emma, 33
    Irene (Sanford) [Emerson], 10–11, 13–15, 17, 19, 21–23, 25, 27, 33–35, 37–39, 41–44, 88, 101–102, 118, 122–123, 127, 129, 132–133
Chambers, Stephan, 96
Chandler, Belle [Cross], 81
Charles (slave), 23
Charless, Charlotte (Blow), 7–8, 130–131
    Joseph, Jr., 7–8, 29, 130–131
    Joseph, Sr., 131
Charless, Blow & Company, 131
Charleston, Marsulite [Madison], 96
Chevalier, Ellen, 23
Cholera epidemic of 1849, 20
Chouteau, —, 23
    Auguste, 17
    Auguste P., 23
    Emilie (Gratiot), 133
    Emilie [Sanford], 11, 132–133
    Francois, 23
    Gabriel, 23
    Gabriel S., 23
    Henry, 23
    Louis, 23
    Pierre, 23, 133
    Pierre Jr., 21–23, 38, 133
    Pierre Sr., 23
Chouteau and Company, 21
Chouteau and Sanford, 19
Civil War, 43, 53, 62, 81, 88, 131, 133
Clark, John B., 11, 132–133
    Henrietta (Sanford), 11, 34, 132–133
Coleman, Bessie, 88
Connecticut, Stanford, 133
Corpus Christi, Texas, 2, 14
Court, Iowa Supreme, 13
    Missouri Supreme, 14, 21–22, 25–26, 33, 102
    St. Louis Circuit [Mo.], 14, 17, 19, 21–23, 27, 32–33, 39, 42–43, 49, 102
    U.S. Circuit [federal], 30, 35
    U.S. Supreme, 22–23, 26, 30–31, 35–38, 42, 44, 88, 100, 102
Covington, Louisiana, 131

Crane, Arbra, 47
Cross, Alexander, 81
  Belle (Chandler), 81
  Charles A., 81
  Christopher, 81
  Grace [Madison], 6, 80–83, 85–86, 88–90, 93–95, 105, 110–111

—— *D* ——

Daily Ohio Statesman, 42
Daniels, Etta, 98
Davenport, Iowa, 8, 11, 13, 41, 102
Davenport Gazette, 11
Davis, Isabella [Sanford], 11, 132–133
Deed of Emancipation, 32, 39, 42; *see also* Writ of Emancipation
Dickson, Moses, Rev., 99
Dowling, Edward, Rev., 93–94, 103
Drake, Charles D., 7, 18, 29, 130–131
  Martha (Blow), 7, 29, 130–131
Dred Scott's Advocate, 12
Dred Scott Decision, 35, 49, 53, 88, 93–94, 96–97, 102–103, 118–119
Dred Scott Heritage Foundation, 98
Dred Scott v. Emerson, 21
Dred Scott v. Sandford, 31
Dyer, Wendy, 118

—— *E* ——

Eads Bridge, 81
East Moline, Illinois, 8
East St. Louis, Illinois, 81
Eighth Street Baptist Church, 66, 70–71
Eiler's Survey, 100
Elijah Lovejoy Society, 95
Emerson, Eliza Irene (Sanford) [Chaffee], *see* Chaffee, Irene
  Frank, 34
  Henrietta, 13, 34, 39, 41, 102
  Irene (Sanford) [Chaffee], *see* Chaffee, Irene
  John, Dr., 8–11, 13, 15, 18–19, 29, 41, 101–102, 122, 131–133
Eugene Field House, 118–119

—— *F* ——

Farnam, Tom Campbell, 118–119
Field, Alexander P., 20
  Eugene, 30
  Martin, 30
  R. M., 117
  Roswell, 29–30, 35–36, 47, 93, 122, 125
First Presbyterian Church, 8
Fitzgibbons Gallery, 47, 75
Florence, Alabama, 2, 7, 15, 101
Fort Armstrong [Illinois], 2, 8–9, 15, 18, 101
Fort Armstrong Chapter DAR, 8
Fort Jesup [Louisiana], 2, 10–11, 13–15, 101
Fort Snelling [Minnesota], 2, 9–11, 15, 18, 101–102
Fort Sumter [South Carolina], 53
Fort Towson, West Choctaw Nation [Oklahoma], 132–133
Francis family, 83
Frank Leslie's Illustrated Newspaper, 43, 46–48
Free Negro License, 49, 54
Freedom Suits, 20, 22
Freemont, J. C., Major-General, 55
Friends of Dred Scott Committee, 119
Friends of Greenwood Cemetery Association, 98
Fugitive Slave Law of 1850, 100

—— *G* ——

Galveston Bay, 133
Gateway Arch, 87
Gathright, Stephanie, 96
Gist, Eliza [Blair], 31
Granby Mining and Smelting Company, 131
Grand Court Order of Cyrenes, 95
Gratiot, Emilie [Chouteau], 133
Great Depression, 83, 95
Greenwood Cemetery, 66, 70–71, 88, 92, 95–98, 103, 113, 115
Greneaux, C. E., 10
Grimsley, Minerva [Blow], 7, 130–131
Gypsy [steamboat], 6, 11, 101

—— *H* ——

Hall, David N., 20
Hager, Ruth Ann (Abels), 103
Hamilton, Alexander, Judge, 19, 23, 25, 38, 42
Hampden County, Massachusetts, 41
Harriet's Hill, 97, 103
Harris-Stowe State University, 87
Harrison, Charles C. Jr., Mrs., 95, 103
Hempstead, C. J., 23
Hicks Alley, 63–64, 66, 70–71
Hollyday, Edith, 118
  Richard C. III, 118

Homer G. Philips Hospital, 88
Howard, Henry F., 100
Isabella, 100
James, 100
Luke, 99–100
Hrdlicka, George, 94
Humphrey, Henry S., 11, 132–133
Mary (Sanford) [Bainbridge], 10–11, 14, 132–133
Huntsville, Alabama, 5, 131

— *I* —

Illinois, East Moline, 8
East St. Louis, 81
Fort Armstrong, 2, 8–9, 15, 18, 101
Moline, 8
Pulaski County, 81
Rock Island, 2, 8, 18, 101
Villa Ridge, 81
In re Ralph, 13
Interstate I–170, 12
Iowa, Bettendorf, 8–9
Davenport, 8, 11, 13, 41, 102
Iowa Supreme Court, 13
Iowa Territory, 13, 15
Iron Mountain Railroad, 131
Isador (slave), 23

— *J* —

J. H. Harrison Funeral Home, 88
Jackson, Brian, 96
Claiborne, Governor, 54
Lynne (Madison), 95–96, 119
Jefferson Barracks, Missouri, 10, 13–15
Jefferson Barracks National Cemetery, 96
Jefferson Barracks Park, 10
Jefferson Hotel, 7, 101
Johnson, Rose (Madison), 6, 80, 83, 87, 93–94
Jones, John, 7

— *K* —

Kaufman, Kenneth, 12
Keemle, C., 41
Kentucky, Allensville, 81
Todd County, 81
Key, John, 7, 130
Mary Ann (Blow), 7, 130
King George County, Virginia, 2, 9
Kirby, Bruce, 119
Knox, Ellen, 50

— *L* —

LaBeaume, Charles Edmund, 29, 131
Eugenia [Blow], 7, 130–131
Louis Alexander, 20, 131
Louis Tarteron, 29, 131
La Grange, Francois, 23
Lambert-St. Louis International Airport, 12
Lauderdale County, Alabama, 7, 15, 101
LeClaire Hotel, 11
Lee, Robert E., 133
Librarian of Congress, 79
Library of Congress, 118, 120, 123, 126–127
Liggett & Myers, 69
Lincoln, Abraham, 95
Lincoln University Law School, 87
Lindell's Grove, 52, 54–55
Louisiana, Covington, 131
Fort Jesup, 2, 10–11, 13–15, 101
Natchitoches, 10, 133
Louisiana [steamship], 133
Louisiana State Historic Site, 10
Loving, Joyce, 119
Lucas, James H., 12
John B., Judge, 17
Lyon, Nathaniel, Captain, 54

— *M* —

Madison, Alma [Miller], 1, 6, 80, 83, 85–87, 89, 93–94
Catherine, 59, 73
Charles, 6, 83, 85, 89
D. Scott, 87
Dred Scott, 6, 83, 87, 93–94
Dred Scott II, 96
Edw., 6, 66–67, 73, 103
Eliza (Scott), 6, 11, 14–15, 18, 20–21, 24–27, 29–32, 37–39, 41–42, 47, 49–50, 53–55, 57, 59, 61–64, 66, 68–71, 73–79, 88, 90, 97, 99–101, 103, 107
Elizabeth (Scott), 6, 50–51, 64, 71–73, 105; *see also* Madison, Eliza
Felicia, 96
Grace (Cross), 6, 80–83, 85–86, 88–90, 93–95, 105, 110–111
Harry, 6, 71, 73, 75–80, 83, 87–88
Harry H., 79

Madison *(continued)*
Henry, 78
John A., 71, 73, 75–79, 81–83, 105, 110–111
John A., Jr., 1, 6, 80, 83, 87, 93–96
John A., Sr., 6, 83, 85, 88–89, 93, 103
Joshua, 49, 70–71
Joshua W., 49, 70–71
Koiana, 96
Lates W., 6, 55–58, 61, 66, 73, 102
Lizzie (Scott), 6, 61; *see also*, Madison, Eliza
Lynne [Jackson], 95–96, 119
Marsulite (Charleston), 96
Michael, 96
Michael A., 96
Pauline, 6, 83, 87
Rose [Johnson], 6, 80, 83, 87, 93
Seales W., *see* Madison, Lates W.
W., 81
Wilson, 6, 27, 49–51, 54, 57–59, 61–64, 66, 68–71, 73–79, 81, 88, 103, 105, 107
Madison County, Alabama, 2, 5, 7, 15, 101
Marguerite (slave), 23
Marie (slave), 23
Marshall, Elizabeth, 86, 112
Freeman, 85
Henry, 85
Lizzie, 84–91, 103, 105, 112
Richard, 85
Mary Charlotte (slave), 23
Maryland, Baltimore, 133
Massachusetts, Hampden County, 41
Springfield, 19, 21, 34, 36, 41, 43, 102, 120, 123, 126–127, 133
McKinstry, J., Major, 55
Menard, Pierre, 23
Merchandise Mart, 69
Mexican War, 13–14, 133
Middlebury College, 30
Miller, Alma (Madison), 1, 6, 80, 83, 85–87, 89, 93–94
Pamela Jean, 94
Phyllis, 96
Raymond Scott, 94, 96
Wendell Curtis, 94
Mineral Point, Washington County, Missouri, 131
Minnesota, Fort Snelling, 2, 9–11, 15, 18, 101
St. Paul, 9
Minnesota Historical Society, 9
Minnesota River, 9
Mississippi River, 6, 8–9, 11, 13, 15, 17, 55, 81
Missouri, Bridgeton, 11–12
Carondelet, 13, 99–100
Jefferson Barracks, 10, 13–15
Mineral Point, 131
Owen's Station, 11
St. Louis, 1–2, 7–8, 10–11 13–14, 17, 19–23, 27, 29–30, 36–37, 43, 47–55, 57–58, 60–62, 64, 66–67, 69–71, 78–81, 83, 86–88, 92, 96, 98–103, 106–112, 114–116, 118, 131, 133
St. Louis County, 10, 11–15, 17, 20, 23, 41, 49, 51, 55, 66–67, 70, 79, 81, 83, 92, 95, 98, 100–103, 106–108, 115, 119
Washington County, 131
Missouri Compromise, 9, 31
Missouri Enabling Act, 13
Missouri Gazette, 22, 131
Missouri River, 13
Missouri Senate, 7, 131
Missouri State Archives, 103
Missouri State Militia, 54
Missouri Supreme Court, 14, 19, 21–22, 25–26, 29–30, 33, 102
Moline, Illinois, 8
Moore, Bob, 118
Morris, George, 41
Murdoch, Francis B., 17–18

—— *N* ——

Natchitoches, Louisiana, 10, 133
National Era, 30
National Historic Landmark, 10
National Park Service, 87, 96
National Register of Historic Places, 98
New Haven Register, 42
New York, Albany, 133
Nunda, 36
New York (city), 133
Saratoga Springs, 131
New York (city), 133
Newfane, Vermont, 30
Northwest Ordinance, 14, 18–19
Northwest Territory, 18
Nunda, New York, 36

—— *O* ——

Oklahoma, Fort Towson, 132–133
Order of the Eastern Star, 88, 95
Owen's Station, Missouri, 11

—— *P* ——

Pennsylvania, Pittsburgh, 81
  Villanova, 95, 103
Peter Blow Inn, 7, 101
Phillis (slave), 7
Phyllis Chapter, Order of the Eastern Star, 88
Pierre (slave), 23
Pittsburgh, Pennsylvania, 81
Pratt, B., 23
Pulaski County, Illinois, 81

—— *Q* ——

Quad Cities, 8

—— *R* ——

Rachel (slave), 19
Rachel v. Walker, 19
Ralph (slave), 13
Ransom, Lydia [Sanford], 11, 132–133
  S. H., 133
  Samuel Henry, 11, 132–133
  Virginia [Sanford], 11, 132–133
Republican Party, 42
Robinson, Harriet [Scott], *see* Scott, Harriet
Rock Island, Illinois, 2, 8, 18, 101
Rombauer, Robert J., 52
Russell, Adeline, Mrs., 19, 21
  Mrs., 19, 21
  Samuel, 14, 18–19

—— *S* ——

St. Louis Association of Colored Women's Clubs, 95
St. Louis Circuit Court [Mo.], 14, 17, 19, 21–23, 27, 32–33, 39, 42–43, 49, 102
St. Louis Convention Center, 50
St. Louis County, Missouri, 10, 11–15, 17, 20, 23, 41, 49, 51, 55, 66–67, 70, 79, 81, 83, 92, 95, 98, 100–103, 106–108, 115, 119
St. Louis County Parks and Recreation Department, 10
St. Louis County Sheriff, 15, 19–22, 25, 37–38, 42, 81, 102, 131
St. Louis Courthouse, 17, 20, 87, 93, 96, 118
St. Louis Daily Evening News, 25–26
St. Louis Fire of 1849, 20
St. Louis Globe-Democrat, 71, 73, 76–78
St. Louis, Missouri, 1–2, 7–8, 10–11, 13–14, 17, 19–23, 27, 29–30, 36–37, 43, 47–55, 57–58, 60–62, 64, 66–67, 69–71, 78–81, 83, 86–88, 92, 96, 98–103, 106–112, 114–116, 118, 131, 133
St. Louis Post-Dispatch, 98
St. Louis Recorder of Deeds, 39
St. Louis Republican, 25, 37
St. Louis Union Station, 1, 85–86
Saint Louis University, 54
Saint Louis University Law School, 93
St. Louis University Law School Student Bar Association, 93
St. Paul, Minnesota, 9
St. Peter's Agency, 9
St. Peter's Cemetery, 78
Sally (slave), 23
Sanders, Henry, 78
  Mattie, 78
Sanford, Alexander, 11–13, 19, 34, 102, 132–133
  Benjamin Chouteau, 133
  Charlotte [Barnes], 11, 19, 34, 132–133
Eliza Irene [Emerson/Chaffee], *see* Chaffee, Irene
Emilie (Chouteau), 11, 132–133
  Henrietta [Clark], 11, 34, 132–133
Irene [Emerson/Chaffee], *see* Chaffee, Irene
Isabella (Davis), 11, 132–133
  John F. A., 11, 15, 19, 21–22, 27, 29, 31, 35–36, 38–39, 102, 120–122, 126, 132–133
  Joseph Perry, 11, 132–133
  Lydia (Ransom), 11, 132–133
  Mary, 34, 132
  Mary [Bainbridge/Humphrey], 10–11, 14, 132–133
  Virginia [Ransom], 11, 132–133
Sarah-Belle Pharmacy, 87
Saratoga Springs, New York, 131
Scott, Charles, 70
  Dred, 2, 5–8, 11, 13–15, 17–23, 25–33, 35–39, 41–43, 47–49, 54, 56–59, 62, 64, 66, 68, 70–71, 75–77, 79, 86–90, 92–97, 99–103, 113–114, 118, 120, 125, 129, 131
  Eliza, 6, 69, 74, 76–77, 79, 105, 109; *see also* Scott, Elizabeth and Scott, Lizzie
  Eliza [Madison], *see* Madison, Eliza
  Elizabeth, 6, 14, 50–51, 72–73, 79, 83–84, 89, 105–107; see *also* Scott, Eliza and Scott, Lizzie
  Harriet (Robinson), 6, 9–11, 13–15, 17–23, 25–26, 29–33, 35, 38–39, 41–42, 47–50, 53–54, 58, 60–62, 64–71, 75–77, 79, 87–90, 92–93, 95–103, 105–108, 113, 115, 118, 131

Scott *(continued)*
 Harriotte, 50–51, 105–107
 Lizzie, 6, 14–15, 18, 20–21, 24–27, 29–32, 37–39, 41–42, 47, 49, 51, 53–54, 62, 68–69, 74, 76–77, 85, 90, 102, 109; see also Scott, Eliza; Scott, Elizabeth; and Marshall, Lizzie
 Lizzy, *see* Scott, Lizzie
 Mary [Blow], 5
 Polly, 70
 Walter, 83, 89
 William, Missouri Supreme Court Justice, 22
Scott v. Emerson, 21–22, 33, 38, 42
Scott v. Sandford, 28, 31, 38, 102, 133
Scypion family, 22
Seminole War, 11, 102
Shenandoah Valley, Virginia, 133
Sigerson Farm Cemetery, 100
Silver Plate Family Award, 95
Simmons, Samuel, 54
South Carolina, Fort Sumter, 53
Southampton County, Virginia, 2, 5, 15, 101, 131
Southern Illinois University, Carbondale, 81
Spanish American War, 88
Springfield Argus, 35, 42, 88, 102
Springfield, Massachusetts, 19, 21, 34, 36, 41, 43, 102, 120, 123, 126–127, 133
Stanford, Connecticut, 133
Stockton, ——, 19
Stowe Teachers College, 87
Sumner High School, 88

—— *T* ——

Taliaferro, Lawrence, Major, 9, 15, 18, 101
Taney, Roger, Chief Justice U.S. Supreme Court, 31
Taylor, Elizabeth [Blow], 5, 7–8, 101, 129–131
 Etheldred, 5
Texas, Corpus Christi, 2, 14
Theotiste (slave), 23
Thompson, James L., Lieut., 9
 Mrs. James L., 9
Todd County, Kentucky, 81
Tunstall, Sarah [Blow], 7, 130–131

—— *U* ——

Union and Advertiser, 36
Union Station, *see* St. Louis Union Station
U.S. Arsenal, 54
U.S. Circuit Court, 11, 30, 35
U.S. House of Representatives, 7, 33, 35, 43, 131
U.S. Postal Service, 87
U.S. Supreme Court, 22–23, 26, 30–31, 35–38, 42, 44, 88, 100, 102

—— *V* ——

Vermont, Newfane, 30
Villanova, Pennsylvania, 95, 103
Villa Ridge, Illinois, 81
Ville Neighborhood, 83
Virginia, Alexandria, 118
 King George County, 2, 9
 Shenandoah Valley, 133
 Southampton County, 2, 5, 15, 101, 131
 Winchester, 133

—— *W* ——

Wahrendoff, Eliza [Blow], 7, 130–131
Walker, William, 19
War of 1812, 8
Washington, D.C, 31, 36, 43, 79, 118, 122, 125
Washington County, Missouri, 131
Washington Park Cemetery, 83, 85, 95, 103
Webster, Julia [Blow], 7, 99, 130–131
Werden, William, 62, 105, 108
Wesleyan Cemetery, 49, 52, 54–59, 78, 102–103, 131
Wesleyan Cemetery Association, 57
West Choctaw Nation [Oklahoma], 133
West Point Military Academy, 43, 133
Whipple Fire Insurance Map, 63, 84
Whitesides, Phebe, 14
Winchester, Virginia, 133
Winn, Ken, 103
Winny, 14
Winny v. Phebe Whitesides, 14
Wisconsin Territory, 6, 9, 15, 18, 101
World War I, 88
World War II, 88
Writ of Emancipation, 27; *see also* Deed of Emancipation

—— *X, Y, Z* ——

Young, Nathan B., 80